VISUAL QUICKSTART GUIDE

iMOVIE HD 6
& iDVD 6

FOR MAC OS X

Jeff Carlson

Peachpit Press

Visual QuickStart Guide
iMovie HD 6 & iDVD 6 for Mac OS X
Jeff Carlson

Peachpit Press

1249 Eighth Street
Berkeley, CA 94710
(800) 283-9444
(510) 524-2178
(510) 524-2221 (fax)

Find us on the Web at: www.peachpit.com
To report errors, please send a note to errata@peachpit.com
Peachpit Press is a division of Pearson Education

Editor: Nancy Davis
Production Coordinator: Lisa Brazieal
Composition: Jeff Carlson
Copyediting: Liane Thomas
Proofreading: Tracy O'Connell
Illustrations and photos: Jeff Tolbert, Laurence Chen, Jeff Carlson
Indexer: Caroline Parks

ISBN 0-321-42327-5

9 8 7 6 5 4 3 2 1

Printed and bound in the United States of America

Dedications:

To Leonard, whose one-month film class at Whitworth instilled in me an appreciation of movies beyond mere popcorn entertainment.

To my sister Lisa, ever encouraging and cheerful.

Special Thanks to:

Nancy Davis, for knowing when to ask, "How are you doing?" and making the author's end of producing a book much easier.

Liane Thomas, for not hesitating to jump into the project when asked, and for her razor-sharp editing eyes.

Caroline Parks, for producing the index in such a way that I didn't have to ask about it or worry about its status. As with the other indexes she's created for me, it just appeared like magic, fully formed and ready to go.

Laurence Chen and **Gena Morgan,** who provided the photos for the lighting examples in Chapter 4.

Jeff Tolbert, for updating my embarassing line drawings of computer and video equipment, and for creating the lighting renderings in Chapter 4.

Don Sellers, for getting me up to speed with shooting, lighting, sound, composition, and providing a real-world reference.

Derick Mains, Paul Towner, Keri Walker, and **Theresa Weaver** at Apple for answering my questions and providing resources when I needed them.

The folks at the **University Village Apple Store (Seattle)** for providing answers, assistance, and letting me test some things on their equipment.

Glenn Fleishman, Kim Ricketts, and **Melody Clark** (plus the various **long-distance inhabitants from earlier office incarnations**) at the Fremont nook for being the best reasons to go to the office every day (well, nearly every day). They're good inspiration and reassurance that this freelance thing actually works.

Nancy Aldrich-Ruenzel, Lisa Brazieal, Gary-Paul Prince, and even some non-hyphenated folks like **Kim Becker, Marjorie Baer, Cliff Colby, Rebecca Ross, Sara Jane Todd, Scott Cowlin,** and **Paula Baker** at Peachpit Press.

And, of course, **Kim Carlson,** who never hesitates to ask, "How can I help?" and keeps me inspired to do what I do each day (and who wrangles a garden into beautiful submission better than anyone I know).

TABLE OF CONTENTS

TABLE OF CONTENTS

INTRODUCTION

I was at Macworld Expo when Apple introduced the first version of iMovie, and seeing it in person was a bona fide "a-ha" moment for me and most of the people in attendance. Video editing, a skill that people spend years mastering in specialized schools, had arrived on the average user's Mac. *Of course* this was going to work. When Steve Jobs presented a short video of two children playing, I knew the days of long, choppy, unedited videotape recordings were coming to a close. Not only can you easily—let me repeat that: *easily*—capture video footage and transfer it to your computer, you can now edit out all the bad shots, the awkward moments, and those times when the camera was inadvertently left recording while dangling at your side.

Now, in 2006, Apple has helped redefine the whole notion of home movies. With built-in support for the high-definition HDV video format (as well as widescreen digital video and native MPEG-4 formats), iMovie HD 6 gives you the chops to make your own independent feature film without appearing as if you made it in your basement—even if that's exactly what you did.

And when you're done editing the movie, send it to iDVD 6 to create a professional-looking DVD that can play on most home DVD players. Your friends and family will be the ones saying, "A-ha!"

Who Should Read this Book

iMovie HD 6 & iDVD 6 for Mac OS X: Visual QuickStart Guide is aimed at the beginning or intermediate videographer who wants to know how to quickly and easily edit movies in iMovie and create DVDs using iDVD. Perhaps you've just purchased your first camcorder and want to turn your home movies into little masterpieces, but don't have the time or money to invest in a professional video editing application. Or maybe you're an old hand at shooting video but new to editing the footage on a computer. Then again, maybe you're a budding Spielberg with scripts in your head and a passion for telling stories on film—the movie business is a tough one to crack, but it's entirely possible that your iMovie-edited film could be the springboard for a career in Hollywood. (In fact, one of the official entries at the 2004 Sundance Film Festival was edited in iMovie.) Or you could also be the owner of a new Macintosh, and want to know why Apple is going to the trouble of giving you a powerful video editing application *for free*.

Since iMovie's introduction, we've seen a boom in digital video editing. Sure, it was possible before, using much more complicated and expensive programs such as Final Cut Pro or Adobe After Effects (and you can still take that route). But with iMovie and iDVD, *anyone* can make a movie and burn it to a disc that can be played in nearly any consumer DVD player.

What's New in this Edition

The book has been updated to cover the changes in iMovie HD 6 and iDVD 6, including iMovie's new Themes and iDVD's Magic iDVD feature. I've also created a new chapter on scoring your movie in GarageBand, revamped the Web-related material to account for iWeb and making video podcasts, and added new tips throughout.

An iMovie and iDVD Toolbox

A full-size movie crew can be unbelievably large and take up a city block. You probably won't require that much gear, but a few items are necessary to use iMovie and iDVD.

◆ **Mac OS X 10.3.9 or later.** iMovie HD 6 and iDVD 6 run under Apple's now and future operating system, Mac OS X, version 10.3.9 or later, though version 10.4.4 and later is recommended. You also need a Mac with a PowerPC G4, PowerPC G5, or Intel Core processor running at 733 MHz or faster.

◆ **iMovie HD 6 and iDVD 6.** If you've purchased a Mac sometime after January 2006, you probably have iMovie HD and iDVD already—look in the folder named *Applications*. The programs are also available as part of the $80 iLife '06 package, which includes iTunes 6, iPhoto 6, Garage-Band 3, and iWeb.

◆ **A digital camcorder.** This handy and compact device records the raw footage that you will edit in iMovie. If you own a camcorder that's not digital, you can still import video into iMovie using a third-party analog-to-digital converter. That said, I can't stress how much easier it is to work when you have a digital camcorder. See Chapter 7 for details.

◆ **Lots of hard disk space.** Storage is getting cheaper by the day, which is a good thing. You'll need lots. I don't mean a few hundred megabytes tucked away in a corner of your drive. Realistically, if you don't have at least 10 GB (gigabytes) of storage (on the low side) to use for iMovie and iDVD, shop for a bigger hard drive. See Chapter 7.

The Moviemaking Process

Creating a movie can be a huge spectrum of experience, but for our purposes I'm going to distill it as follows.

1. **Preproduction.** If you're filming a scripted movie (with actors, sets, dialogue, etc.), be sure you hire the actors, build the sets, write the script, and otherwise prepare to shoot a film. See Appendix B for some resources on where to learn more about the process of getting a movie before the cameras. On the other hand, if you're shooting an event or vacation, preproduction may entail making sure you have a camcorder (see Chapter 1), its batteries are charged, and that you have enough tape available.

2. **Capture footage.** With preproduction out of the way, it's time to actually film your movie. The shooting part is when this book starts to come in handy. Chapters 2 through 5 discuss methods of composing your shots, lighting the scenes, and capturing audio.

3. **Import footage into iMovie.** Your tape is full of raw video waiting to be sculpted by your keen eye and innate sense of drama. The next step is importing it onto your computer and into iMovie. See Chapter 7.

4. **Edit your footage in iMovie.** Before iMovie, average folks had no simple way to edit their footage. The result was endless hours of suffering as relatives were forced to watch every outtake, flubbed shot, and those 10 minutes of walking when you thought the camera was turned off. iMovie changes all that. See Chapters 8 through 13 to learn how to edit your video and audio, plus add elements such as transitions, titles, and special effects.

5. **Export video.** The movie is complete, and it's a gem. Now you need to share it with the world. Using the information found in Chapters 14 through 18, you can record the movie onto a videotape, export it to a QuickTime movie for downloading from the Web, email it to another person, or transfer it to a device (such as a cellular phone) using Bluetooth networking; or onto a DVD (using iDVD).

The DVD Creation Process

iDVD provides a clear path to customizing the appearance of your DVD, adding more content, and burning the DVD disc.

1. **Choose a theme.** iDVD's professionally designed themes provide a menu system that your viewers interact with to watch your movie. Chapter 20 shows you how to expand the menu's organization by adding submenus and AutoPlay movies.

2. **Customize themes and add more content.** With the bare bones in place, change the theme's settings to personalize the menus. Learn how to change buttons, replace background images, modify text formatting, build slideshows, and more in Chapters 21 and 22.

3. **Burn, baby, burn!** Choose an encoding method and burn your disc, or create a project archive that can be moved to another computer for burning there (such as a faster Mac). The smoke rises over Chapter 23.

This Book's Companion Web Site

I maintain a frequently-updated iMovie blog that includes additional tips, pointers to software, examples from the book, and other iLife-related information. Check often at `http://www.jeffcarlson.com/imovievqs/`.

INTRODUCTION

What You Can Accomplish by the End of this Book

To say, "Prepare your acceptance speech" would be exaggerating a bit, but the truth is, you can theoretically use iMovie to create a feature film, award-winning documentary, or even just the best darn vacation video you've ever seen. As you delve deeper into digital video and nonlinear editing (NLE), you'll realize that more options and more control can be had with more sophisticated (and pricey) systems, such as Final Cut Express and Final Cut Pro. But nothing says you can't do what you want with iMovie.

Stepping out of the clouds, you should easily (there's that word again) be able to shoot, edit, and distribute your movie. In the process, you'll find a new respect for film and video—you can't help it. After using iMovie for a few hours, you'll start watching television with a new eye that picks up aspects like pacing, framing, transitions, and audio that you may never have noticed before.

That's been my experience, and now look at me: I've written five editions of this book. And assembled some of the best darn vacation movies you've ever seen.

Part 1
Shooting

THE DIGITAL CAMCORDER

Ages ago, my copy of iMovie 1.0 sat neglected on my hard drive for months because I had no easy way to import video footage. I could have used an analog-to-digital converter to bring in the contents of old videotapes (see Chapter 7), but it would have been a hassle. What I needed was a digital camcorder.

Although digital camcorders cost more than analog models, you can get a good quality model these days for less than $400. You can also easily spend $5,000 or more, with plenty of models falling between those ranges.

iMovie HD gives you another option: high-definition (HD) digital camcorders that capture video at a much higher resolution for playback on HD televisions. Surprisingly, you can get one for around $1,500 currently, a bargain compared to full-fledged HD systems (more on that in this chapter).

For the money, you also get a host of features—and gimmicks. If you've not yet purchased a digital camcorder, this chapter will help you decide which combination of features is right for you. Note that I'll give some examples, but won't be recommending any particular model because (like all technology) the field changes pretty quickly. If you already own a camcorder, skim this chapter to see which features are important and which you should turn off.

Buying a Camcorder

If you don't yet own a digital camcorder, you need one. Here's a look at the important characteristics of these devices.

HD or DV format

iMovie HD offers you an important choice: should you shoot in standard DV (digital video, also sometimes referred to as SD, or standard definition), or in HD (high-definition video)?

Prior to 2004, shooting in HD required expensive cameras costing tens or hundreds of thousands of dollars. Now, you can get an HD camcorder for less than $1,500. As of this writing, a few HD cameras are available that work with iMovie HD, such as JVC's GR-HD1 and Sony's compact HDR-HC1 (**Figure 1.1**).

HD video captures more image information than standard DV, and comes in two variations (**Figure 1.2**): *720p* measures 1,280 by 720 pixels, and captures each frame in its entirety (known as "progressive" capture, the "p" in 720p); *1080i* measures 1,920 by 1,080 pixels, and interlaces each frame (hence the "i"; see **Figure 1.3**). HD also shoots in a 16:9 widescreen aspect ratio. As you might expect, video shot with HD cameras looks great on an HD television.

iMovie HD supports the HDV (High Definition Video) format, a consumer-level version of HD that uses MPEG-2 compression designed to minimize the data rate and work on consumer-level hardware. For example, you can connect an HDV camera to your Mac using a FireWire cable and import the footage onto regular hard drives. By comparison, working with uncompressed 10-bit HD video requires massive amounts of storage, around 500 GB per hour of footage (see Chapter 7 for HDV storage requirements).

Figure 1.1 Sony's HDR-HC1 high-definition camcorder costs less than $1,500 (which is cheap compared to most HD camcorders).

DV: 720 by 480 pixels

HD 720p: 1,280 by 720 pixels

HD 1080i: 1,920 by 1,080 pixels

Figure 1.2 HD uses much more image information than standard DV video. Also note that HD features a 16:9 widescreen aspect ratio, while SD uses the television standard 4:3 ratio.

Progressive frame

Interlaced frame   *Next interlaced frame*

Figure 1.3 A progressive frame is captured in its entirety, the way each frame of film is recorded. Interlaced video captures every other line (exaggerated here for clarity) so that as the frames are played back, your eye sees the image as a solid picture. Interlacing can capture larger images because it's actually storing about half of the image information for each frame. (Interlacing is also the way most televisions operate.)

So although you're not getting the same super-high quality as someone shooting with a $200,000 setup, you still end up with beautiful HD footage. Another bonus HDV offers the average shooter is that it stores 60 minutes of footage on a standard MiniDV tape, the same as shooting with a DV camera.

✔ Tips

- Once edited in iMovie, your HD movie must be exported back to the camera (see Chapter 15) and then hook the camera up to an HD television to view it in HD.

- iDVD handles incoming HD video, but it can't currently burn the HD-quality version to a DVD. Two competing high-definition DVD formats are jostling for position in the entertainment and computer industries: HD-DVD and Blu-Ray DVD, each backed by major corporate entities. Considering that the Hollywood movie studios now make more money from DVD sales than from theatrical screenings, it's a hotly contested fight for dominance. Apple is on the board of Blu-Ray, so it's likely (but not guaranteed) that the SuperDrives in future Macs will be capable of burning HD video to Blu-Ray discs. But until the discs begin appearing, iDVD compresses the HD video to make it fit onto today's DVD media.

- To edit HD in its native resolution, you need a computer monitor at least 23-inches or larger, such as Apple's Cinema HD Displays.

- The full scope of HD video production is enough to fill several books. For hands-on, in-the-trenches coverage of HD, I turn to Mike Curtis's *HD for Indies* weblog (www.hdforindies.com). Also check out *HD Info Net* (www.hdvinfo.net), and, of course, the companion Web site for this book (jeffcarlson.com/imovievqs/).

NTSC or PAL

Standard-definition video is broadcast in one of two formats, depending on where you live. In the Americas and many Asian countries, the standard is NTSC (National Television Systems Committee), which runs at 30 frames per second (actually 29.97 fps). In several European and some Asian countries, the standard is PAL (Phase Alternating Line), which runs at 25 fps. In most cases, you don't need to choose one or the other—it's whatever is predominant in your area. However, some people prefer to shoot in PAL because it's closer to the film projection rate of 24 fps. Either way, iMovie automatically detects the type of camera that is connected and adjusts its settings to accommodate.

Camcorder size

Ah, camcorder envy. You're carrying a new, tiny, handheld camcorder, but then you spy someone whose camcorder is even more compact. For those of us who've had to lug shoulder-mounted VHS cameras back in the day, the miniaturization of camcorder technology is amazing. Although the majority of digital camcorders aren't super small, they're remarkable nonetheless—many fit into a large pants pocket or small purse (**Figure 1.4**).

The small sizes are ultra convenient, but have two drawbacks. You're paying a premium for compactness, so expect to shell out more money for a smaller device. Also, a small camcorder that doesn't weigh much can be harder to keep steady when shooting. If you're looking for something portable to use for grabbing footage anywhere and anytime, go as small as you can afford. If you anticipate more staged shots, where a camera can sit on a tripod for hours, size becomes less of an issue.

Figure 1.4 Today's digital camcorders are small enough to fit in your palm.

MicroMV and DVD Camcorders

Don't be tempted to buy very small camcorders that record to MicroMV tapes or directly to smaller-size DVD discs. There's a catch.

To get a decent amount of data on such small tapes, the MicroMV format uses MPEG compression to shrink the image data, resulting in image quality that isn't as good as MiniDV. (HDV cameras also use MPEG compression, but it tends to produce higher-quality footage.) And due to the way MicroMV data is stored, whenever you stop recording, the camera takes the last frame and creates a still photo that occupies a few seconds of tape.

Currently MicroMV only works under Microsoft Windows, and only when using special software. So as an iMovie-using Mac owner, there's no easy way to import your footage and edit it.

The DVD camcorders also use MPEG compression, which degrades the image quality and can't be imported into iMovie. These models are primarily designed for people who have no intention of editing: they'd rather just pop the tiny disc into a DVD player and watch what they shot right away.

Figure 1.5 As part of the miniaturization of digital camcorders, the tape media is smaller, too. But despite the size, MiniDV tapes store roughly one hour of high-quality video. The new HDV camcorders use the same tapes and store the same amount of footage.

MiniDV tape format

To capture the best quality footage, get a camcorder that uses the MiniDV format. MiniDV tapes are compact, store 100 percent digital information, and record between 60 minutes (at standard playing, or SP, speed) or 90 minutes (at long playing, or LP, speed) of footage (**Figure 1.5**). They're not particularly cheap, but they're not too expensive either. An online search shows you can find them in bulk for around $3 to $5 per cassette.

MiniDV can store roughly 500 horizontal lines of resolution, which means you're capturing more information than other formats (televisions display about 330 lines). It can also record 16-bit audio at 48 kHz, which is slightly better than CD-quality. What's more, MiniDV tapes retain that quality when you record over them, or make copies from other MiniDV tapes. The same can't be said for VHS tapes, which degrade in quality each time you make a copy.

Flash memory

To make cameras even smaller, manufacturers are avoiding tape altogether and releasing cameras that store footage on flash memory (usually CompactFlash or SD cards), the type found in digital still cameras. In fact, some still cameras feature movie modes that shoot nearly as well as a dedicated camcorder. iMovie can import this footage (see Chapter 7), but the data is shrunk using MPEG-4 compression, which degrades the image quality.

✔ Tip

- It doesn't seem to matter which brand of tape you choose—only that you stick with the same one. Companies use different lubricants on their tapes, so mixing brands can potentially lead to a sticky, camera-damaging mess.

Wait...Tape?

Isn't a digital camera supposed to avoid tape altogether? Yes and no. Although the camcorder is capturing footage and storing it digitally, tape is still the dominant medium for storing large quantities of data. Future camcorders will probably include small high-density hard drives (such as the 60 GB drive used by Apple's current high-end iPod, or even the much smaller-sized 4 GB drive in the iPod nano), but for now tape is the best solution. The data is still stored as a series of ones and zeros, resulting in better image quality than other tape formats.

Charge-coupled device (CCD)

A traditional movie camera records light onto a strip of film as it passes through the lens. In a digital camcorder, the light comes through the lens and is recorded by a charge-coupled device (CCD), containing arrays of thousands or millions of tiny sensors that note the color of light that's striking them. When you put the sensors all together, they create the image you see on video.

Most camcorders come with a single CCD, varying in size and resolution. In general, more resolution is better, even though video output is the same—you're paying for better image fidelity, not necessarily a higher number of pixels, as with digital still cameras.

FireWire/i.Link

As you'll soon discover, digital video data is massive, occupying about 3.6 MB *per second* for standard DV footage (see Chapter 7). Even a short movie would take forever to transfer from your camcorder to your Mac if not for the FireWire connection between the two. Also known on Sony camcorders as i.Link, FireWire is necessary to import movies into iMovie. If the camcorder doesn't include a FireWire port, find another model that does (**Figure 1.6**).

✔ Tip

■ Most digital camcorders don't come with a FireWire cable, even though they include a FireWire port. Check the packaging that came with your Mac—Apple includes this cable with most models (**Figure 1.7**). If you need to buy one (as a spare, for example), it will likely be labeled as an IEEE 1394 (the standard on which FireWire is based) cable, and has a smaller plug on one end. Expect to pay around $30 for this essential add-on.

FireWire/DV port

Figure 1.6 The 4-pin FireWire port on a digital camcorder is smaller than the one on your Mac.

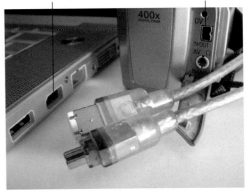

Mac's FireWire port   *Camera's FireWire/DV port*

Figure 1.7 Use a high-speed FireWire connection to import your footage into iMovie on your Mac. You may need to purchase a cable like this one, which has both sizes of FireWire plugs.

Three-CCD Camcorders

Top-of-the-line camcorders feature three separate CCDs, each of which captures a specific color: red, green, or blue. You're not gaining any more image resolution, but the overall color quality is better than that offered by single-CCD cameras. However, three-CCD devices cost significantly more.

Figure 1.8 Canon's XL H1 is a high-definition MiniDV camera with all the trimmings. The microphone is mounted above the unit to record what you're shooting, not the sound of the camera itself.

Figure 1.9 An LCD viewfinder lets you shoot at odd angles. Rotate the screen to view the shot.

Microphone

Every digital camcorder has a microphone, usually built into the body of the camera, but sometimes mounted to the top or front of the camera (**Figure 1.8**). One thing to watch out for is where the microphone is housed: if it's too close to the camcorder's motors, it could pick up the sound of the camera operating (including the motors used for zoom control). Whenever possible, experiment with a few different camcorder models to check their audio output. You can also attach an external microphone to the camera. See Chapter 5 for more information.

LCD viewfinder

Most digital camcorders include a liquid crystal display (LCD) viewfinder that pops out from the side of the camera and shows you what the lens sees. LCDs vary in size, from 2.5 inches (diagonal) on up. You can use it in place of the built-in viewfinder, which is often advantageous when you need to hold the camera above your head or near your feet (**Figure 1.9**), or if you're filming yourself and want to make sure your head hasn't slipped out of frame.

The LCD is especially useful when you want to review the footage you've taken, or show some video to a few people looking over your shoulder. And you'll find it invaluable for fast-forwarding to the end of your footage to make sure you don't accidentally shoot over your existing video.

✔ Tip

■ Remember that it takes power to light up the LCD's pixels and backlighting. Using it often will drain your camera's batteries faster than using the built-in viewfinder. Some cameras now include a switch to turn off or reduce the LCD's backlight to conserve battery power.

BUYING A CAMCORDER

Electronic image stabilization

It's likely that I'll spend this entire book saying, "You know what else is great about digital?" So I'll help you get used to it now. Another great thing about a modern digital camcorder is that the software running it can help you stabilize your image and prevent the shaky footage associated with small handheld cameras. To do this, the camcorder uses an outer portion of the total image as reference, then compares movement of objects within the field of view to the outer area (**Figure 1.10**). If most of the image moves together, the software assumes that the whole camera is moving instead of just the objects, and compensates by shifting the active image.

Electronic image stabilization is helpful, but certainly has its drawbacks. It doesn't record the entire screen, so in some cases you may find that objects on the periphery don't show up in the final footage. It's also not good if you're intentionally moving the camera, such as when you pan or zoom, because the software has to figure out that your motion is deliberate; the end result is sometimes blurry motion that would otherwise be clearer. Still, compared to footage that looks like it was shot during an earthquake, these trade-offs become more acceptable.

✔ Tip

- Of course, image stabilization isn't so good that it will make the shot you took while running down the street look like it was filmed with a Steadicam. If you need to put the brakes on seriously shifty video, consider software such as Slick Stabilize (part of GeeThree's Slick volume 8 package of iMovie effects) or iStabilize (see Appendix B). Both programs do an admirable job of stabilizing the footage after the fact.

Guide area

Image shifted, prompting the camera to compensate

Figure 1.10 In this *massively* simplified diagram, the original image (top) is shifted to the right (bottom) by the camera operator's nervousness around such towering animals. The camera compares the image to the pixels in the unrecorded guide area and compensates by shifting the main image to match. (In reality, the camera doesn't use such a huge guide area—it divides the entire image into several quadrants and continually compares each guide area to its corresponding image area.)

Light enters prism *Variable-bend prism adjusts to refracted light* *CCD*

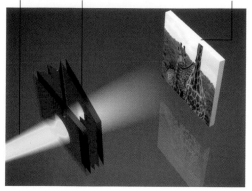

Figure 1.11 An optical image stabilization system uses two lenses to detect light refraction.

Optical image stabilization

Another option for stabilizing your video is to buy a camera with *optical* image stabilization. Unlike the digital method, optical stabilization uses a prism composed of two lenses with silicon fluid between them. The prism determines whether the light coming into the lens is refracted (think of how a stick poking halfway out of water appears to bend below the water's surface). If it is, the camcorder adjusts the lenses to remove the refraction (**Figure 1.11**). An optical stabilizer can work a bit slower than electronic stabilization—since it's performing mechanical, not digital, adjustments—but tends to be a bit smoother overall.

Lens optics

The camera's lens is your eye to the footage you'll shoot, so optical quality is an important consideration. The lenses in the majority of cameras are of good quality, but more-expensive models tend to feature better optics. I'm not saying that more expensive lenses are always better, of course. Research different models and read owner reviews online to learn more.

Remote control

It's not like you don't have enough remote controls lying around the house. I thought having a remote control for a camera was a dumb idea until I realized its two main purposes: playing back video when the camera is attached to a television or monitor, and controlling recording when you can't be near the camera (such as when you're in the frame). The remote ends up being more important than I thought.

Features Worth Noting

Electronics manufacturers love to make bulleted lists of features. Some you may never need or want, while others can help you improve the footage you shoot.

Focus

It's a safe bet that you want the subjects in your video to be in focus—but which subjects, and when? Camcorders feature automatic focus control, which is great when you're shooting footage on the fly. Who wants to try to manually focus when following animals in the wild (**Figure 1.12**)?

However, sometimes the automatic focus can be too good, bringing most objects in a scene into focus—which is why camcorders include an option for manually focusing the lens. (Higher-end models include a focus ring built around the lens, like on a 35mm still camera. Most smaller camcorders sport small dials or scroll wheels to control manual focus.) Manual focus is essential for some situations, such as interviews, when you're not moving the camera (see Chapter 2).

Shutter speed

The term "shutter speed" is a bit misleading here, since a digital camcorder doesn't technically have a shutter (a door or iris that opens quickly to allow light to enter the lens). However, it's possible to duplicate the effects of different shutter speeds by changing the setting on the camera. This is good for filming action with movement that would otherwise appear blurry (such as sporting events). Shutter speed is measured in fractions of a second, so a setting of 1/60 is slower than 1/8000 (see Chapter 3).

Figure 1.12 Gratuitous vacation footage inserted here. But really, when you're shooting video on the run, trying to focus manually tat the same time would have meant losing the shot. You can view this movie clip at this book's companion Web site (jeffcarlson.com/imovievqs).

Normal

Low-light setting

Figure 1.13 Some camcorders feature a low-light setting, which boosts the effectiveness of the available light.

Night vision/low light

You have a few options for filming in low-light conditions. You could always carry around a full lighting setup, but that's not realistic. To compensate, some cameras include a night-vision mode that picks up heat from objects near the camera and displays a greenish representation of the scene.

Other cameras may include a low-light setting, which boosts the amount of available light that's picked up by the camera's image sensors (**Figure 1.13**). It's surprisingly effective, though the playback can be stuttered or blurry if a lot of movement is in the scene.

S-Video port

All camcorders offer some type of output port so you can hook up a television or monitor to play back your footage. Usually, RCA-style plugs are included, but some models also offer an S-Video port. Hooking up your camera to a TV with an S-Video cable provides a clearer picture than with other AV cables. Use it if you've got it.

Features to Ignore/Avoid

Just as there are features you should pay attention to, some features should be ignored or outright avoided. Most of these are included for buyers who don't have the means to edit their movies after shooting. But iMovie does all of the following better than a camera. Most importantly, these effects permanently alter your footage, which you can't correct later in iMovie.

Figure 1.14 Digital zoom creates lots of pixelation as the camera tries to interpolate the image.

◆ **Digital zoom.** One of the first features you'll see on a camera is that it has a 200X (or higher) digital zoom. The technical interpretation is that the computer inside the camera digitally enlarges the image it's seeing, and it appears as if the camera is zoomed beyond its optical capabilities (**Figure 1.14**). The real-world interpretation, at least for now, is that some marketer somewhere is smiling and thinking about the wisdom of P.T. Barnum. Digital zoom isn't pure hokum, but it's also not a mature enough technology to be used in your movies. I expect that as cameras become more powerful and the image processing chips and software speed up (as they inevitably will), digital zoom will become a powerful tool. But not yet.

◆ **Special effects.** Before iMovie, you couldn't apply "sophisticated" techniques such as fade-in or fade-out without using an expensive professional editing system. So, camcorder makers added the capability to apply fades, wipes, and image distortions such as sepia tones or solarization (**Figure 1.15**). Well, forget special effects entirely—you can do them better in iMovie, with more control, and without degrading your footage.

Figure 1.15 In-camera special effects are really only good for ruining otherwise good footage. And not to sound mean, but the Mosaic (top) and Wave (bottom) effects shown here aren't even that interesting. Let iMovie handle your effects (see Chapter 13).

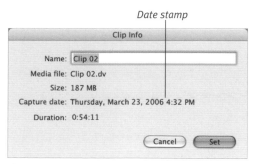

Date stamp

Figure 1.16 iMovie notes the date and time a clip was shot, so you don't need to use a date stamp feature that permanently adds it to the footage.

◆ **Date stamp.** You can optionally display the date and time on your footage, which would appear to be helpful if not for the fact that the information remains on the tape. Even with this feature disabled, your camcorder is recording (but not displaying) this data, which shows up in iMovie when you view information about a clip (**Figure 1.16**). Similarly, avoid built-in options for adding titles.

◆ **Still photo.** Most cameras now include the capability to take still photos. This is a good idea in theory, but the execution varies widely. Some cameras can capture progressive-scan images—which means every pixel is grabbed—and then save them to a separate memory card (such as SD or Sony Memory Stick cards). These result in better images, depending on the camera, but still not as good as what you'd get from most digital still cameras. A few models now include separate CCDs (and even separate lenses) to take higher quality images.

The technology is always improving, so it's possible that soon you may be able to buy a still photo and video camera combination that works well for both tasks. But personally, I'm more comfortable carrying two cameras that each excels at its appointed tasks.

COMPOSITION AND COVERAGE

Camcorder in hand, it's time to start shooting. Where to start? The easiest route is to point the lens at something and start recording. You're bound to get some good footage. However, by learning how to improve your video as you shoot it, you'll end up with better source footage when it's time to edit.

The material in this chapter (and the rest of the chapters in this section of the book) isn't rocket science. If you've grown up watching television or movies (as we all have, to varying degrees), some of it may be too obvious to warrant mentioning. And yet, when it comes time to shoot, it's all too easy to forget the basics and just let the camcorder run—again, perfectly acceptable, but you might kick yourself when you start working with your footage in iMovie. Remember, with iMovie you can edit your clips into a professional-looking movie, but it can't help you improve mediocre source material.

In this chapter, I'll touch upon the basics of getting a shot, and introduce you to some techniques for framing your scenes and shooting plenty of coverage to work with later. Depending on what you're shooting, some or all of this material may apply—you may have control over aspects such as lighting and how the subjects act, or you may be on safari trying to film elephants while avoiding getting eaten by lions.

Preproduction

In general, the term *preproduction* refers to everything done before the camera starts rolling. I think it's safe to assume that you know how to operate your camcorder, and you probably know roughly what you want to shoot. The following steps—except for the first one, which I consider essential—are optional, depending on the type of movie you're shooting. (For example, feel free to storyboard your baby's first steps, but she'll ultimately be the one to decide how that scene plays out.)

+ **Imagine the end result.** Before you even turn on your camcorder, think about how the video will be seen. Will it be viewed on a television, movie screen, computer monitor, or maybe a combination of them all? This decision will help you when shooting. For example, if your movie will only appear on the Web, you may want to shoot more close-ups of people, to make sure they're identifiable in a 320 by 160-pixel window on your computer screen. If it's going to be shown on a big-screen television, on the other hand, you could frame your shots with wider vistas or complex background action in the shot.

+ **Write the script.** If you're shooting a fictional story, with scenes, sets, actors, and the like, you're going to need a script. Sure, the bigwigs in Hollywood don't always start movies with a script, but you've no doubt seen one of those stinkers and wondered if entire sections of Los Angeles underwent covert lobotomies. A good movie starts with a good script, without exception. Even in the low-budget world of digital video filmmaking, a good script can often overcome bland direction, lighting, staging, acting, sound, etc.

An Afternoon, A Life

Shortly after starting work on the first edition of this book, I spent an afternoon with a colleague of mine, who also happens to be an Emmy-winning filmmaker, to pick his brain about filmmaking. "Anything in particular?" he asked me.

"Shooting, lighting, sound…," I replied.

He laughed. "Some people spend their entire lives learning just *one* of those skills."

Filmmaking is an evolutionary art, and involves far more than I can include in this book. I'll cover the basics, but I highly recommend consulting Appendix B for resources on where to learn more about shooting.

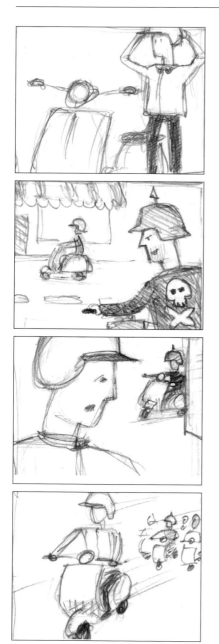

Figure 2.1 Drawing up a storyboard will help you visualize your shots and save time. If you're shooting casually or on the go, create a list of shots you want to try to capture. (Your storyboards are likely to run left-to-right, like most, but I'm working in a vertical layout here.)

◆ **Create storyboards.** Another step in producing a good fictional movie is creating storyboards: shot-by-shot sketches of what you want to shoot (**Figure 2.1**). In fact, you can use storyboards for documentary-style shooting, too. The point of storyboarding is to formulate your idea of what to shoot before you actually shoot; this process will save you time and help ensure that you're capturing all the visuals you want. At the very least, make a list of things you want to shoot, even if you're grabbing vacation video.

◆ **Prepare your equipment.** Do you have plenty of MiniDV cassettes? Spare batteries—and are they charged? Power cord or battery charger? Lens cleaning cloth? Tripod? "Going to shoot video" can simply mean bringing your body and camcorder; or, it can involve hauling truckloads of equipment. In either case, make sure you have what you'll need to accomplish the job.

PREPRODUCTION

Understanding Timecode

As you shoot, you're recording video to the MiniDV tape. If you ever want to find that footage again, you need to understand timecode, the method all camcorders use to label and keep track of footage. You'll use timecode constantly in iMovie, to the point where it becomes as natural as breathing.

As the tape advances, the camcorder notes at which point on the tape that footage is being recorded and displays a numeric tracking code in the viewfinder or on the LCD screen (**Figure 2.2**). A full timecode notation looks like this:

    01:42:38:12

The interpretation of those numbers is a lot like telling time on a digital clock, except for the last two digits:

    Hours:Minutes:Seconds:Frames

So, our timecode number above is read as 1 hour, 42 minutes, 38 seconds, and 12 frames. NTSC digital video records at 30 frames per second (fps), so the last number starts at :00 and ends at :29; for PAL video, which records at 25 fps, the range is between :00 and :24.

When you're recording, you typically won't see all of those numbers. More common is something like 0:03:31 (zero hours, 3 minutes, and 31 seconds), because the camera doesn't split out partial seconds (so no frame numbers are shown). In iMovie, however, you can split clips between frames, not just between seconds, so the full notation becomes important (see Chapter 8).

Timecode indicator

Figure 2.2 The camera assigns a timecode to each frame of film, which is used to manage your footage later in iMovie.

iMovie Timecode versus Real-World Timecode

Video pros may bristle when I talk about timecode in iMovie, because the concept of timecode in iMovie is a bit different from the timecode used in the industry at large.

For the sake of simplicity, say you import a 5-minute clip into iMovie that appeared halfway through your MiniDV tape, or roughly 00:30:00:00 (zero hours, 30 minutes). When you select that clip in the Shelf, its timecode begins at 00:00:00:00 and ends at 00:05:00:00 (I'm using full-length timecode notation for this example; in iMovie, it appears as 0:05:00).

In professional editing programs like Final Cut Pro, the timecode for that clip would begin at 00:30:00:00 and end at 00:35:00:00 to reflect precisely where on the tape the clip originates. This is important if the editor needs to recapture an exact section of footage.

However, iMovie was designed for people who don't necessarily need to know exact timecode, which is why iMovie timecode remains relative to the length of the clip.

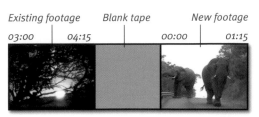

Existing footage   Blank tape   New footage

03:00   04:15   00:00   01:15

Figure 2.3 Broken timecode occurs when blank tape exists between sections of footage. The camcorder uses the last known timecode marker (in this example, 04:15) to compute the time for later frames. However, the portion of blank tape before the new footage has reset the timecode back to zero (00:00).

Keeping timecode intact

The camcorder's timecode indicator ticks away as you shoot, so in theory you can reach the end of a 60-minute tape with a timecode value of 59:59:29 (or thereabouts; I don't think I've ever actually wrapped up a tape that was exactly 60 minutes in length).

However, depending on how you've been shooting, you may notice that the timecode has started over at zero at some point. If this happens, your timecode is broken.

Before you complain to the manufacturer, look at how you were shooting. If you rewound the tape to review some footage, then started again a few seconds after the end of that clip, you inadvertently broke the timecode. The camera counts forward based on the last timecode recorded. If you move into an area of tape that hasn't been marked with a timecode, the camera doesn't know where to begin counting, and starts over at zero (**Figure 2.3**). Fortunately, there's a way to fix broken timecode as you're shooting— but you'll record over any video recorded after the breaking point.

To fix broken timecode:

1. With your camera in Play (VCR) mode, rewind the tape until you see the last footage with unbroken timecode.

2. Advance the tape until you're about two seconds from the end of that footage.

3. Switch the camcorder to Camera mode and begin recording from that point.

I Broke It. So What?

It's not essential that you maintain unbroken timecode throughout your video. Such breaks aren't going to damage your footage, or even confuse iMovie. They will make it more difficult for you to go back and locate specific scenes that you've shot, however. It's far easier to insert your tape and advance to 0:27:18 than to remember that your scene is at 0:02:24 somewhere in the middle of the tape.

✔ Tips

- iMovie doesn't use timecode to work with the tape in your camera. Most high-end video editing packages let you specify a timecode value and then the program advances or rewinds the tape to that point. In iMovie, that task is up to you. If you have unbroken timecode on your tape, it's a lot easier for you to find the footage you're looking for without having to review every minute.

- To ensure that your timecode doesn't break, *prestripe* your tapes before you begin shooting. Load a tape into the camcorder, keep the lens cap on, and record until the tape ends. That gives you an unbroken timecode stream over the entire tape, which you can record over when it's time to shoot the real footage.

- Maintaining unbroken timecode means less wear and tear on your camera. When you search by reviewing your footage, the tape is in contact with the playhead inside the camera. A camcorder's life span is based on the number of hours the playhead is used, so repeatedly scanning the video using the fast-forward and rewind features while it's playing contributes to the wear of the playhead. Instead, forward or rewind the cassette without playing it, when the tape is not in contact with the playhead. This doesn't mean you're going to kill the camera by viewing your footage, just that you are helping to speed the process a little.

Shooting Video Without Disruption

I'm always a little self-conscious when I'm shooting, because often I have to make myself conspicuous in order to get the shot I want. On vacation, this isn't always a problem (my little camcorder is much less intrusive than that other guy's honkin' 35mm lens), but some occasions—for example, weddings—call for discretion. You can take a few different approaches to shooting without disruption.

For one, you don't have to shoot with the camera in front of your face. You can rotate the LCD screen and film from your hip (or even shoot behind you). If it's inevitable that your camera is going to be noticeable, don't be rude about it. People will understand if you need to step softly into view for a few seconds to get a shot, then retreat to a neutral location. Depending on the circumstances, try to ingratiate yourself into the scene so the people involved will trust that you won't be obnoxious.

Or, you could take the route of a professional still photographer who was on a recent vacation I took: not only was he taking great pictures, he offered to sell the resulting photos to fellow vacationers. People (at least the ones whom I assume bought the album) no longer seemed to mind so much if he blocked their view.

Footage for movie

Footage for reference

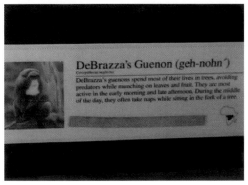

Figure 2.4 In lieu of keeping a notebook, take shots of signs or other identifying markers.

Take Notes

When shooting, you may think you'll remember that the panda bears were located at roughly the 24-minute mark of the Panasonic tape with the purple label, but in reality you'll find yourself scanning through the footage and wishing you'd taken the time to take notes. Get a simple binder and make columns for the tape, timecode, and notes. Then, as you're shooting, jot down what you've just filmed. It doesn't have to be complicated, as long as it offers a quick reference to where your scenes occur. Taking notes is also essential when you need to keep track of locations and the names of people who appear in your video.

✔ Tips

- Label your tapes. They add up quickly, tend to look alike, and are guaranteed to fall off your desk in a cluttered heap just before you need to grab the right one in a hurry.

- Listen, I hate taking notes, too. With digital video, however, you have an advantage: before or after a shot, simply keep the camera running and speak your details. It won't help you find a clip in the middle of a tape, but it will give you the important details of what was recorded.

- Another suggestion is to use a few seconds of your video to record informative signs or other helpful visual indicators (**Figure 2.4**). You don't need to use this footage in your movie, but it helps as a reference when you're editing.

Composing Your Shots

If you really want to, you can hold the camcorder up in the air and hit record—with your eyes closed. But by putting a small amount of thought into the composition of your shots, you can give them a much more professional look.

Shoot large

I had the opportunity to see a 70mm print of *Lawrence of Arabia* a few years ago on the massive screen at Seattle's Cinerama theater. The movie is filled with sweeping desert vistas where you can see miles in every direction, taking full advantage of a large-screen experience.

Most likely, your video will instead play on a television screen or as a QuickTime movie on a Web page (**Figure 2.5**). For that reason, try to "shoot large"—make sure the subject is large enough in the frame that it's instantly recognizable even on a small screen. Getting closer also reveals more detail than can be seen from a distance.

Maintain an axis

Most people are fluent enough in the language of film that they aren't thrown by sudden cuts or changes in a scene. But visually crossing an axis tends to freak them out. The idea is this: if you have two people in a scene, and you're switching between close-ups of each one, they should both remain on their own sides of the screen (**Figure 2.6**). If character A is on the left side of the table, but then you move the camera so that he appears on the right side of the *screen*, the viewer is left wondering how he moved so quickly. At the very least, she'll notice that something odd has happened, which distracts her from the movie's content.

Figure 2.5 Sweeping vistas don't always work in small movie windows, so try to shoot large when you can. Don't abandon wide shots, however. Tape is relatively cheap, so grab the shot when it's available; you can intercut the wider shots later when you're editing in iMovie. See "Coverage" later in this chapter.

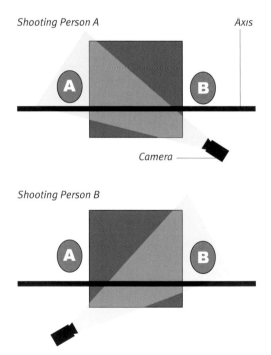

Figure 2.6 Keeping the camera on the same side of your axis line helps the viewer maintain a mental geography of the scene.

Figure 2.7 The train's engine appears in the first third vertical portion of this shot.

Figure 2.8 When your subject faces toward the middle of the frame, he remains engaged with the rest of the shot, rather than looking outside the frame at something else (which is then where your viewers will want to look).

Balance your shots

As I look through still photos I've taken over the years, I notice an annoying consistency: everything is centered. People, monuments, sunsets—all evenly positioned between the edges of the frame. Perhaps it's just our nature to center objects, but it's a good habit to break. Go watch television or a movie and you'll see that almost nothing is centered.

Positioning elements slightly askew of center makes them more interesting. Another take on this positioning is called the *rule of thirds*: the focus of your composition should appear one third of the way from the edge of the frame (**Figure 2.7**). Also make sure that the subject is facing into the frame, not toward the outside (**Figure 2.8**).

✔ Tips

- As you're shooting, be aware of everything in your field of view—don't just focus your attention on the subject. If something else is distracting or disturbing elsewhere in the frame, viewers will likely gravitate toward that, and away from your subject.

- Similarly, take your environment into consideration when possible. Because video is interlaced (every other horizontal line on the television screen is displayed), some objects such as window blinds may create distracting patterns onscreen.

- Many cameras today have the capability to shoot in a 16:9 aspect ratio, also known as widescreen mode. On the camera, it looks as if the image has been squished in from the sides, but iMovie can interpret the ratio correctly (see Chapter 7).

Focus

Pity the poor UFO watchers of days gone by, with their bulky cameras and—most distressingly—manual focus. It's hard enough to spot a saucer in the sky, but to also keep it in clear focus was a daunting task.

I suspect that today's sky-watchers are thrilled with modern camcorders, if for no other reason than the inclusion of *automatic focus control*. Thanks to millions of calculations processed while shooting, a camcorder can do an amazing job of keeping objects in focus. Sometimes, however, the camera performs its job too well.

Automatic focus versus manual focus

Digital camcorders use automatic focus by default. Although they include some sort of manual focus control (which is often a small dial that's hard to adjust in the middle of shooting), most likely it's not the type of focus ring found on your 35mm still camera. Nonetheless, don't be tempted to let automatic focus dominate your shots.

Auto focus tends to focus everything in view, causing footage to appear hyper-real at times (**Figure 2.9**). Your eyes don't bring everything into focus as you look around, so video that is predominantly focused can be distracting.

In an ironic twist, automatic focus can actually contribute to blurry images. The camera generally attempts to focus the objects in the foreground (which may appear on the periphery of the image and not be immediately visible to you), but that can throw off the focus in the rest of the shot and leave your subjects blurry (**Figure 2.10**).

If your camera is mostly stationary, experiment with manual focus to ensure that the objects you want to capture remain in focus.

Figure 2.9 Camcorders do a good job of focusing—sometimes too good. In this shot, Greta is competing with the chair and the firepit in the background for the viewer's attention.

Figure 2.10 Objects in the foreground, such as the branches of this tree, can throw off your camcorder's automatic focus and obscure what you wanted to capture (in this case, a rhino in the wild).

Figure 2.11 The background is out of focus and less vibrant compared to the foreground, which helps to visually separate the two.

Depth of Field

We usually want to keep things in focus, but when everything appears sharp, most scenes begin to look flat. Instead, highlight objects in the foreground by keeping them in focus, and separate them from the background by keeping it soft. When you increase this depth of field, you're more effectively simulating how a viewer's vision works, and subtly influencing what they should see. This works particularly well during interviews or scenes where a character is occupying the frame.

To increase depth of field:

1. Position the camera as far away from your subject as possible.

2. Use the camcorder's zooming controls to zoom in close to the subject.

3. Set the manual focus so that the subject is clear (**Figure 2.11**).

✔ Tip

■ If you're shooting a fixed object where the camera won't move (such as a person being interviewed), use manual focus. Sometimes the motion of the person talking (if they move forward slightly when making a point, for example) will trigger the camera to adjust its automatic focus, causing other elements in the frame to "bounce."

DEPTH OF FIELD

Coverage

With some basics under your belt about framing your shots, we come to a bigger question: what shots are needed to create a movie? If you're shooting a family event, you may think the question doesn't apply to you; after all, you shoot whatever happens, right?

Well, shooting the event itself is a good start, but you need more than that. And you need to make sure you have enough *coverage*, the footage that will give you plenty of room to work when you're editing in iMovie.

Shoot to edit

At the beginning of this chapter, I advised you to imagine the end result of your movie before you begin shooting. A similar notion is *shooting to edit*. In the days before anyone with a Mac could edit their movies, amateur filmmakers shot "in the camera," meaning they structured their shot process so that scenes fell sequentially in the order they would appear when the tape was played— "editing" was done in advance by planning what to shoot.

Now, you're shooting with the knowledge that your raw footage is going to be edited in iMovie. You don't have to shoot things in order, limit yourself to the main subject, or even use footage from the same session.

By way of example, suppose you're filming a family reunion. Immediately following the pick-up basketball game (where Uncle Barney surprised everyone with 32 points and a slam dunk), you shoot a few minutes of a wood-pecker perched on a nearby tree. Then you return to the festivities. The woodpecker has nothing to do with the family reunion, so you may not even use it in your final video—or perhaps you'll pop a few seconds of it into the beginning to show what a beautiful, nature-filled location everyone enjoyed.

Figure 2.12 An establishing shot gives the viewer a sense of where the scene is beginning, such as this shot of the campsite, where the next scenes will occur.

As another example, to round out your movie you want to show the sunset and then fade to black. Unfortunately, the sunset footage you shot wasn't as memorable as you remembered, so instead you grab 20 seconds of sunset footage you took on another location and insert that into your movie. Unless it's painfully obvious that the two locations are different (the presence of a sandy beach where before you were in the middle of a forest, for example), no one will know the difference, and your movie will end stronger. In each example, you had extra footage at your disposal because you were shooting to edit.

Types of coverage

When shooting a feature-length motion picture, a director will use multiple camera setups to shoot as much coverage as possible. So in one scene, the camera may shoot both actors in the frame, each actor from one or more different positions, and various combinations of points of view. The goal is to present a scene in the edited movie where the camera position is integral to the scene's mood or content.

◆ **Establishing shot.** This is usually an overview shot that's wide enough to let the viewer know the setting and which characters inhabit the scene (**Figure 2.12**). It can be a sign reading "Welcome to Twin Falls," a shot of someone's house, or a shot of a room. The important thing is that the establishing shot provides a physical geography of where objects appear. (This technique is used to great effect in dozens of movies and television shows: you see an establishing shot of the Chicago skyline and assume that the action takes place there, even though actual filming took place in Vancouver.)

continues on next page

COVERAGE

◆ **Medium shot.** Most shots end up as variations of medium shots. Generally, this shot is large enough to frame two or three people's torsos, although it can vary between a shot of a single person or half of a room (**Figure 2.13**).

◆ **Close-up.** The screen is filled with part of a person or object (**Figure 2.14**). Close-ups usually show a person's head and shoulders, but can also push in closer (known as an extreme close-up) so you see only the person's eyes. Other examples of close-ups include shots of a person's hands, or any object that occupies the entire frame.

◆ **Cut-away shots.** Sometimes referred to as B-roll footage, cut-aways are shots of associated objects or scenes that aren't necessarily part of the central action in a scene. An example would be the view from a ship traveling through a passage, which cuts away to a shot of the darkening sky, then returns to the ship safely emerging from the passage. The woodpecker footage mentioned in the family reunion example earlier could easily be used as a cut-away shot. Cut-aways often prove invaluable when you need to cover up a few frames of a glitch or when cutting and shortening interviews.

◆ **In points and out points.** If possible, give yourself some shots that can be used to enter or exit a scene, sometimes known as in points and out points. For example, if you're shooting an interview and your subject has just declared his intention to walk on Mars, don't immediately stop recording. Hold the camera on him as he finishes speaking, then perhaps pan down to his desk where a model of his rocket ship is mounted.

Figure 2.13 A medium shot is typically close enough to include two or three people.

Figure 2.14 A close-up focuses on one person or object that occupies most of the frame.

COVERAGE

Figure 2.15 Resist the temptation to rotate your camcorder as you would a still camera to take "vertical" shots, because in video they'll look like this.

✔ Tips

- Linger on shots when you can. It's far easier to cut footage out than to add it back in later (especially if it's vacation footage or something similar...unless you *really* need to rationalize a trip back!).

- How long should you hold on to a shot? First of all, don't automatically shut off the camcorder just when the action has stopped. Stay for a few seconds or minutes to let the emotion of a scene dissipate. This is true when you're doing interviews or shooting wildlife. You can always trim it later in iMovie.

- Remember that a camcorder isn't like a still camera. I've seen people rotate the camcorder 90 degrees as they would a still camera in an effort to shoot a "taller" image (**Figure 2.15**). Unfortunately, no matter how you shoot, the end result will still be a horizontal image—it's not a print that you can view vertically.

  (That said, your footage *can* be salvaged. See Chapter 8 to learn how.)

- Here's a tip I came across while on a soggy camping trip. When shooting in poor weather, you'll need to protect your gear. You can buy hoods and covers and other accessories, which are fine but add bulk. Instead, I have a fleece vest that I use to cover the camera: the lens points through one arm hole, protecting it from the rain but still giving enough room for me to operate the camera.

COVERAGE

THE CAMERA
IN MOTION

3

My digital camcorder is small enough that I can take it almost anywhere. While we're driving to work, my wife will occasionally grab the camera out of my bag and start shooting anything that catches her eye: a brilliant sunrise, the way Seattle's skyline materializes on a foggy morning, rows of orange-tipped trees alongside the roadway in the fall. Although we initially bought the camera to take with us on vacation, it has turned into an unofficial chronicler of our lives.

One of the advantages of a small camera is that it easily moves with you. However, when you're shooting, motion can become a character in its own right. Slowly moving across a scene imparts a different feeling than quickly scanning your surroundings, for example. This chapter addresses the most common ways of moving the camera to add motion to your movie, including the number one rule: don't move.

Don't Move

It's time to go watch TV again (hey, this moviemaking stuff is easy!). Turn to a scripted dramatic show and note how often the camera moves. I don't mean how often the *camera is moved*, which provides different angles of the same scene, but how often the camera is actually moving—not much. When it does move, such as when following a character through a set, the movement is smooth and measured.

As much as possible, limit your camera's movement. You want action that emotionally affects the viewer, which is more likely to happen when the camera is stationary and focused on the contents of a scene. A shot that's bouncing, zooming, or otherwise sloshing about like a drunk at happy hour is a scene where the movement is distracting from the action. Of course, there are times when motion is called for: can you imagine reality-television shows like *COPS* or *The Amazing Race* using stationary cameras? I imagine it's difficult enough to chase a suspected criminal down a dark alley and over a chain-link fence without asking him to pause for a few minutes while the crew sets up its lights and tripods.

Staying still has another practical benefit: excess movement causes blurring in your images (**Figure 3.1**). Our eyes do a good job of pulling detail out of motion blur, but there's a limit to how often they can tolerate fuzzy swabs of color streaking across the screen.

✔ Tip

- To move the camera and keep it steady, consider building your own Steadicam-like rig. You can find instructions in Dan Selakovich's book *Killer Camera Rigs that You Can Build* (www.dvcamerarigs.com).

Figure 3.1 Sudden camera moves introduce blurriness to your footage. Try to keep the camera stationary for most of your shots, if possible.

But If You Must Move...

Okay, you don't have to remain completely still when shooting. In fact, motion can be particularly effective—in moderation. A little motion can go a long way.

Case in point: film director Steven Soderberg. If you watch one of his movies, you'll notice that the camera is almost always in motion, but just barely. A scene in *Ocean's Eleven* stands out in my mind, where a group of main characters steals a device from a research university. In the shot, you're looking down the side of their getaway van toward a set of doors where the crooks will emerge with the device.

It would have been simple to lock the camera down in a fixed location and shoot the actors coming out of the doors. Instead, Soderberg *very slowly* pushes in on a dolly (see "Dollying," later in this chapter). The camera only moves perhaps one or two feet, but the subtle motion draws your attention to the door in a way that a motionless shot would not.

Figure 3.2 Optical zoom and automatic focus can be a great combination when you're shooting something from far away.

Start with the camera zoomed out...

...and slowly zoom in...

...then hold on the zoomed-in image before slowly zooming back out.

Figure 3.3 Quick zooms in and out are effective ways to instill headaches in your viewers. Instead, slowly zoom in, hold, then slowly zoom out. This technique gives you good, clear footage at several distances.

Zooming

Now that I've lectured on the evils of moving your camera, let's get into the realities of the types of motion you'll encounter. To start, let's look at one of the most common trouble-makers, the zoom control.

When you bought your camera, the first thing you probably did was play with the zoom control. It's usually a rocker switch that moves between W (wide) and T (telephoto), and enables you to view distant objects. Combined with a camera's automatic focus feature, especially when shooting in the field, zooming can get you closer to your subject (**Figure 3.2**).

However, the control can be sensitive, leading to abrupt or too-quick zooms in and out. A better approach is to smoothly zoom in on your subject, hold for a bit, then slowly zoom out (**Figure 3.3**). Practice with the control to get a feel for how much pressure is needed, and try to run through the shot a few times before you actually record it.

✔ Tips

- If you missed the memo in Chapter 1: turn off the digital zoom feature of your camera. The camera tries to enlarge the pixels, thereby appearing to zoom beyond its optical limit. All you really end up with is large blocky pixels.

- Sometimes you want an abrupt zoom, either because it enhances the action or because you don't have time to shoot, stop recording, zoom in, then begin recording again. In the latter case, zoom quickly and hold onto the shot—you can edit out the actual zoom later in iMovie.

- A good zoom can be handy when you're not recording. If you're not toting a pair of binoculars, your camcorder will help you see objects in the distance.

Dollying

Dollying is similar to zooming, in that the camera moves in toward (or away from) a subject. However, a dolly shot doesn't use the zoom control at all. In feature film shoots, a dolly is a platform that holds the camera and rides on rails similar to railroad tracks. When filming, one or more people (known as grips) push the dolly, resulting in a smooth shot.

When you zoom, the camcorder's lens is simulating the appearance of moving closer to your subject. When dollying, you're moving the camera physically closer. The difference is especially pronounced in the background (**Figure 3.4**).

✔ Tips

■ As with zooming, you want to ease in and out of a dolly shot. Grips aren't just people who push equipment around. A good grip can accelerate and decelerate smoothly and, often more importantly, *consistently* during multiple takes.

■ A dolly shot is a professional-looking camera move, but it's likely you don't have a dolly setup or want to spend the money to rent one. Instead, choose from a number of alternative dollies. Wheelchairs are great (and comfortable for filming!), and skateboards also work in a pinch. It doesn't matter so much *how* you get the shot, only that the shot turns out the way you want it.

Zoomed in

Pushed in on dolly, no zoom

Figure 3.4 These two shots are similarly framed, but look at the orange building in the background to see how the two approaches differ.

Automatic

1/2000 shutter speed

Figure 3.5 Higher shutter speeds can make fast-moving objects appear clearer.

Changing Shutter Speed

Your camcorder doesn't have a shutter in the traditional sense. There's no little door that opens and closes quickly to control the amount of light that gets through the lens. However, camcorders can simulate shutter speed by controlling how quickly the CCD sensors refresh the image being recorded, which is measured in times per second. A normal shutter speed is approximately 1/60th of a second, meaning the CCD samples an image 60 times per second.

Why change shutter speed? Using a higher setting is good for capturing fast-moving action like sporting events. The blur caused by moving objects is substantially reduced at speeds of 1/4000 or 1/8000, creating frames that contain very little blurring (**Figure 3.5**). You'll need to experiment with your camera's settings, though; a high shutter speed can also make the image appear to strobe, or flash artificially.

✔ Tips

- Faster shutter speeds require more light. If you think of a traditional shutter, not as much light enters the camera when the shutter is closing more times per second. So a dimly lit room can appear even darker at a high shutter speed.

- Your camcorder is probably changing shutter speeds without your knowledge. On Auto setting, it detects what kind of light is present, and if it detects fluorescent lighting—which flickers imperceptibly to our eyes, but can cause havoc on a digital recording—the shutter speed automatically changes to compensate.

Panning

Film has the great advantage of width: its wider aspect ratio captures landscape images in a way your regular video camcorder can only dream about. (One of the advantages of shooting in HD is that it's always widescreen.) However, you can pivot the camera left or right to shoot that landscape and not disrupt the scene with too much motion. This side-to-side movement is called panning, and is a common tool in a director's box of shots. A similar shot, tilting, moves the camera up and down, though it's not used as frequently.

To pan a scene:

1. Mount your camera on a tripod for best results, or hold it as steady as you can.

2. Determine where the pan will begin and end.

3. Begin recording at the first point, and pivot the camera left or right at an even pace. If your camera is not on a tripod, swivel your body steadily at the hips.

4. When you reach the end point of your pan, stop recording.

Pan ahead of subjects

A panning shot often follows a subject from one side of the screen to the other, but think of your composition as you do this. Don't just center the subject in the frame. Instead, provide space into which the person can walk by panning ahead of him (**Figure 3.6**).

Figure 3.6 Frame your shots when panning so that subjects walk into the shot, not out the edges.

Figure 3.7 It's either you or the camera—the world just doesn't naturally tip like that.

✔ Tips

- To help stabilize the camera while you're holding it, pull your elbows in close to your body, hold the camera with both hands, and keep a wide stance.

- If you're using a tripod, be sure to get a fluid-head tripod. It's more expensive than your standard unit, but allows for much smoother motion.

- As it turns out, the biggest problem with panning isn't moving the camera smoothly. Your top concern should be: is the horizon level? If the camera isn't exactly even with the horizon, panning will give the effect of moving uphill or downhill (**Figure 3.7**).

- Panning doesn't have to involve rotating the camera around a central axis. Use a dolly setup (see "Dollying," earlier) to move the camera from side to side.

4

LIGHTING

Unless you plan to shoot with the lens cap on, you'll have to come to grips with lighting in your videos. Put simply, you want to have enough light to see what's being filmed, but not so much that it blows out the camcorder's sensors with pure white. You also don't want scenes that are so dark you can't see what's going on.

When a Hollywood film crew shoots a movie, the lighting you see is enhanced (or outright artificial—even the most natural-looking sunlight coming through a window is likely a big spotlight on the other side of the wall). You don't need to go to those extremes, of course. Most often your lighting rigs will entail the sun, some lamps, and maybe a spotlight or two.

What's important is that you know how basic lighting works, and how to take advantage of it to ensure that the objects you're shooting don't turn out to be dark, talking blobs when you're editing.

Hard and Soft Light

There are infinite possible combinations of light, which can seem daunting when you're shooting video. Fortunately, for our purposes we can break light down into two broad categories: hard and soft.

◆ **Hard light.** The term hard light refers to the light produced by a direct source, which creates shadows with clearly defined edges (**Figure 4.1**). Hard light tends to be bright, like the sun at midday.

◆ **Soft light.** In contrast, soft light isn't as direct, and produces shadows that are blurred at the edges or fade away (**Figure 4.2**). Soft light is typically light that's filtered by artificial means (such as hoods and filters attached to the light) or by natural means (such as clouds, fog, or shade).

In general, soft light is better to film by, because it gives you more levels of brightness and accentuates natural textures. Hard light creates a lot of contrast, limiting the brightness levels because you see either high-intensity light or deep, dark shadows.

✔ Tip

■ If lighting is particularly important to a scene, add a video monitor to your list of equipment to bring on a video shoot. Although your camcorder offers a viewfinder and an LCD, you won't know how the image will look on a TV screen until you see it projected on a monitor. The camera's LCD is great for viewing the content you're capturing, but LCDs can often display images brighter than they're being recorded; or, if you're outside, the LCD's pixels can get washed out by the sunlight.

Figure 4.1 Hard light creates sharp, clearly defined shadows. A bright halogen lamp is providing the light.

Figure 4.2 Soft light diffuses the shadows, making them blurry or even fade out gradually. In this case, a white t-shirt was put in front of the halogen bulb to dampen its intensity. (Hey, we're real high-tech at the Carlson world headquarters.)

White balance, indoors

White balance, outdoors

Figure 4.3 Many camcorders feature the capability to adjust the color temperature they display.

Color Temperature

White light is a combination of all the colors of the spectrum, as you've seen when playing with a prism or looking at a rainbow. As such, it's not going to always be white while you're filming—a myriad of factors can make images appear with a colored cast, leading to video footage that looks a little too green, or blue, or any number of shifts.

Your camcorder automatically adjusts to compensate for this *color temperature* of the light by setting the white balance. Essentially, this is the color that the camera sees as white, causing the camera to adjust the display of the rest of the colors based on this setting. You probably have a few basic controls for changing the setting, such as Auto, Indoor, or Outdoor presets (**Figure 4.3**).

You may also be able to specify the white point manually by selecting Manual and filming a sheet of white paper in the environment where you'll be shooting; the camera uses the values it captured as the basis for displaying the other colors.

Three-Point Lighting

If you have more control over the way your scene is lit, try to use a basic three-point lighting setup. This allows for plenty of light to illuminate the scene, while also reducing deep shadows. A three-point setup consists of a *key light*, a *fill light*, and a *back light* (**Figure 4.4**).

The key light is the primary light source in your scene, and usually the brightest. The fill light is softer, filling in the shadows and adding texture, and is often dimmer than the key light to avoid washing out the image and flattening it. The back light is often small, focused, and used to help separate the scene's subject from the background.

As an easy example, let's say you're setting up to shoot an interview (**Figure 4.5**). Remember, this is just a basic configuration—you can position the lights any way you choose.

To set up three-point lighting:

1. With the camera facing the interview subject, position the key light to the right and slightly forward of the camera. Raise the light so that it's at a 35- to 45-degree angle, pointing down at the subject.

2. Position the fill light to the left of the camera and subject, approximately halfway between the two. The fill prevents deep shadows caused by the key.

3. Place the back light behind the subject, raised a bit higher than the key light, and aimed so that it illuminates the back of the subject's head and shoulders.

Fill light — Back light — Key light

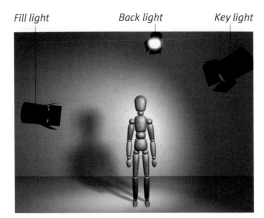

Figure 4.4 A basic lighting setup involves three lights, though of course you can use more (or less).

Key light only

Key light and fill light

Key, fill, and back lights

Figure 4.5 You could use just a key light, a fill and key, or any other combination of lights. Shown here is the progression of adding lights.

Figure 4.6 A strong light source behind your subjects can easily make them appear as silhouettes.

✔ Tips

- Your camcorder is programmed to automatically adjust the exposure (the amount of light coming in) by opening or closing its iris. You've probably seen this happen when you move from a bright area to a dark one, as details come into view after a second or two. To minimize this extreme change of contrast, break up your shots so that the camera can make the adjustment when you're not filming.

- You've seen the silhouettes. When the key light is behind your subject—whether it's the sun, an especially bright white wall, or a lamp in the background—the camera picks up on the light area in favor of the dark, and pretty soon the person in your video looks like a mob informant protecting his identity (**Figure 4.6**). Try to shoot with the light coming from behind you or from one side, so the light falls on the person or object you're filming.

- When a back light spills directly into the frame, you get the visual artifact known as lens flare. Repositioning your light usually fixes the problem.

- Keep in mind that you don't need to raid a professional camera store and stock up on lighting equipment. You probably have all the lights you need at home or in your office, if you're willing to move things around a bit. Just be careful not to shed too much light onto a scene, which will make it appear flat and less interesting.

- Three-point lighting is a good minimum starting point. On some productions, dozens of light sources may be used to light a scene properly.

THREE-POINT LIGHTING

Bounce Cards and Reflectors

You don't need a truckload of lights to illuminate your scene. A common and easy solution for shedding more light on your subject is to use a bounce card or reflector. These are either pieces of cardboard, cloth, or wood that are colored white, gray, or silver to reflect light into shadowy areas. You can buy inexpensive flexible reflectors that twist into a compact circle for storage. You could also create your own reflectors—white poster board covered with aluminum foil on one side, for example.

Have someone hold the reflector, or mount it on something, and aim its reflection as you would with a fill light.

✔ Tips

- Bounce light onto a person's face, but don't bounce it into their eyes. Yeah, it's a mean thing to do, but more importantly (for our purposes, anyway), it makes him squint, hiding the eyes, which are often a subject's most compelling feature.

- iMovie includes an effect for adjusting the brightness and contrast in a movie clip, but it won't fix a poorly lit scene. In fact, cranking up the brightness often washes out the image, because the setting is applied evenly throughout the frame. See Chapter 13 to learn how to apply effects in iMovie.

Figure 4.7 Shooting in the middle of the day can create sharp shadows.

Shooting Outside

It's one thing to configure lighting in a dark room where you have absolute control. But the rules become much more slippery when you're filming outside, where the sun and clouds can change the lighting from moment to moment. No matter where you're filming, you can make choices that take advantage of the weather.

◆ Avoid shooting in the middle of the day when the sun is directly overhead. A key light from above casts shadows down across the face, which obscures a person's eyes and can give the appearance of a hung-over Frankenstein (**Figure 4.7**).

◆ Clouds are your friends. A good layer of cloud cover is an excellent diffuser of sunlight, providing a more even level of light in your scene. Coupled with a few well-placed bounce cards and a fill light, a typical cloudy day can provide warmer tones than you might expect.

◆ Shade is also your friend. Again, you want to minimize high-contrast key light-ing and enhance the balance between shadows and fill light. Move to the shade of a tree (which can also provide its own unique shadow textures, depending on the tree) or to the side of a building.

◆ To maximize natural light, shoot early or late in the day, when the sun is near the horizon. The light isn't as harsh, you can get some very intriguing shadows, and the color of the scene is generally warmer and more inviting.

✔ Tip

■ If you must shoot in the middle of a sunny day, put some light-colored fabric above your subject to act as a diffuser.

SHOOTING OUTSIDE

CAPTURING AUDIO

Video gets all the attention. When new camcorders are released, companies hype the image resolution, the color fidelity, the zoom ratios, optics...oh, and there's a microphone in there somewhere, too.

Well, you'll discover soon enough how important audio is. You can spend hours setting up your lighting and composition, but if the sound is poor, your scene is poor. The good news is, for most casual shooters, the built-in mic will capture what you're filming. Some cameras include controls for varying input levels, while most others offer automatic gain control (AGC) to manage the input without your involvement. However, even if you're going to be filming informally, consider purchasing a separate microphone.

As with lighting, you can spend your life learning the complexities of audio production. This chapter is intended as an overview of some options available for capturing audio.

Headphones

If sound is at all important to you, pack a pair of headphones when you go shooting (**Figure 5.1**). You can use almost any old pair (earbud-style headphones, for example, are extremely portable), but what's important is that you can hear what your camcorder is recording.

When you're standing behind the camera, your ears are naturally picking out the audio in the scene and ignoring other ambient noises. Your camera's microphone isn't nearly as sophisticated, and does its best to maintain a level input based on all the noise in the immediate vicinity. Camcorder mics can also be sensitive to movement, picking up the sound of you shifting the camera or adjusting the focus.

A pair of headphones screens out the noise around you and gives you a direct bead on what the camera is hearing. And, it's the best audio troubleshooting device on the market: if you can't hear your subject, you'll know right away, instead of later on when you're editing in iMovie.

Figure 5.1 Wearing headphones while shooting is the only accurate way to know what your camera is recording.

Built-in microphone

Figure 5.2 The camera's built-in microphone is good, but it's susceptible to picking up noise from the camera and doesn't record distant subjects too well.

Your Camcorder's Microphone

I don't want to give the impression that a camcorder's built-in microphone is a flimsy afterthought. On the contrary, it's a sophisticated device that does the best it can, given the circumstances. Where it falls flat at times is with its placement: Because camcorders are so small, there isn't much room for a microphone (**Figure 5.2**), so you're bound to pick up sounds that the camera is making (such as the motor advancing the tape, or the zoom control adjusting the lens).

Another limitation is distance. The most important factor when recording audio is the distance between the microphone and subject—the closer the better. If you're filming a birthday party, for example, you're likely to be right in the action and will pick up audio pretty well. But what about when you're doing an interview? You want the person's comments to be picked up clearly, but you don't want the camcorder to be in her face. If you're shooting from a moderate distance away (see "Depth of Field" in Chapter 2), the microphone won't pick up the sound clearly.

✔ Tip

- Camera manufacturers are starting to realize that audio recording can be a compelling selling point. Sony now offers a camcorder that records in Dolby 5.1 stereo surround sound, and I expect other companies will follow suit in the future.

12-bit versus 16-bit audio

Most likely, your camcorder includes the option to record in 12-bit or 16-bit audio. When you're recording in 12-bit, the microphone is grabbing sound in stereo and saving it to two separate channels (left and right), leaving two more channels to record more audio in the camera later.

If you choose to record in 16-bit audio, the quality is a bit better than what you'd hear from a CD—you're sampling more audio data than in 12-bit mode. However, that extra data occupies the available channels, so you can't add more audio to that footage (but see the tip at the end of this chapter). More data also means that your footage will take up more disk space in iMovie than 12-bit footage.

Now, with the definitions out of the way, *forget about 12-bit audio*. Although 16-bit takes up more disk space, iMovie prefers it; 12-bit has been known to cause audio dropouts and other problems. Plus, iMovie ignores 12-bit's two separate stereo tracks anyway, so from the software's perspective, it's just one audio stream.

Wind Screen mode

Here's a good general tip: read your camcorder manual before you go on vacation. If I hadn't been in such a hurry to take a break, I would have discovered the Wind Screen feature of my camcorder, which does a decent job of cutting down the extra noise produced by wind blowing into the microphone. It's not a perfect solution (what is?), but it would have made some of my footage sound less like I was in the middle of a tornado.

✔ Tip

- The Noise Reducer audio effect in iMovie HD 6 can do a fair job of cutting down exactly this type of noise. See Chapter 13.

Ambient Sound

Your biggest concern is likely to be capturing the audio of your main subject, but don't forget about ambient noise. The sounds that surround you can be just as important as the main audio to establish mood or place. It's also good for maintaining *consistent* noise. For example, I took some footage on the airplane en route to my aforementioned vacation, but when I brought it into iMovie, the engine noise differed depending on when the video was shot (when we started to descend) and even what side of the plane I was filming. However, I was able to use a sample of ambient noise in the background to provide an even level of noise (and also to adjust the audio so it wasn't as dominant). Record ambient noise whenever you can—you can spend a few minutes before or after your primary shooting and get plenty of material to work with later in iMovie.

This applies to "quiet" rooms as well. Even an empty room has its own audio signature—it's never completely silent. Grab a minute or two of quiet noise, too.

Figure 5.3 A simple clip-on lavalier microphone can greatly increase the quality of your recorded audio.

Directional microphone

Figure 5.4 Higher-end digital camcorders are outfitted with directional microphones that aren't as likely to pick up camera (or camera operator) noise.

Microphones

Remember earlier how I said you could spend years mastering the art of capturing audio? As with any specialized field, you could also spend a fortune on microphones and audio equipment. The good news is that you can also spend around $20 at Radio Shack and get what you need. Since it's unlikely that you'd spend tens of thousands of dollars on microphones to use with a $500 camcorder, I'm going to stick with a few realistic options.

Lavalier

A simple and portable solution is to purchase a lavalier microphone (**Figure 5.3**). It clips to your subject's shirt or tie, and often has a small battery-powered amplifier, making it a condenser mic, which is how your camcorder's documentation refers to it.

Directional

Directional microphones come in a number of shapes and sizes, and are built to pick up sound in some areas and not others. For example, cardioid microphones minimize sound coming from the sides and block sound from behind.

A shotgun mic, like the ones found on higher-end camcorders (**Figure 5.4**), picks up audio only in front of the camera (or whatever the mic is pointed at) while ignoring sound from behind the mic (therefore reducing the likelihood of recording camera noise).

An omnidirectional microphone, on the other hand, picks up sound from all sides and is good to use when you're not focused on any one particular subject.

Wireless

Wireless microphones also come in a variety of shapes and sizes, but aren't tied to an audio cable that snakes back to the camcorder. They're portable, allowing you more freedom to shoot your video while moving, or from anywhere in the room. The biggest drawback to using a wireless mic is that it's more likely to pick up interference from other radio sources, so be sure to test the output before you start filming, and use headphones to monitor the recording while shooting.

✔ Tips

- Check your camcorder's specifications for attaching external microphones. Some require that the mic is amplified, calling for an external power source. Other cameras can use the camcorder's battery to provide power.

- If you don't entirely trust your camcorder's mic, or just want to be sure you have a backup source of audio, consider purchasing a MiniDisc recorder so you can make an additional recording of a scene's audio while you're filming. It stores audio digitally, which you can import into iMovie and add to your movie, or use in place of audio that didn't record clearly (due to the placement of the microphone, for example). Another option, if your audio doesn't need to be at high quality, is to use a Belkin voice recorder (www.belkin.com) attached to an iPod.

  If you're dubbing dialogue, you may have to break the audio into several clips in iMovie and synchronize the timing often, but that's a better solution than trying to re-create the original shoot. See Chapter 10 for more on editing audio.

Part 2
Editing in
iMovie HD

iMovie Overview

Being a fan of the moviemaking process, I enjoy reading "behind the scenes" articles about how films are produced. In nearly all cases, the reporter interviews cast and crew at the movie set during shooting (and invariably makes it sound more exciting than it usually is). But filming is only one part of the production.

Rarely reported on is the editing stage, when the editor (often with the director) spends long hours in a dark editing room—sometimes for many months—shaping hours of raw footage into what we eventually see in a theater. They grab the best takes from each day's shooting, assemble them according to the storyline, and then add transitions, audio, special effects, and whatever else is required for that particular flick.

The process of making your digital video is the same (minus the reporters). By this point you've shot your footage, but that doesn't mean you have a movie. Here's where iMovie and digital non-linear editing can take your mass of video and audio and turn it into a movie. This chapter introduces iMovie, making sure you have the tools you need to get started, and giving you an overview tour of the program's unexpectedly powerful yet simple interface.

Getting iMovie

If you've purchased a new Macintosh within the last couple of years, you should have a free copy of at least one version of iMovie on your hard disk or on an accompanying CD-ROM. If you bought a Mac after January 2006, iMovie HD 6 should already be installed.

Otherwise, you need to purchase iLife '06, Apple's $79 suite of digital hub applications (www.apple.com/ilife/), which includes iMovie HD 6, iDVD 6, iPhoto 6, iTunes 6, GarageBand 3, and iWeb.

Working with Projects

The first thing to do is launch iMovie. This step may seem absurdly obvious, but stick with me for a minute. Go to your Applications folder in the Finder and launch iMovie by double-clicking its icon. A dialog offers the following options (**Figure 6.1**):

◆ **Create a New Project** starts an iMovie project from scratch. After clicking the button, give your project a name and decide where it will live on your hard disk.

◆ **Open an Existing Project** loads a project in progress. In the dialog that appears, locate the project file on your hard disk.

◆ **Make a Magic iMovie** creates a new project and starts the process of automatically importing footage from your camcorder (see Chapter 7 for details).

◆ **The Question Mark (?) button** launches iMovie's help system in the Help Viewer application.

◆ **Quit** exits the program.

✔ Tips

■ In addition to the Help Viewer files, an iMovie manual in PDF format is located in the Library > Documentation > Applications > iMovie folder (note that this is Mac OS X's main Library folder, not the Library folder that exists in your Home directory). It's basically the same information as the help files, but in an easily printed format.

■ .Mac members can watch free iMovie and iDVD training movies at www.mac.com.

■ iMovie HD 6 runs only under Mac OS X 10.3.9 or higher; Mac OS X 10.4.4 or later is required to use iMovie HD's new themes (see Chapter 8).

Figure 6.1 Launching iMovie for the first time gives you five simple options.

Upgrading from Previous Versions of iMovie

Upgrading to iMovie HD is easy, but I recommend keeping a copy of earlier iMovie versions available, too. Before you run the iMovie installer, locate the iMovie program in your Applications folder and copy it to another hard disk, or duplicate it (press Command-D in the Finder) and rename it as "iMovie HD 5".

Why make a copy? The iLife '06 installer looks for "iMovie HD" in your Applications folder and replaces it. If you want to go back to a previous version for whatever reason, you'd have to reinstall it. Instead, make a separate copy to have on hand.

If you're upgrading and the iLife '06 installer has already replaced it, the situation is a little more complicated. Locate the Software Restore discs that came with your Mac; these let you install a fresh Mac OS X system—the entire thing. Instead, download the shareware utility Pacifist (www.charlessoft.com), and use it to locate the iMovie HD installation package on one of the Software Restore discs.

WORKING WITH PROJECTS

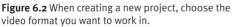

Figure 6.2 When creating a new project, choose the video format you want to work in.

NTSC and PAL Projects

iMovie's General preferences include the option to choose the project's frame rate: either 29.97 fps (NTSC) or 25 fps (PAL). When you change this preference, it applies to *new* projects, which means you can't switch rate in the middle of editing.

Although you can manually apply this setting, iMovie will override your choice depending on the camcorder you connect. For example, suppose you have a PAL project that contains footage, and you connect an NTSC camera. iMovie recognizes the camera when you click the Camera Mode popup menu, but notes that it is "Incompatible With Project." If you try to select the camera, you get an error message.

However, if you create a new PAL project that does not yet contain content and then plug in an NTSC camera, iMovie changes the project to 29.97 fps.

Creating a new project

One of the great features of iMovie HD is the capability to work with several video formats. When you create a new project, you have the option of choosing the format.

To create a new project:

1. At the iMovie launch screen, click the Create a New Project button. You can also choose New from the File menu (or press Command-N) at any time.

2. In the dialog that appears, choose a location for your project. iMovie uses the Movies folder in your Home folder as the default, but you can also choose another disk (for example, a larger external FireWire hard drive).

3. If a camcorder is connected to your Mac, the appropriate video format is pre-selected for you. However, you can choose another—click the Video format expansion triangle to reveal format options (if they're not already visible).

4. Choose a format from the Video format popup menu (**Figure 6.2**).

5. Give your project a descriptive file name.

6. Click the Create button to save the new project.

✔ Tips

- Even if you don't own an HDV camcorder, you can create an HDV (1080i or 720p) project. It's great for making high-resolution slideshows (see Chapter 9).

- You can always look to the project title at the top of the window to see the project's format and frame rate ("DV–NTSC").

- See Chapter 7 for information on mixing and matching different video formats within the same project.

WORKING WITH PROJECTS

Opening projects

A new iMovie project is saved to your hard disk as a single file (**Figure 6.3**). The next time you want to work on it, simply double-click the project file in the Finder to open it.

However, you might not need to open it at all: iMovie remembers which project you were working on between sessions, so the project you were working on the last time you used iMovie automatically loads the next time you launch the program, thereby skipping the initial dialog.

Also, in iMovie HD 6, you can (finally) open more than one project at a time.

Saving copies of the project

The Save Project As command under the File menu creates a copy of your project at its current state. This feature is good if you want to explore some editing ideas without destroying the work you've put in so far. Saving a copy duplicates all the media, too, so be sure you've got the hard disk space to accommodate the new copy.

Closing projects

In previous versions of iMovie, when you closed a project file, the program quit. Thankfully, that confusing behavior is gone; now, when you close a project, the initial dialog appears and the program continues to run. You can then create a new project, open an existing one, or quit the application.

Burning projects to disc

The Burn Project to Disc command under the File menu enables you to create a backup of your iMovie project to a writeable CD or DVD disc; it doesn't create an iDVD project (see Chapter 18 for that). However, if your project size is larger than what the disc will hold, iMovie won't create a backup.

Figure 6.3 A project file (left) is a package that stores all of the data for your movie (right).

Turn Off FileVault!

Mac OS X 10.3 Panther introduced FileVault, a feature that encrypts your Home folder to secure your data—as you work, the files are decrypted on the fly. For many types of files, this is no big deal. However, when dealing with massive digital video files, it can make iMovie unusable. Not only does it slow down performance, but because iMovie prefers to save its project files in the Movies folder of your Home directory, the encrypted FileVault image on your disk can quickly balloon in size to several gigabytes.

Go to the Security preference pane in Mac OS X's System Preferences and click the Turn Off FileVault button if it's on. FileVault isn't a bad idea by itself, but its current incarnation (as of Mac OS X 10.4) is poorly implemented.

Figure 6.4 Opening a project created in an older version of iMovie results in this dialog.

Opening Old Project Files

When you open a project file created with an earlier version of iMovie, a dialog informs you that the files will be upgraded and that you won't be able to open it in the older version (**Figure 6.4**). To ensure that it behaves like other iMovie projects in the Finder, close the project after it's converted, and then append the text ".iMovieProject" to the end of the project's folder name (the folder "Testing" becomes "Testing.iMovieProject", for example).

However, I don't recommend converting old projects if you don't have to. Some users report odd behavior with converted data. Conventional iMovie wisdom recommends finishing a project in the same version you started.

✔ Tips

■ Users of earlier versions of iMovie might wonder where all the media files disappeared to. Formerly stored in separate folders, everything now lives in the project file, which isn't just a normal file—it's a *package*. To view its contents, go to the Finder, Control-click the project file, and choose Show Package Contents from the contextual menu that appears. A new window displays the files and folders within the package (**Figure 6.3**).

■ iMovie 3 introduced a QuickTime movie file in the project folder, which was a DV-format rendition of the movie you were assembling. It was a handy shortcut for adding movies to iDVD without going through the hassle of exporting from iMovie. That movie still exists within the project file's package in iMovie HD 6 (in the Cache folder, called "Timeline Movie. mov"), but you can ignore it from now on. Now you can just drag an iMovie project file into iDVD to add it (see "Creating a New iDVD Project" in Chapter 19).

■ One weirdness that results from opening old iMovie projects (version 4 and earlier) in iMovie HD 6 deals with clips that have been sped up or slowed down using the Clip Speed slider. That control is now gone, replaced by the Fast/Slow/Reverse effect (see Chapter 13). Unfortunately, the speed-adjusted clips still retain their settings, but the only way to set them to normal speed is to try to counteract the speed using the Fast/Slow/Reverse effect. So, for example, if a converted clip was twice as fast in iMovie 4, and you want it to be only a quarter as fast as the original clip, you need to apply Fast/Slow/Reverse to *slow down* the clip by 25 percent. You can also re-import the original footage from tape (see Chapter 7).

iMovie's Interface

In iMovie, everything happens in one big window (**Figure 6.5**). Use the resize control in the lower-right corner to change the window's size, or click the green Zoom button in the upper-left corner to maximize the window.

The interface comprises three main areas: the Monitor, where you view video clips; the Clips pane, where clips are stored; and the Timeline, which toggles between the Clip Viewer and Timeline Viewer, where you assemble your movie.

✔ Tips

■ To help improve performance, try reducing iMovie's window to its minimum size. If the Monitor is smaller, iMovie doesn't need to expend as much processing power drawing video on the screen.

■ If you're fortunate enough to have a large display, such as Apple's giant Cinema HD Display, the Monitor enlarges when you increase the size of iMovie's window. However, the Clips pane doesn't display more columns, which would be a treat.

■ Choose Show Full Video Resolution from the Window menu to view your movie in a pixel–accurate-sized view.

Figure 6.5 iMovie is broken down into three main sections: the Monitor, the Clips pane, and the Timeline, which can switch between the Clip Viewer and the Timeline Viewer (shown here).

Monitor window   *Scrubber Bar*

Camera Mode/   *Playback*
Edit Mode switch   *controls*

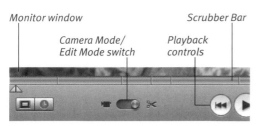

Figure 6.6 The left side of iMovie's Monitor controls.

Playback   *Playhead*   *Volume*
controls   *slider*

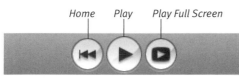

Figure 6.7 The right side of iMovie's Monitor controls.

Home   *Play*   *Play Full Screen*

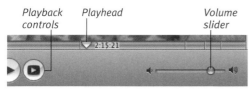

Figure 6.8 Use these playback controls when you're in iMovie's Edit Mode. To rewind or fast-forward through a clip or movie, use the Scrubber Bar.

The Monitor

The Monitor is where you view and edit clips. A few controls, such as the Scrubber Bar, affect how you edit your clips (**Figures 6.6** and **6.7**). The playback controls are context-sensitive, and can play clips (**Figure 6.8**) or control a camcorder (**Figure 6.9**, next page).

Monitor controls

◆ **Monitor window.** View clips and incoming video from a camcorder.

◆ **Camera Mode/Edit Mode switch.** Toggle between these modes to either import or edit video footage. If multiple cameras are connected, click the Camera Mode icon and choose one from the popup menu that appears.

◆ **Volume slider.** Set the playback volume by dragging the knob or clicking a spot on the slider; this doesn't affect clip volume.

◆ **Playhead.** Drag the Playhead to any point within your movie or clip; the numbers beside it indicate the time location within the movie.

◆ **Scrubber Bar.** When viewing an entire movie, the Scrubber Bar includes lines marking clips and transitions. This is also where you can select portions of clips and cut, copy, or crop them (see Chapter 8).

Playback controls (Edit Mode)

◆ **Home.** Click here to move to the start of the movie (or to the beginning of an individual clip if selected in the Clips pane).

◆ **Play.** Click this button to play the video in real time. Click it again to stop playback (or hit the spacebar).

◆ **Play Full Screen.** This button plays the video using the entire screen. Click the mouse or press any key to stop playback and return to the normal window.

Playback controls (Camera Mode)

◆ **Import.** With a camera attached, click this button to begin saving the video to your hard disk. Click it again to stop capturing.

◆ **Rewind/Review.** Click this button to rewind the camcorder's tape. If the tape is playing, click and hold to review (play backwards) the footage quickly. Release the button to resume normal playback.

◆ **Stop.** This button stops the camcorder's tape and ceases playback.

◆ **Play.** Click this button to play the video in real time.

◆ **Pause.** Click this button to pause, but still view, the camera's playback. Click it again to resume.

◆ **Fast Forward.** Click to advance the tape without playing it. As with the Rewind/Review control, if the tape is playing, click and hold to view the footage accelerated, then release the button to resume normal playback.

✔ Tips

■ If playback in Edit Mode seems stuttery, try changing the playback method. Choose Preferences from the iMovie HD menu (or press Command-comma), and click the Playback icon. Choose a quality setting by clicking its radio button (**Figure 6.10**), then close the Preferences window.

■ In Edit Mode, the spacebar activates and deactivates the Play button. In Camera Mode, the spacebar activates the Import button.

■ Use the left and right arrow keys to move the video in one-frame increments when you're in Edit Mode. Hold Shift and use the arrow keys to move 10 frames at a time.

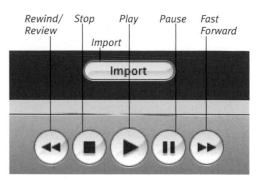

Figure 6.9 With Camera Mode enabled, the buttons control the camera's playback functions.

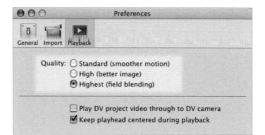

Figure 6.10 Experiment with the Quality settings in iMovie's preferences if your playback is choppy while editing.

Review and Fast Forward

In Edit Mode, there are no buttons for reviewing (rewinding) and fast-forwarding your movie during playback. However, the functionality is there: press [(left bracket) to review, press] (right bracket) to fast-forward. To stop playback, hit the keys again or press the spacebar. (Note that these steps differ from iMovie 3, which required using the Command key. Now, pressing Command and a bracket key navigates bookmarks. See "Using Bookmarks," in Chapter 8.)

These features are always good for a laugh, too, when you've been editing for hours without a break: the audio plays at the same sped-up rate.

iMOVIE'S INTERFACE

Figure 6.11 The Clips pane, in addition to storing clips, serves as the area for controlling other features such as transitions, effects, and titles.

List buttons

Figure 6.12 Click a button at the top of a pane to access lists of media or editing features.

The Clips pane

Think of the Clips pane as a big rack filled with lots of videocassettes, photos, and audio reels (but much better organized); this is where you store your raw footage in preparation for editing (**Figure 6.11**). It's also where you find controls for working with themes, photos, audio, titles, transitions, effects, and chapter markers for iDVD or GarageBand.

Clips pane components

- **Clips pane.** The purpose of the Clips pane is to store your clips, which are arranged in a grid. Use the scroll bar at right to view more clips.

- **Pane buttons.** The Clips pane doubles as the control center for working with themes, photos, audio, titles, transitions, and effects. Click one of the buttons at the bottom to activate a pane. (Each is discussed at length throughout the book.)

- **List buttons.** In iMovie HD 6, the Media and Editing panes include separate lists for functions such as photos, titles, and effects. After you click a pane button, click a list button at the top of the pane to narrow your choices (**Figure 6.12**).

✔ Tip

- You may know the Clips pane by its former clever moniker, the Shelf, if you've used a version of the software prior to iMovie HD 6.

The Timeline

The Clips pane may hold all of your raw video clips, but you don't have a movie until you start moving them to the Timeline, which encompasses the Clip Viewer and Timeline Viewer. The viewers are two different ways of looking at the structure of your movie.

The Clip Viewer displays clips in the order that they play, with large thumbnail previews to help identify them (**Figure 6.13**). The Timeline Viewer arranges the clips in order and also depicts their lengths (**Figure 6.15**, opposite page).

Speaking of length, you can always view the duration of your movie at the bottom of the iMovie window (**Figure 6.14**). With nothing selected, you see the total duration; with one or more clips selected, iMovie displays the amount of time they represent.

The Timeline also includes audio tracks and controls for changing aspects of a clip, which I discuss in the next few chapters.

Clip Viewer components

◆ **Clip Viewer button.** Click the filmstrip icon to display the Clip Viewer, or press Command-E to toggle between viewers.

◆ **Transitions.** When you add a transition to your movie, an icon indicates which clip(s) it's attached to (see Chapter 11).

Clip Viewer button   Clip

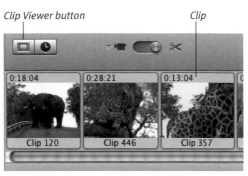

Figure 6.13 Using the Clip Viewer is often easier than the Timeline Viewer when adding clips.

Nothing selected

One clip selected

Multiple clips selected

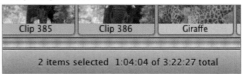

Figure 6.14 Look to the bottom of the main window to view lengths of specific clips and of the total movie.

Timeline Viewer button   *Video clip*   *Audio clip*

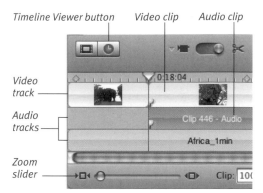

Video track

Audio tracks

Zoom slider

Figure 6.15 The Timeline Viewer offers a better sense of how much time a clip occupies.

Clip-specific sound control

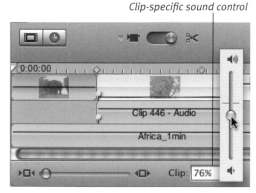

Figure 6.16 The sound control at the bottom only applies to selected clips.

Timeline Viewer components

- **Timeline Viewer button.** Click the clock icon to bring this viewer to the front, or press Command-E.

- **Video track.** The top horizontal bar represents the video track, where clips are displayed according to their lengths. Transitions also appear here, with an icon similar to those found in the Clip Viewer.

- **Audio tracks.** iMovie gives you two separate audio tracks to work with, just below the video track. Audio can be extracted from video clips or imported and edited on these tracks.

- **Zoom slider.** This control determines how much of the Timeline is shown in the viewer: with the slider at the left, the entire movie appears in the Timeline; with the slider button at full right, you may see only a few seconds, depending on your movie's length. Zooming in is helpful when you're editing small clips or transitions.

- **Clip-specific sound controls.** The volume control slider only applies to a selected clip (**Figure 6.16**). See Chapter 10 for more on editing audio.

- **Mute switches.** Uncheck a box to turn off the volume in its associated video or audio track (**Figure 6.17**, next page). This doesn't affect any volume adjustments you've made to particular clips.

Project Trash and free space indicator

- **Project Trash.** When you delete clips, they're sent to the Project Trash; the amount of data in the trash is indicated to the right of the icon (**Figure 6.17**). Clicking the Trash gives you the option to empty it or pull items out (see Chapter 7).

- **Free space indicator.** The numbers indicate the amount of available space on the hard disk where your project is stored. When the text turns yellow, you're getting low; red text means you're critically low on space.

✔ Tip

- iMovie HD no longer features the Clip Speed slider, which used to be below the Timeline Viewer and enabled you to speed up or slow down clips. Instead, that functionality has been moved to the Fast/Slow/Reverse effect in the Effects pane (see Chapter 13).

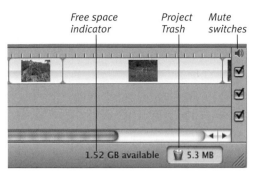

Free space   Project   Mute
indicator   Trash   switches

Figure 6.17 Mute switches turn audio on and off for an entire track. The Project Trash and free space indicator appear in the Clip Viewer as well.

Changing View Preferences

You can tweak some of the ways clips are displayed by setting options in iMovie's preferences (**Figure 6.18**).

- **Automatically resize window to fit project.** This option depends on the project's video format.

- **Only show audio locking when selected.** You can lock audio clips individually, which are then shown with a pin icon (see Chapter 10). This option shows the icon only when the clip is selected.

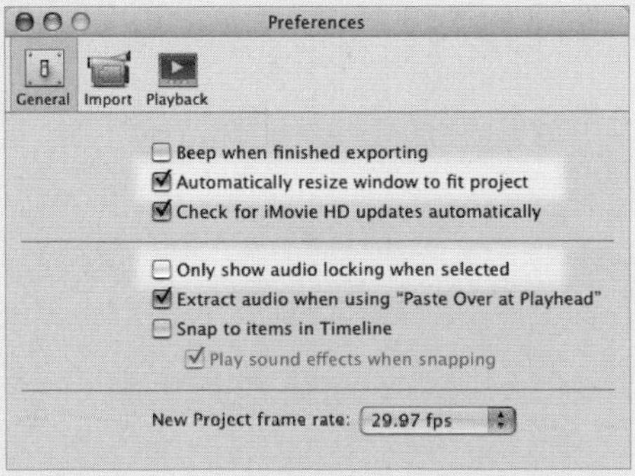

Figure 6.18 A few of iMovie's preferences affect how clips appear in the Clip Viewer and Timeline Viewer.

Monitoring Your Movies

iMovie's Monitor window is invaluable, and the Play Full Screen feature is helpful when you need to get a better feel for how the movie will display. However, consider hooking up an external television or AV monitor so you can see how your movie will really look to your audience (**Figure 6.19**). (If your movies are destined only for display on the Web or via email, you may not want to go to this trouble.)

You'll need your computer, a television or AV monitor with RCA-style input jacks, and your digital camcorder. You'll also need the FireWire cable to hook up your camcorder to your Mac, and the AV cable that came with your camcorder, which allows you to view movies on a TV (it normally has three connectors on one end—yellow, red, and white—and a single connector that plugs into the camera, though some models work with S-video cabling, too).

To hook up an external monitor:

1. Connect the camera to your computer via the FireWire cable.

2. Connect the television to your camera using the AV cable.

3. Switch the television's mode from TV to Video, if necessary.

4. In iMovie, choose Preferences from the iMovie menu.

5. Click the Playback icon, and then click the checkbox labeled Play DV project video through to DV camera.

6. Close the Preferences window. Your movie should now appear on the TV.

✔ Tips

- Monitoring works only with DV projects, not HDV or MPEG-4.

- Plug in the camera's AC adapter while you're working, so you don't drain the battery.

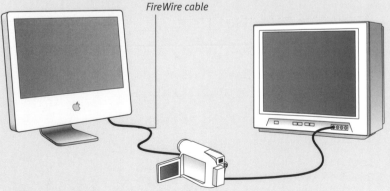

FireWire cable

Figure 6.19 Adding an external television or AV monitor to your iMovie setup lets you see how the video appears on a real video screen.

IMPORTING FOOTAGE

Whatever the source of your video—DV or HDV camcorder, digital still camera with a video recording feature, DVD, an iSight camera, or just movie files on your hard drive—it's easy to bring the footage you shot into iMovie for editing.

For the least amount of hassle, the video should be digital. I realize you can buy inexpensive analog camcorders these days, but since the footage will need to be digitized anyway, you may as well start with digital originals. (If you already own an analog camcorder, don't go scrambling for a credit card to buy a new camera; I talk about importing that video, too.)

Speaking of less hassle, let's start with the easiest method of importing footage: the Magic iMovie feature.

Making a Magic iMovie

The Magic iMovie feature automates the process of importing and building a movie.

To make a Magic iMovie:

1. From iMovie's title screen, click the Make a Magic iMovie button. Or, if you already created a new project, choose Make a Magic iMovie from the File menu.

2. In the Movie title field, type a title that will appear at the beginning (**Figure 7.1**).

3. Mark the first checkbox to automatically rewind the camera's tape.

4. iMovie will import until the camera reaches the tape's end or 10 seconds of blank tape. To instead specify a section of tape to import, mark the second checkbox and enter the number of minutes.

5. If you want iMovie to add transitions between each scene, mark the third checkbox and choose a style from the popup menu.

6. If you want music to play during the movie, mark the fourth checkbox and click the Choose Music button.

   ▲ In the Choose Music dialog, drag songs from your iTunes Library to the column on the right (**Figure 7.2**).

   ▲ Use the slider to define the volume level of the music. If you set it to Music Only, the audio from the video footage is muted. Click OK.

7. If you want to create a DVD of the Magic iMovie, mark the last checkbox.

8. Make sure your camcorder is connected and contains a tape, then click the Create button to begin. iMovie rewinds the tape (if you opted for that step) and begins importing.

Figure 7.1 Set up your movie's title, transitions, and music in the Magic iMovie dialog.

Figure 7.2 Drag songs from your iTunes Library (left) to the column on the right, and set a volume level.

Pretty Prestidigitation

The Magic iMovie feature is geared toward those who want to just shoot and share without editing. If you want to make a slick-looking chronicle of your child's soccer game, this is the easiest route to take.

Magic iMovie can also be helpful as a base to get you started, automating the first part of the editing process.

However, since you bought a book about editing video in iMovie, I think it's safe to ignore Magic iMovie and press on.

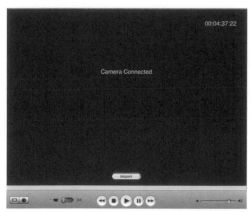

Figure 7.3 Connecting the camera to your Mac via FireWire automatically switches iMovie's Monitor to Camera mode.

Click the Import button...

...to create clips in the Clips pane.

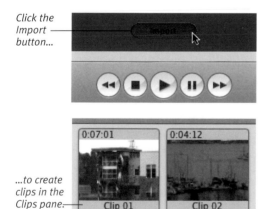

Figure 7.4 iMovie automatically detects when scenes begin and end, and splits them into separate clips.

Importing Clips

Getting video footage into iMovie is a snap: connect your digital camcorder to your Mac via FireWire, and start importing. You don't even need to shut down your Mac to plug in the FireWire cable (as we needed to do way back in the days of SCSI devices). Your only practical limitation is space on your hard drive—make sure you have plenty (see the sidebar on the next page).

To connect via FireWire:

1. Quit iMovie if it's running. Apple recommends quitting iMovie before you plug in or unplug FireWire cables.

2. Plug the FireWire cable into the Mac and the camcorder.

3. Switch the camcorder to VCR or Play mode.

4. Launch iMovie. If you don't have a project file yet, create a new one and name it. The Monitor switches to Camera mode and displays "Camera Connected" (**Figure 7.3**).

To import footage from the camcorder:

1. Use the Monitor's Playback controls to rewind or forward the camcorder's tape to the spot where you want to begin.

2. Click the Import button. The imported footage is stored as clips in the Clips pane (**Figure 7.4**).

3. Click the Import button again to stop.

✔ Tip

- If you're importing from an HDV camcorder, clicking the Import button to stop the capture process may not work as you expect. See "Importing HDV footage" later in this chapter.

Automatic scene detection

By default, iMovie creates a new clip for each scene, which is calculated based on the time stamps stored on the tape. If you prefer, the video can be stored in fewer clips, giving you the option to *manually* control where clips are split. If you want, you can import all your footage as one gigantic clip. However, I've found that leaving iMovie's automatic scene detection turned on saves time later when I'm editing.

To turn off automatic scene detection:

1. Choose Preferences from the iMovie menu to open iMovie's preferences.

2. Click the Import icon.

3. Deselect the option labeled Start a new clip at each scene break.

4. Close the window to exit preferences.

✔ Tips

■ iMovie supports having more than one video source attached to your Mac. Click the Camera Mode button and select a camcorder from the popup menu (**Figure 7.5**).

■ Control-click anywhere in the Monitor to choose a camera as the input source.

■ Are are you you hearing hearing double double? There's a slight lag between the camera and the Mac when importing. Turn the volume all the way down on either the camcorder or in iMovie.

■ If you hear audio problems during import (popping, etc.), enable the Filter audio from camera option in iMovie's Import preferences.

■ If you want to import your video to an external FireWire hard drive, get one with a speed of at least 7,200 RPM.

Figure 7.5 If you have multiple video sources, choose one from the Camera Mode button's popup menu.

The Biggest Hard Drive Isn't Large Enough

When you begin working with digital video, your concept of hard disk space changes forever. For example, one second of DV footage equals 3.6 MB on disk.

Fortunately, hard drives are cheaper every day: a quick search for a 200 GB internal drive turns up prices between $80 and $120 as of this writing (try www.dealmac.com). (To compare, that amount of money bought a 60 GB drive just a few years ago.) Here's one way to estimate how much storage you need, courtesy of Jay Nelson's *Design Tools Monthly* newsletter (www.design-tools.com):

To determine a disk's DV capacity:

1. Divide the disk capacity by 3.6 MB, which is the amount of space required to save one second of digital video.

2. Divide that result by 60 to convert from seconds to minutes.

For example, a 60 GB hard disk can hold 277.77 minutes of digital video (60,000 MB / 3.6 MB = 16,666.67 seconds / 60 = 277.77 minutes).

Figure 7.6 Choose the Movie Timeline radio button to import footage directly to the Timeline.

In addition to importing video from the camcorder's tape, you can grab live footage directly from the camera.

To import live footage from the camera:

1. Connect the camera to your Mac, and ensure that it has no tape inserted.

2. Launch iMovie.

3. Switch the camcorder to Camera or Record mode.

4. Switch iMovie to Camera mode and click the Import button. You don't need to use the camera's Record button.

5. Click the Import button again to stop.

As clips are imported, they're stored in order in the Clips pane with the expectation that you're going to crop and rearrange them when they are put into the movie. But suppose you're importing footage that's already been edited, or is otherwise in the correct order. You can save a few steps by importing the clips directly to the Timeline.

To import to the Timeline instead of the Clips pane:

1. Open iMovie's preferences.

2. Click the Import icon.

3. Click the Movie Timeline radio button (**Figure 7.6**). Close the window.

4. Click the Import button to begin capturing the footage, then click Import again to stop.

✔ Tip

■ When importing directly to the Timeline, either the Clip Viewer or the Timeline Viewer can be active.

RAID Storage

Most likely, buying one or two external hard drives will provide the storage you need. However, if you find yourself doing a lot of iMovie editing, consider buying or assembling a RAID (redundant array of inexpensive disks). By making two or more hard drives work in tandem, you can view their combined storage capacity as one volume, and potentially speed up performance.

A hardware RAID system, such as Apple's Xserve RAID, includes the hard drives in some type of enclosure, and handles all the data exchange among the drives by itself. You can also connect a few drives via FireWire and configure them as a RAID using Apple's Disk Utility, or the $130 SoftRAID (www.softraid.com).

IMPORTING CLIPS

Importing HDV footage

Importing high-definition video works the same as importing DV, with one difference. iMovie transcodes the HDV footage into AIC (Apple Intermediate Codec) for editing, so importing does not happen in real time on many machines. This causes a lag between what you see on the camera's screen and in iMovie—the incoming video is stored in a buffer and then transcoded. The import speed is indicated below iMovie's Monitor (**Figure 7.7**).

For this reason, don't use iMovie's playback controls to stop importing unless you're capturing in real time—you won't get the footage you expect. Instead, use the camera's LCD screen as a guide and press the camera's Stop button when you reach the end of the footage you want to capture. iMovie then transcodes the rest of the footage in its buffer (**Figure 7.8**).

✔ Tips

■ When the HDV camcorder is in Record mode (i.e., the camera's picture is being fed directly to iMovie), you may still experience a lag. iMovie displays "Previewing HD at [X] speed" below iMovie's Monitor.

■ The transcoding process applies when you're exporting video back to the tape; in fact, it takes even longer for the Mac to go from the Apple Intermediate Codec to MPEG-2 (see Chapter 15).

Figure 7.7 iMovie indicates the speed at which the video is being captured (MacBook Pro shown here).

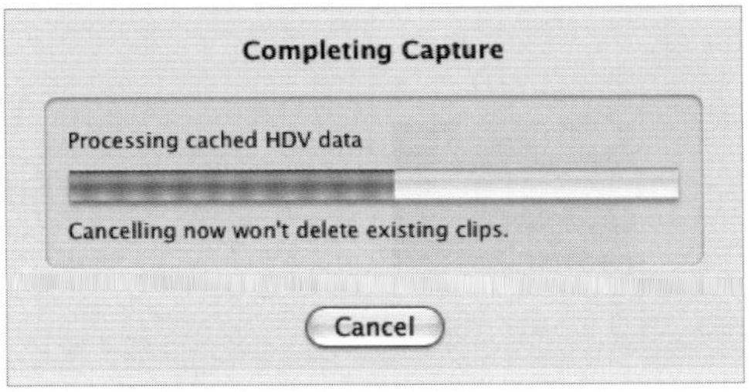

Completing Capture

Processing cached HDV data

Cancelling now won't delete existing clips.

(Cancel)

Figure 7.8 After you stop importing from an HDV camcorder, iMovie needs to finish transcoding the footage that's still in the program's buffer.

How Much Disk Space for HDV?

A couple pages ago, I mentioned that DV footage takes up 3.6 MB of hard disk space for every second of video. So how does HDV compare?

HDV video is compressed in-camera using MPEG-2 compression, so the final size on disk depends on how much compression was applied to the footage, which itself depends on the type of footage you shot.

Members of Apple's iMovie HD discussion board did some testing and came up with a figure: between 38 GB and 50 GB of disk space for one hour of HDV video (discussions.info.apple.com/).

Figure 7.9 If you own an Apple iSight camera, or your Mac features a built-in iSight, you can record directly into iMovie.

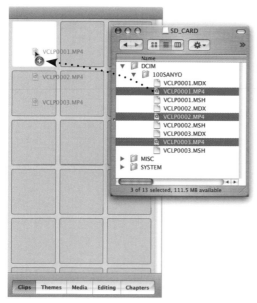

Figure 7.10 Drag MPEG-4 movie files from the memory card mounted on your Desktop to iMovie's Clips pane.

Backing Up Video

Just as it's important to back up your computer's data (you *do* have a backup system in place, right?), you want a video backup, too. Due to the sheer amount of data, I recommend purchasing external hard drives for keeping copies of your iMovie project files. If that's too pricey, remember that the footage you shot on tape is also a backup, though it doesn't save the work you put into editing it.

Importing from an iSight

Apple's iSight video camera was designed for videoconferencing using iChat, but you can record directly to iMovie, too.

To import iSight footage:

1. Connect an iSight to your Mac and launch iMovie.

2. Switch to Camera mode; if more than one camera is attached, choose iSight from the Camera Mode popup menu.

3. Click the Record With iSight button to begin recording (**Figure 7.9**). Click the button again when you want to stop.

Importing MPEG-4 footage

The new batch of MPEG-4 camcorders store footage on memory cards, not tape. When you connect one to your Mac (via USB), it shows up on the desktop as a mounted disk. In this case, you need to import the clips into iMovie by dragging them.

To import MPEG-4 footage:

1. Connect the camera to your Mac, or use a USB memory card reader to mount the card on your Desktop.

2. Locate the movie files on the card; you may have to navigate down a few folders in the hierarchy (**Figure 7.10**).

3. Drag the movie files to the Clips pane or Timeline to add them to your project.

✔ Tip

■ When you mount a memory card, don't be surprised if iPhoto automatically launches: the Mac thinks you're importing photos. To change this behavior, open the Image Capture progam (in your Applications folder), go to its preferences, and change the option labeled "When a camera is connected, open [application]."

Importing Movies from iPhoto

Movies you shoot using a digital still camera can be imported into iPhoto, making it the best route to bring such videos into iMovie.

To import movies from iPhoto:

1. Click the Media button and then the Photos button.

2. Locate a video file in the list (**Figure 7.11**).

3. Drag the file to the Timeline.

Importing Movies from Other iMovie Projects

In iMovie HD 6, you can open more than one project at a time, enabling you to share clips (see "Managing Clips," later in this chapter).

To import movies from other iMovie projects:

1. Open more than one iMovie project file.

2. Drag one or more clips from one project to the Clips pane or Timeline of the other project (**Figure 7.12**).

Or

1. Select a clip in one project and choose Copy from the Edit menu (or press Command-C).

2. Switch to the other project and choose Paste from the Edit menu (or press Command-V).

✔ Tips

- You can import movies from iTunes, too, via the Audio list in the Media pane.

- See Chapter 9 for more information on importing pictures from iPhoto, and Chapter 10 for more on adding music.

- If you're importing an MPEG video and it has no sound, convert it using the free MPEG Streamclip (www.squared5.com).

Figure 7.11 Movies you shoot using a digital still camera are stored in iPhoto. In this example, I set up a smart album in iPhoto to list movie files.

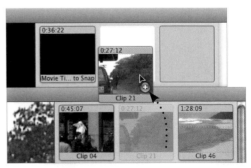

Figure 7.12 Drag clips from one iMovie project to another to easily share them.

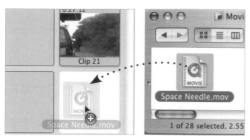

Figure 7.13 Add a QuickTime-compatible movie to your project by dragging it to the iMovie window.

Figure 7.14 To compare image resolution, I exported some DV footage (top) as a QuickTime file, then imported the file back into iMovie (bottom).

Importing Other Movies

iMovie is built on QuickTime, Apple's technology for playing and creating all sorts of digital audio and video. You can drag and drop other movie files that QuickTime reads into the Clips pane or the Timeline.

To import a movie file into iMovie:

◆ Drag a QuickTime-compatible movie file from the Finder to iMovie's window (**Figure 7.13**).

Or

1. In iMovie, choose Import from the File menu, or press Command-Shift-I.

2. Locate the file in the Import dialog, then click the Open button. The clip appears in the Clips pane.

✔ Tips

■ See www.apple.com/quicktime/ for a list of movie formats QuickTime can read.

■ Most movie files are small in size and compressed, which is great for viewing on the Web but not so good-looking compared to a DV clip taken from a video camcorder (**Figure 7.14**).

■ As you'll learn in the next chapter, nonlinear editing means you don't have to stick to the chronology of the camcorder's tape. What if you want to insert the great bear sighting you filmed days earlier? Simply locate the media file on your hard disk that contains the footage you want (see "Managing Clips," later in this chapter, for more information), and drag it into iMovie. You can also export one or more clips out of one project as DV-formatted files, then import them into another project (see "Combining Movie Segments" in Chapter 16).

IMPORTING CLIPS

Mixing Video Formats

One of iMovie HD's signature features is its capability to handle different video formats, but what's especially cool is that you can mix and match different formats within the same project. However, keep a few things in mind.

Importing from the camcorder:

◆ In an HDV project, you can't import footage from a DV camera (and vice-versa). The Camera Mode popup menu reads "[Camera] Incompatible With Project".

◆ If you import DV Widescreen footage into a DV project, the clips are letterboxed (black bars above and below the image, **Figure 7.15**).

◆ Similarly, in a DV Widescreen project, standard DV clips are pillarboxed (black bars to the left and right of the image, **Figure 7.16**).

◆ You can import iSight footage into a project of any format.

Importing individual clips:

◆ When importing clips by dragging them in from the Finder or using the Import dialog, iMovie converts them to the project's format (for example, an HDV 1080i clip brought into a DV project is sampled down to 720 x 480 pixels and letterboxed).

✔ Tip

■ To prevent iMovie from adding black bars to your footage, open the program's preferences, click the Import icon, and turn off Automatic DV Pillarboxing & Letterboxing (**Figure 7.17**).

Figure 7.15 This widescreen footage was imported into a standard DV project and letterboxed.

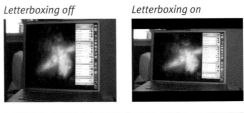

Figure 7.16 This standard DV footage was pillarboxed after being imported into a DV Widescreen project.

Letterboxing off   *Letterboxing on*

Figure 7.17 Turning off Automatic DV Pillarboxing & Letterboxing let me import widescreen footage into a standard-definition project without conversion.

Figure 7.18 The quality of VHS tapes deteriorates dramatically, as evidenced by this 10-year-old clip. (The damage is more dramatic full-size; see it at www.jeffcarlson.com/imovievqs/vhs.html.)

Importing Old VHS Tapes Using a DV Camcorder

If you own a digital camcorder, but still have some older VHS (or other format) tapes, you can bring that footage into iMovie to edit or even just store digitally. Connect your VCR to your camcorder and record the contents of the VHS tape to the DV tape. Then you can import your footage into iMovie normally. (Or, use an analog-to-digital converter between the VCR and your Mac.)

Another option is to use a recent Sony DV camcorder, which performs an in-camera analog-to-digital conversion.

Analog tape doesn't last forever—save your wedding/graduation/school play on disk. As a gift to my wife on our tenth wedding anniversary, I digitized the video from the ceremony (shot by my uncle on VHS), cut together the highlights, and burned it to a DVD. I'm glad I did—the image and sound quality had severely deteriorated (**Figure 7.18**).

Importing Footage from an Analog Camcorder

The process of importing footage from an analog camcorder in iMovie is much the same as when importing from a digital camcorder. However, you need a go-between device that converts the camcorder's analog signal to digital information on the Mac. Products from companies such as Canopus (www.canopus.com) or ADS Technologies (www.adstech.com) feature a FireWire port for connecting to your computer and RCA-style inputs for connecting to your camera; some devices also include an S-Video port.

To import from a non-DV camcorder:

1. Connect the conversion device to the Mac via FireWire, and to the camera using RCA or S-Video cabling.

2. Switch the camcorder to VCR or Play mode.

3. Push the camcorder's Play button.

4. Click the Import button in iMovie.

5. When finished, click Import again to stop capturing video, and press the Stop button on the camcorder.

✔ Tip

■ Since you're importing converted analog data, iMovie doesn't automatically split clips according to scenes. You'll have to use iMovie's editing tools to trim and organize the clips, or manually start and stop importing according to scenes.

How iMovie Manages Clips

If you're casually flipping through this chapter, I'll understand if you skip everything else—*except this section*. It's important to understand how iMovie handles clips as you're working with them, especially when you begin deleting unused clips.

Clips can be made up of either video footage or imported still pictures. Each clip includes a thumbnail image of the clip's first frame, a timecode noting the clip's duration, and a title that you can edit (**Figure 7.19**).

When you import footage, iMovie creates a new clip for each scene, which also adds a new clip file to your hard disk. However, even if you rename, split, or otherwise edit a clip in iMovie, *the media file stays the same* (**Figure 7.20**). iMovie actually records only the *changes* made to the clip, and doesn't alter the clip's original media file.

This clip management style comes in handy in several ways as you use iMovie.

Advantages of iMovie's method of managing clips

◆ **Undo.** iMovie offers virtually unlimited levels of Undo, enabling you to recombine split clips, move clips back to their original locations, and other actions.

◆ **Deleting clips.** When you split a clip and throw away one of the portions, that discarded section can either be retrieved from the trash or pulled from the piece you kept (see "Direct Trimming" in Chapter 8).

◆ **Reverting clips.** If you're not happy with your edits, or something has gone horribly wrong, you can always restore the clip to its original state, because the original data is always on file. See the next chapter to learn how to restore clips.

Timecode   Title   Thumbnail   Split clip

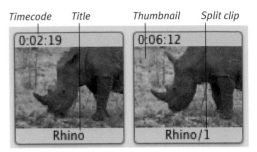

Figure 7.19 Each clip contains a thumbnail image of the first frame in the video. If a clip has been split, iMovie adds a number to indicate it's a section from the original.

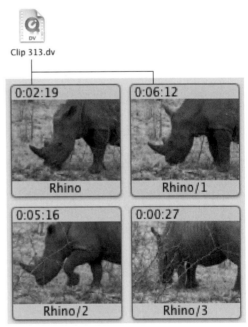

Figure 7.20 The original clip, "Clip 313.dv," was renamed "Rhino" and split into four separate clips, but the Clip 313.dv source file located in the project's package on the hard disk is not renamed or split.

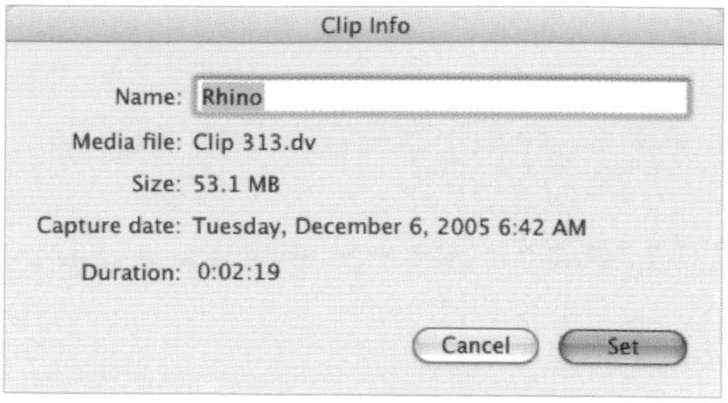

Clip Info

Name: Rhino

Media file: Clip 313.dv

Size: 53.1 MB

Capture date: Tuesday, December 6, 2005 6:42 AM

Duration: 0:02:19

Cancel | Set

Figure 7.21 Double-clicking a clip displays the Clip Info dialog, which reveals the media file's name.

Figure 7.22 Click and drag your pointer in the Clips pane's background area to select multiple clips.

Managing Clips

Clips are named sequentially during import (such as "Clip 01"), but you can rename them with more meaningful titles. If you split a clip (explained in the next chapter), iMovie adds a slash and a number to indicate it's part of the original, such as "Rhino/1".

To rename a clip:

1. Click the clip's title and then select the text. Or, you can double-click the clip or press Command-I to display the Clip Info dialog (**Figure 7.21**).

2. Type a new name and press Return or click Set.

The Clips pane features slots for storing clips, but it doesn't matter in what order they appear. You'll find yourself moving them frequently as you assemble your movie.

To reorder clips in the Clips pane:

1. Click the clip(s) you wish to move. To grab a range of clips, Shift-click multiple clips or click and drag a box around them with the pointer (**Figure 7.22**).

2. Click and drag the clip(s) to a new location in the Clips pane.

✔ Tips

- Renaming a clip only changes its name in iMovie. The original media file is still named "Clip 313.dv" (or similar). Do not rename the media file on disk or iMovie will lose track of it.

- Since you can drag clips anywhere in the Clips pane, use this capability to visually group scenes or related materials before you add them to your movie.

- Select several clips and look beneath the Timeline to see how much time they occupy.

MANAGING CLIPS

Working with the Trash

One of the few elements of iMovie that used to vex me was the Trash. You could easily delete clips, but there was no way to open the Trash and pull out a deleted clip. Finally, iMovie HD changes that behavior.

To delete a clip:

1. Select a clip.

2. Press the Delete key, or click and drag the clip to the Trash icon (**Figure 7.23**).

So far, so simple. Remember that iMovie isn't actually deleting any file from your hard disk, only keeping track of which portions of clips have been sent to the Trash (**Figure 7.24**).

To retrieve a clip from the Trash:

1. Click the Trash icon to open the iMovie Trash window (**Figure 7.25**).

2. Drag a clip from the window to the Clips pane or the Timeline. You can preview a clip by selecting it and playing the thumbnail movie in the upper-right corner.

3. Close the iMovie Trash window.

✔ Tip

- Levels of Undo don't transfer between your editing sessions. When you quit iMovie then launch it again later, your last actions are forgotten.

Figure 7.23 To delete a clip, drag it to the Trash; or, simply select the clip and press the Delete key.

Figure 7.24 As clips are added, the Trash indicates how much footage is marked for deletion.

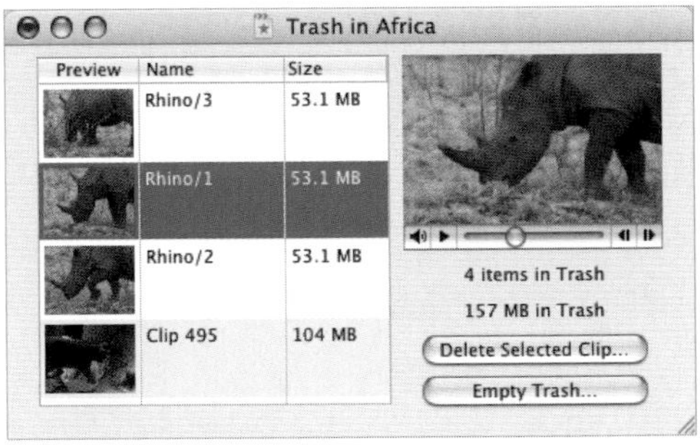

Figure 7.25 Preview clips in the Trash by playing them in the upper-right corner.

Figure 7.26 I usually think reminder dialogs are annoying, but this is one I always pay attention to.

iMovie HD Does Not Rewrite Media Files

Unlike older versions of iMovie, emptying the Trash in iMovie HD does not rewrite the media files to account for portions that have been deleted. So, if you deleted "Rhino/2" (a split portion of the original "Rhino" clip) and you empty the Trash, the entire "Rhino" clip is still available to you as long as one portion is still in the Clips pane or the Timeline.

However, if you delete an entire clip and empty the Trash, that clip is gone for good. You'd need to re-import it to get the footage back.

This also means that iMovie HD projects tend to take up more disk space, because the full clip data remains in the project's package on disk.

Emptying the Trash

If you know (if you're *certain*) you're not going to need any of the deleted clips later, you can empty the Trash or delete selected clips in the iMovie Trash window. (See the sidebar below to learn just what gets deleted from your hard disk.)

To empty the Trash:

1. Choose Empty Trash from the File menu, or click the Trash icon and click the Empty Trash button. To delete just some of the clips in the Trash, select them in the list and click Delete Selected Clips.

2. iMovie displays a warning (**Figure 7.26**). Click Empty Trash and Save Project, or click Cancel to leave its contents untouched.

✔ Tips

- Don't forget that even if you empty the Trash, you still have a backup of your clips: the original footage stored on your camcorder's tape.

- When you use Direct Trimming to edit a clip in the Timeline, the Trash grows according to the amount of footage you've trimmed. However, that footage can be "pulled out of the Trash," as it were, by exposing it using the Direct Trimming editing method. (If you have no idea what I'm talking about—since I haven't covered it yet—see Chapter 8 for an explanation of Direct Trimming. Sorry to jump ahead, but you'll soon see how cool this tip is.)

- Rather than risk deleting footage accidentally, I make a point of never emptying the Trash until a project is completely finished—and maybe not even then.

WORKING WITH THE TRASH

Extracting Footage from a DVD

So you burned a movie to DVD last year and want to snag some of that footage without trying to find the original MiniDV tape.

Cinematize (www.miraizon.com), and DropDV (www.dropdv.com) can each extract the MPEG-2 video files stored on DVD discs. You can then import the footage into iMovie. DropDV is the more straightforward option (it converts everything, whereas Cinematize offers more options for choosing which footage to grab), so I'll use that as the example program here.

To extract video from a DVD:

1. Insert a DVD disc into your Mac. If the DVD Player application launches, quit it.

2. Open the DVD's volume on the Desktop and locate the folder called VIDEO_TS.

3. Open the VIDEO_TS folder and locate the MPEG video files, which end in the suffix .VOB (**Figure 7.27**).

4. Drag the .VOB file onto DropDV. Depending on the movie's length, the conversion process could take a while (**Figure 7.28**).

5. Drag the .DV file that was created to your iMovie project to add it.

✔ Tips

■ Keep in mind that video you pull from a DVD is compressed, and will therefore be of less quality than the original. But sometimes that's better than not having any footage at all.

■ Be good, use copyrighted video footage legally, and only extract video from discs you own or have the rights to use. You know the drill.

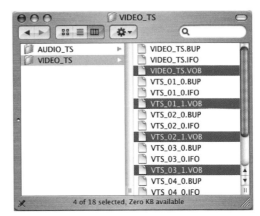

Figure 7.27 Video and audio on a DVD are stored in the VIDEO_TS folder as .VOB files.

Figure 7.28 DropDV converts MPEG-2 formatted video files to DV files in a minimal interface.

Copy-protected DVDs

Some DVD extraction utilities won't work with commercial DVDs that have copy protection applied, but there's a workaround. Download the free utility HandBrake (handbrake.m0k.org) to pull even "secure" footage off most discs.

You can then use DropDV or Cinematize to convert the footage from MPEG-2 to DV format. Obviously, I'm not advocating movie piracy here. But there are legitimate occasions when you might want to use a section of a movie (in a multimedia school report, for example), or copy a movie that you own to your laptop's hard drive to watch later without toting along a sleeve of discs when you travel.

8

Editing Video

The first movies were pure documentaries. Armed with new technology, camera operators shot what they saw: trains leaving the station, people at work, the movement of animals. Motion pictures didn't need to tell a story because the story was in the reproduction. The first movie created by brothers Louis and Auguste Lumière was the action spectacular *Workers Leaving the Lumière Factory*, depicting exactly that.

However, filmmakers soon realized that their "flickers" didn't need to be just linear slices of life. They could shoot movies in any order and assemble them to tell a story, or even combine totally unrelated scenes for dramatic effect. Lev Kuleshov, an early Russian filmmaker, filmed a closeup of an actor wearing a neutral expression. He then intercut a scene of an empty bowl, prompting audiences to praise the actor's subtle portrayal of hunger. Kuleshov took the same neutral footage and intercut scenes of a dead woman in a coffin, then a girl playing with a doll, and in each case audiences were amazed to see the actor's grief or joy. Editing became a vehicle for expressing emotions or ideas that weren't necessarily present during filming.

Today, iMovie and non-linear editing give you the capability to use the visual language of film to tell stories, whether fiction or simply a day at the park. The fun begins here!

Chapter 8

Timecode

In Chapter 2, I explained how timecode works as it applies to a camcorder. Although it operates the same in iMovie, you're going to run into slightly different versions of it in various places while editing.

Timecode in iMovie

◆ **At the Playhead.** The Playhead's time-code always shows the time relative to the entire movie. So, for example, positioning the Playhead two seconds into a clip that appears in the middle of your movie displays something like "0:08:04" instead of "0:02:00" (**Figure 8.1**). The only exception is when you select a clip in the Clips pane, which isn't yet part of your movie.

◆ **Beneath the Timeline.** In addition to showing timecode of individual clips, the movie's total length appears beneath the Timeline. The Thumbnail Playhead, a red inverted T, indicates where the Playhead appears.

◆ **In the Timeline Viewer.** Although the Playhead in the Scrubber Bar shows a timecode, you often need to refer to the Timeline Viewer (and its Playhead) when editing (**Figure 8.2**).

✔ Tips

■ When you select multiple clips in the Timeline or Clips pane, their combined duration appears below the Timeline.

■ Need to quickly figure out the total length of your movie if you add a 3:43:19 clip to it? Plug it into the free Hollywood Calculator utility (www.macupdate.com/info.php/id/17042). Timecode math has never been easier.

■ See Chapter 2's sidebar, "iMovie Time-code versus Real-World Timecode," for a timecode refresher.

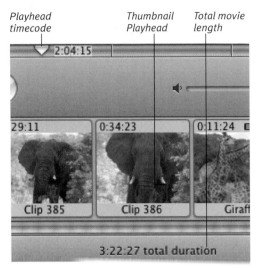

Figure 8.1 The Playhead timecode refers to time location within the context of the movie, even if only a single clip is selected.

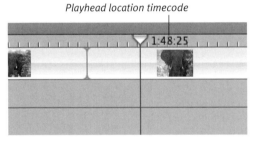

Figure 8.2 The Playhead in the Timeline Viewer includes its own timecode indicator, which is based on the movie's total time.

Figure 8.3 Drag clips from the Clips pane to the Clip Viewer (shown) or Timeline Viewer to add them.

Adding Clips to the Movie

Even with lots of clips in the Clips pane, your movie doesn't exist until you begin building it in the Clip Viewer or the Timeline Viewer.

To add clips to the movie:

1. Select one or more clips in the Clips pane.

2. Drag the clip(s) to the Timeline Viewer or the Clip Viewer (**Figure 8.3**).

✔ Tip

■ If you don't hear any audio as you play clips in the Monitor, go to iMovie's preferences and make sure the option Play DV project video through to DV camera is disabled.

Working through the Video Editing Backlog

One of the most common laments among home videographers is the backlog of footage that piles up, unedited. It's easy to shoot hours of video of your kids or vacation, but editing it into movies takes even more hours. I know people who have so many filled MiniDV tapes that they end up not editing any of it because the task is so huge.

The trick is to break the editing down into smaller components, so that it's not such an intimidating endeavor. Instead of facing an entire video that needs to be finished, approach the process in steps. You can tackle a step each weekend, for example. Here's one suggested approach.

1. In the Clips pane, delete any clips that you know you won't ever use, such as the times when you didn't know the camera was on (yep, everyone does it). Don't try to edit out portions of clips; this step is just to remove the obvious deadwood.

2. Assemble a rough cut by dragging clips from the Clips pane to the Timeline in the approximate order you want them to appear in the movie.

3. Start culling the obviously useless footage from your clips using the techniques described in this chapter.

4. Tighten your movie by trimming clips, paying attention to how it's paced. Start adding music and other additional audio.

5. With a tight edit in place, start applying transitions, titles, and effects.

6. Wrap up any final trimming and polishing.

See, it's not that intimidating after all!

Adding iMovie Themes

iMovie HD 6 introduces themes, pre-made sequences of motion graphics that you can customize with your own video, photos, and text. Like the menu themes in iDVD, iMovie themes can give your movie a bit of snazz and professional feel (and in an amazing coincidence, the themes in iMovie match up with new themes in iDVD 6). Each theme contains *drop zones* where you can add your content and personalize the theme.

To choose a theme:

1. Click the Themes button to display the Themes pane (**Figure 8.4**).

2. Choose a theme from the popup menu at the top of the Themes pane (**Figure 8.5**).

3. Click a theme element from the list. A preview appears in the Monitor. Using the Preview controls, you can (**Figure 8.6**):

   ▲ Click the Play button to start or stop playback of the preview.

   ▲ Click the Loop button to start or stop continuous playback.

   ▲ Drag the Preview playhead in the preview's scrubber bar.

   ▲ Click the Hide Preview button (marked X) to cancel the theme.

   ▲ Click the Apply button (marked with a checkbox) to apply the theme, which adds it to the Timeline.

To add content to a theme:

1. Click the Show Drop Zones button if the Drop Zones palette isn't already visible.

2. Drag content to the slots in the floating Drop Zones palette (**Figure 8.7**): switch to the Clips pane or Media pane while the Drop Zones palette is still visible and drag videos or photos to it.

3. Type text into the title field(s).

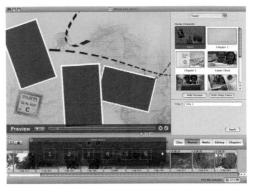

Figure 8.4 When you view the Themes pane, a preview plays within the Monitor, and the Drop Zones palette appears.

Figure 8.5 Choose a motion graphics theme and a theme element to get started.

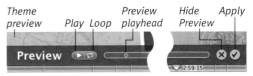

Theme preview   Play Loop   Preview playhead   Hide Preview   Apply

Figure 8.6 Use the Preview controls to see how the rendered theme will appear.

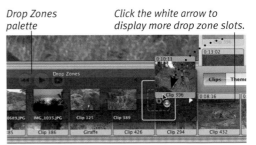

Drop Zones palette   Click the white arrow to display more drop zone slots.

Figure 8.7 Drag clips or photos from the Clips pane or Media pane to the Drop Zones palette.

Figure 8.8 When the theme is ready to go, drag it to the Timeline or click one of the Apply buttons.

Figure 8.9 If you leave a drop zone empty, it appears gray when the theme is rendered.

Theme Glossary

If you're not in the broadcast industry, the theme terms might be confusing.

- **Open:** An extended opening sequence.

- **Chapter:** The beginning of a section, usually with stylized titling to match the theme.

- **Bumper:** A transition between two scenes that's more interesting than a simple iMovie transition.

- **Lower Third:** A graphic element that occupies the bottom portion of the screen.

- **Credits:** A list of people who worked on the movie (or whatever text you want, really).

To delete media from a drop zone:

- With the Drop Zones palette visible, click a slot and press the Delete key.

- Drag an item out of the Drop Zone palette; it disappears in a poof of smoke.

To add the theme to the movie:

- Drag the theme element from the Themes pane to the Timeline (**Figure 8.8**). iMovie renders the theme as a single video file.

- Click the Apply button in the Themes pane or the Apply button in the Preview controls. The rendered theme appears as the last clip in the Timeline.

✔ Tips

- When you add a clip to a drop zone, iMovie uses a copy, not the original clip.

- Once applied, a theme element turns into an ordinary video clip, which can be edited like any other. For example, you can cut down the Open element of the Reflection themes to show only the first appearance of the drop zones.

- However, because a theme becomes a video clip, you can't go back and change the contents of your drop zones—you'll need to re-create the theme element.

- If the theme titles aren't to your liking, leave the fields blank and apply your own iMovie titles (see Chapter 12).

- To make the floating Drop Zones palette go away, click the Hide Drop Zones button in the Themes pane or the close button in the upper-left corner of the palette.

- Any drop zones you leave empty appear blank and gray in the finished theme, so be sure to load 'em up (**Figure 8.9**).

ADDING iMOVIE THEMES

Ordering Clips

The movie's order progresses from left to right in the Timeline, so use the Clip Viewer or the Timeline Viewer to drag and drop clips in the order you wish them to appear; iMovie politely moves existing clips aside to indicate where you can drop your clip (**Figure 8.10**).

✔ Tips

■ You can rearrange clips in the Timeline Viewer (**Figure 8.11**). If you do, however, make sure you drag the clip above the video track to avoid creating a gap (see "Creating Blank Clips," later in this chapter, for more on working with gaps).

■ It's easier to assemble your movie by dragging clips to the Clip Viewer where each clip icon is the same size. The Timeline Viewer displays clips in different sizes based on their lengths (**Figure 8.12**).

■ If you need to determine when a clip was originally filmed, select it and choose Show Info from the File menu (or press Command-I). iMovie notes the date and time the clip was recorded.

■ As editor, you have power over time. Clips can appear in any order, no matter when the events happened chronologically. (Most studio movies are rarely—if ever—shot in chronological order.)

■ With a clip selected in the Timeline, choose Select Similar Clips from the Edit menu (or press Command-Option-A) to select other clips with similar properties. For example, this is an easy way to select all still photo clips in your movie.

Drag a clip in the Timeline...

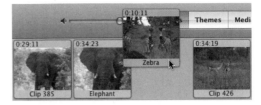

...and drop it in a new location.

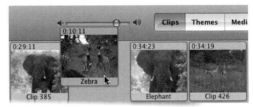

Figure 8.10 When adding clips to the Timeline, the clips in the movie (see "Elephant" above) scoot aside to indicate where you're about to drop the new clip.

Figure 8.11 Move clips in the Timeline Viewer, not just the Clip Viewer.

Clip Viewer

Timeline Viewer

Figure 8.12 The two views shown here are of the same clip. The Timeline Viewer displays an approximation of the clip's length.

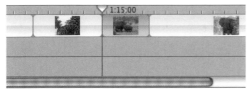

Figure 8.13 The Scroll to Playhead command positions the Playhead in the center of the Timeline, depending on the current zoom setting. Even if it's not centered, it becomes visible (which is more important).

Figure 8.14 Scroll to Selection makes one or more selected clips visible in the Timeline.

Figure 8.15 When you choose Zoom to Selection, the clip selected in Figure 8.14 fills most of the Timeline.

Navigating the Timeline

The Timeline features a cool transition effect that occurs when you switch between the Clip Viewer and Timeline Viewer. But that can also be a problem: it's easy to lose the Playhead when scrolling or zooming the Timeline.

Scrolling and zooming

You can scroll to the Playhead or to a selected clip, or zoom to a selected clip so that it fills the Timeline.

To switch between Viewers:

◆ Choose Switch to [Clip or Timeline] Viewer from the View menu, or press Command-E.

To scroll to the Playhead:

◆ Choose Scroll to Playhead from the View menu, or press Command-Option-P (**Figure 8.13**). The Playhead becomes visible. This command works in both the Clip Viewer and the Timeline Viewer.

To scroll to selected clips:

1. Select one or more clips in either the Clip Viewer or the Timeline Viewer.

2. Choose Scroll to Selection from the View menu, or press Command-Option-S (**Figure 8.14**).

To zoom to selected clips:

1. Select one or more clips in either the Clip Viewer or the Timeline Viewer.

2. Choose Zoom to Selection from the View menu, or press Command-Option-Z (**Figure 8.15**). If the Clip Viewer is active, the Timeline switches to the Timeline Viewer (you can't zoom while in the Clip Viewer).

Timeline snapping

With Timeline snapping enabled, the Playhead sticks to an edit point like a magnet. The advantage is that you can position the Playhead at the exact frame where an edit begins. Snapping also applies to bookmarks (see the opposite page) and iDVD chapter markers (see Chapter 18).

To enable Timeline snapping:

1. Open iMovie's preferences.

2. Mark the checkbox labeled Snap to items in Timeline (**Figure 8.16**). Also mark the Play sound effects when snapping checkbox if you want to hear audible feedback when snapping occurs.

To snap to an edit point:

◆ With Timeline snapping enabled, move the Playhead to an edit point in the Timeline Viewer (**Figure 8.17**). Pop!

✔ Tips

■ Forget the snapping option in Preferences: hold down Shift as you drag to enable snapping temporarily. (Use the preference option to turn the sound on and off, though, even if the feature is disabled in the preferences.)

■ Select a series of clips and click the Play button (or press the Spacebar) to play back only that selection.

■ You can zoom in on a selection, but what about zooming out again? To see your entire movie in the Timeline Viewer without manually adjusting the Zoom slider, press Command-A to select all the clips in your movie, then press Command-Option-Z to zoom to selection.

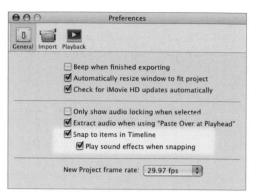

Figure 8.16 Turn on Timeline snapping in iMovie's preferences, and optionally enable the snap sounds.

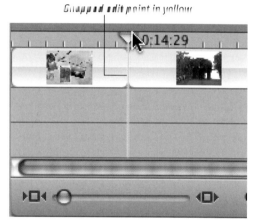

Figure 8.17 With snapping enabled, the Playhead sticks to an edit point when you move near it. The snap point turns yellow.

Bookmark

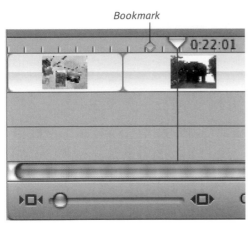

0:22:01

Figure 8.18 Create bookmarks in the Timeline to mark places that are easy to return to later.

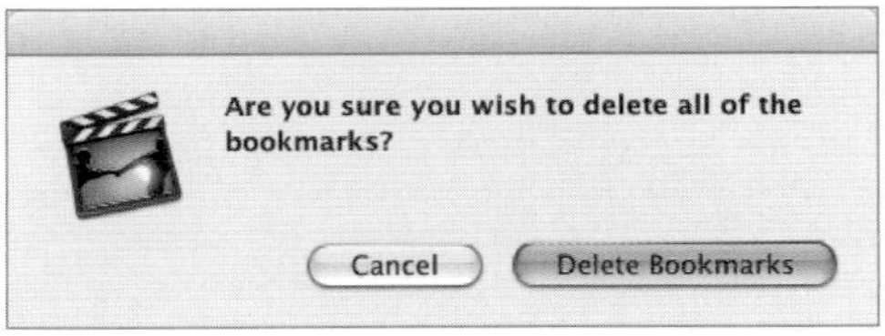

Are you sure you wish to delete all of the bookmarks?

Cancel   Delete Bookmarks

Figure 8.19 This confirmation dialog appears when you choose to delete all bookmarks.

Using Bookmarks

When editing long movies, it's sometimes difficult to locate a particular scene without scrubbing through the movie in the Monitor. iMovie's bookmarks let you set placeholders that are easy to locate. Bookmarks don't appear in your final movie in any way—they exist purely for your organizational pleasure.

To set a bookmark:

1. Position the Playhead where you'd like a bookmark to appear.

2. Choose Add Bookmark from the Markers menu, or press Command-B. A green diamond appears above the Timeline Viewer at that location (**Figure 8.18**).

To delete a bookmark:

1. Position the Playhead at a bookmark.

2. Choose Delete Bookmark from the Markers menu (Option–Command-B).

To delete all bookmarks:

◆ Choose Delete All Bookmarks from the Markers menu. In the confirmation dialog that appears, click the Delete Bookmarks button (**Figure 8.19**).

To jump to bookmarks:

◆ Choose Previous Bookmark or Next Bookmark from the Markers menu. I find it easier to press Command-[(left bracket) or Command-] (right bracket) to go to the previous or next bookmark, respectively.

Editing Clips

Remember in Chapter 2 when I advised you to shoot plenty of footage? Take a moment to look back on those lingering, leisurely days, because in this chapter you're going to chop your film into the smallest pieces you can, and still keep it comprehensible. Part of your job as editor is to arrange the many pieces into a unified whole, but you also want to keep your audience awake.

Direct Trimming

Direct Trimming lets you edit a clip directly in the Timeline in such a way that frames you remove are still available, not made inaccessible in the Trash (see the sidebar on the next page).

Think of Direct Trimming as working with a page of rolled-up blueprints. If you want to view just one portion of the plans, you roll the edges in to hide the rest of the design. In an iMovie video or audio clip, you can hide the frames you choose not to use in your movie. If you need those frames later, you can simply unroll the edges of the clip to display the footage. Direct Trimming works only in the Timeline Viewer, though you'll discover that this style of editing affects cuts made in the Monitor as well.

To edit a clip using Direct Trimming:

1. Switch to the Timeline Viewer, if it's not already active.

2. Position your mouse pointer at the left or right edge of a clip. Rounded corners indicate the end of the clip's available media; straight corners indicate that more footage is available (**Figure 8.20**). The normal cursor icon becomes a horizontal arrow indicating the direction(s) that you can edit.

Straight corner indicates more footage available. *Rounded corner indicates end of clip media.*

Figure 8.20 Direct Trimming allows you to hide frames that you don't want to use, rather than deleting them outright.

Place the mouse cursor at the edge of the clip...

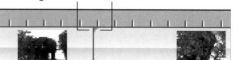

...and drag to hide frames.

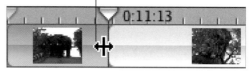

Straight corner *Curved corner*

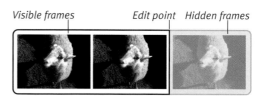

Figure 8.21 Drag the edge of a clip in the Timeline Viewer to edit out the frames you don't need.

Visible frames *Edit point* *Hidden frames*

Figure 8.22 Clips are edited non-destructively in iMovie, so the footage you delete is just hidden from view and available for later.

Command-dragging creates a gap.

Figure 8.23 Hold Command while dragging to prevent the rest of the clips in the Timeline from adjusting as you perform the edit.

Figure 8.24 When you switch to the Clip Viewer, the gap becomes a black clip.

Direct Trimming and Non-Destructive Editing

Direct Trimming is actually a happy byproduct of a revolutionary change within iMovie. iMovie 3 and earlier were *destructive*: cutting out sections of a clip discarded the affected frames. If you needed that footage back, you had to restore the entire clip (see "Reverting Clips," later in this chapter) or hope that you could still undo the change.

In iMovie HD, clips are *non-destructive* (**Figure 8.22**). If you delete a few seconds from the end of a clip, then later decide you need that footage, it's still available to you using the Direct Trimming feature.

---

3. Click the edge of the clip and drag it toward the clip's center (**Figure 8.21**). The Monitor displays the current frame.

4. Release the mouse button at your chosen edit point.

To recover footage using Direct Trimming:

◆ Click and drag the edge of a clip away from the center. The footage that was previously hidden comes into view as you drag. If the clip edge stops moving and has rounded corners, you've reached the limit of the clip's original footage.

✔ Tips

■ Select a clip that you've trimmed, and Command-drag it over the top of the next clip; this trims frames from the adjacent clip, a technique known as a "roll edit."

■ The Timeline Viewer adjusts as you perform a Direct Trimming action, which can look odd. Moving a clip's edge to the left, for example, squishes the clip before it—but once you release the mouse, that clip springs back to regular size.

■ Command-drag a clip's edges to trim without having the rest of the clips on the Timeline automatically fill in the space as you edit (**Figure 8.23**). This leaves a gap, just as if you had tried to move a clip (as described earlier under "Ordering Clips").

■ To fill the gap left by trimming with the Command key, switch to the Clip Viewer and delete the black clip that appears in its place (**Figure 8.24**). Or, Control-click the empty space and choose Convert Empty Space to Clip. A new blank clip is created. Delete it to bring the clips back into tight harmony. (See "Creating Blank Clips," later in this chapter.)

Other editing methods

iMovie also offers four other methods for editing clips: *splitting*, which divides a clip where the Playhead is located; *trimming*, which deletes a selection of frames; *cropping*, which deletes the frames that aren't selected; and *copying and pasting*, which creates a new clip based on selected frames. These actions can be performed on clips that are in the Clips pane or in the Timeline.

To split a clip:

1. Position the Playhead at the point where you want to split the clip.

2. Choose Split Video Clip at Playhead from the Edit menu, or press Command-T. A new clip is created and placed next to the original (**Figure 8.25**). iMovie appends a slash and number to the name to indicate it's a partial clip (such as "Elephant/1").

✔ Tips

■ This command works wherever the Playhead is located—you don't need to select a clip in order to split it.

■ After splitting, the two clips are still selected. To deselect the clips, click the top of the Viewer, or select another clip.

■ If you choose Split Video Clip at Playhead with no clip selected, only the video clip is split, not any audio clips that may appear in tracks below it.

■ After you split a clip, each half still contains all of the frames they had when they were one (thanks to iMovie's non-destructive editing). Use Direct Trimming to reveal the hidden frames.

Single clip

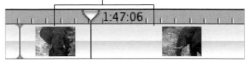

Two clips after splitting

Figure 8.25 Use the Split Video Clip at Playhead command to slice a clip into two separate clips.

Get In, Get Out

There are times when long, lingering shots can define a scene or even an entire movie—but not many. When you're editing, concentrate on making your movies *tight*, showing only the essential shots within your scenes. For example, it's a good idea to have an establishing shot of a room, and perhaps a person opening the door. But you don't need to show him closing the door, walking to the center of the room, and beginning a conversation. Jump right to the conversation, since that's probably the core action of the scene. This advice applies to all types of movies: for your trip to the zoo, jump straight to the lions; we don't need to see you bounce along the pathway looking for directions.

Of course, there are always exceptions (watching *2001: A Space Odyssey* immediately comes to mind), but a tighter film is almost always a better film.

Crop markers

Figure 8.26 Position the mouse pointer just below the Scrubber Bar at the beginning of your selection.

Drag to make a selection.

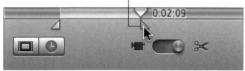

Figure 8.27 Click and drag to create a selection, which appears in yellow.

Right crop marker dragged past left one

Figure 8.28 Dragging one crop marker past the other swaps their positions (right becomes left, or left becomes right). This allows you to make a different selection in only one mouse move instead of several.

To select portions of a clip:

1. Select a clip and place the mouse pointer just below the Scrubber Bar where you want to start the selection (**Figure 8.26**).

2. Click and drag to make a selection, which is highlighted in yellow (**Figure 8.27**) in the Scrubber Bar and in the Timeline Viewer. The Monitor playback follows your pointer so you can see the frames being selected.

   or

   Shift-click in the Scrubber Bar to make a selection.

3. Move the crop markers to fine-tune your selection.

✔ Tips

■ You can click and drag at any point on the Scrubber Bar to make a selection; you don't need to drag the crop markers from the left side of the bar.

■ Click on another clip or at the top of the Timeline Viewer to deselect the frames. You can also choose Select None from the Edit menu (Command-Shift-A).

■ If you move the right crop mark past the left crop mark, it becomes the left mark (**Figure 8.28**). However, if you use the Shift-click method, the selection is extended in the direction based on which crop mark is closest.

■ With a selection made on the Scrubber Bar, choose Select All from the Edit menu (or press Command-A) to highlight all the frames in the clip; conversely, choose Select None from the Edit menu (or press Command-Shift-A) to cancel your selection. This only works when you have a single clip selected; otherwise it selects or deselects all clips in your movie.

To trim a clip:

1. Select a portion of a clip.

2. Choose Clear or Cut from the Edit menu, or press the Delete key. The selection is removed (**Figure 8.29**).

   If you chose to cut the selection, it will be stored in the Mac's Clipboard.

To crop a clip:

1. Select a portion of a clip.

2. Choose Crop from the Edit menu, or press Command-K. The selection is retained, and the rest of the clip's frames are deleted (**Figure 8.30**).

✔ Tips

- Just to be clear, the "trimming" I'm explaining on this page is different from Direct Trimming, discussed earlier. In fact, it's probably more accurate to just say "removing" or "clearing" frames, but trimming is the proper editing term. "Direct Trimming," as you no doubt guessed, is a snazzy term dreamed up by Apple to sound impressive.

- As with the other editing methods described in this chapter, iMovie's non-destructive editing capabilities let you use Direct Trimming to recover "lost" frames that have been trimmed or cropped from a clip.

- You can edit clips in the Clips pane by trimming, cropping, or cutting and pasting them.

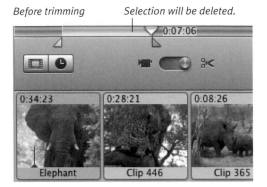

Figure 8.29 Trimming deletes selected frames. The remaining segments become two separate clips. (If you trim from the beginning or end of a clip, you end up with just one smaller clip.)

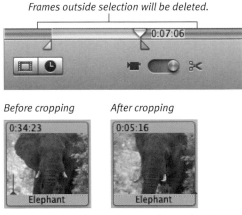

Figure 8.30 Cropping works opposite to trimming. The frames outside the selection are deleted.

Before pasting

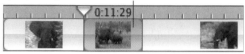

After pasting   *Pasted selection*

Figure 8.31 When pasting a copied selection into your movie, the new clip splits any existing clip at the Playhead and pushes its parts out of the way.

Duplicated clip

Figure 8.32 Duplicating creates an exact clone of the original, so it's a good idea to rename the new clip.

Figure 8.33 In the Clips pane, hold down Option and drag a clip to an empty slot to create a clone of the original.

To copy and paste a selection to a new clip:

1. Select a portion of a clip.

2. Choose Copy from the Edit menu, or press Command-C. The selection is stored in your Mac's Clipboard.

3. Select any clip in the Clips pane, then choose Paste from the Edit menu (Command-V). iMovie creates a new clip.

    or

    Position the Playhead in your movie to the location where you want the clip to appear, then paste it. iMovie inserts the new clip at that point, splitting any clip that was present and pushing its remaining footage to the right (**Figure 8.31**).

To duplicate a clip:

1. Select the clip in the Timeline or the Clips pane.

2. Choose Copy from the Edit menu.

3. Choose Paste from the Edit menu. A new, identical clip appears beside the original (**Figure 8.32**).

To duplicate a clip by Option-dragging:

1. Select the clip in the Clips pane.

2. Option-drag the clip to an empty space in the Clips pane (**Figure 8.33**).

✔ Tips

■ Duplicating a clip makes a copy on disk of the entire media file, not just the edited portion. So even if you use just two seconds of a 200 MB clip, iMovie creates another 200 MB clip in your project file.

■ Consider renaming your new dragged or pasted clip, since it will share the original's name.

Pasting Clips over Clips

In addition to pasting a whole clip into your movie, which inserts it and pushes aside other footage, you can also replace a section of an existing clip (or clips). This is an easy way to show different visuals while retaining a clip's original audio, such as when someone is narrating a flashback (**Figure 8.34**). You can choose to make the sound of both clips editable or not.

To set the audio preference:

1. Open iMovie's Preferences.

2. To be able to edit the audio of the original video clip, enable the Extract audio when using "Paste Over at Playhead" option, if it's not already active (**Figure 8.35**). If you want to substitute in the audio of the pasted clip, disable Extract audio in paste over. Close the Preferences window.

To paste a clip over another clip:

1. Select some footage or a clip, and cut or copy it.

2. Position the Playhead where you want the pasted footage to begin, or select a range of frames to be replaced.

3. Choose Paste Over at Playhead from the Advanced menu, or press Command-Shift-V.

   The pasted clip appears directly on top of the clip that was there before, with its sound clip—colored purple—added to the first audio track (**Figure 8.36**). The audio clip actually belongs to the original clip, and is what you hear when you play the sequence. The clip you inserted still has its soundtrack embedded, and you can hear the volume from each. However, you can now edit the audio levels and control which clip's sound is louder or softer (see Chapter 10).

Figure 8.34 Using the Paste Over feature, you can add a flashback (middle) without interrupting the audio of your subject speaking.

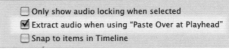

Figure 8.35 To make sure the original clip's audio plays, enable the Extract audio when using "Paste Over at Playhead" option in iMovie's preferences.

Clip pasted over   Audio track from
at Playhead   original video clip

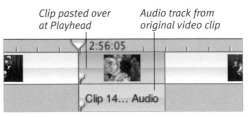

Figure 8.36 The original clip's audio is extracted so you can edit it independently of the pasted-over clip.

Contents pasted
over from Clipboard   Gap created

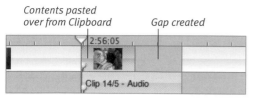

Figure 8.37 iMovie automatically adds black frames if the Clipboard contents are shorter than the selection.

Pasted-over clip

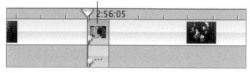

Figure 8.38 If you've made a selection that's shorter than the contents of the Clipboard, iMovie only pastes over as much as will fit.

✔ Tips

■ Selecting a range of frames in the existing clip and then using the Paste Over at Playhead command can create a number of interesting results.

   ▲ If the number of frames in both clips matches exactly, the footage is added with no worries, mate.

   ▲ If the selection is longer than the Clipboard footage, a gap is added to make up the difference (**Figure 8.37**).

   ▲ If the selection is shorter than the footage from the Clipboard, iMovie pastes only as much footage as will fit into the selection (**Figure 8.38**).

■ When you use the paste-over technique, you're actually overwriting the existing footage (versus overlaying something such as a title; see Chapter 12). This means that if you delete the pasted-over clip, the existing footage is hidden. You can recover the "lost" footage by Direct Trimming, using Undo, or by completely restoring the clip media (explained at the end of this chapter).

■ If you're looking for a Robert Altman-esque audio effect where the audio from both clips plays simultaneously, use the Paste Over at Playhead command. Click the pasted clip (which retains its embedded audio track if the Extract audio in paste over option is enabled), then edit its volume (see Chapter 10).

PASTING CLIPS OVER CLIPS

Creating Blank Clips

When you add clips to your movie, they're inserted end to end without any gaps. But sometimes you want to start a clip at one specific point. While you're experimenting with the timing of your movie, you can insert placeholder clips consisting of black frames to pad sections of the movie. iMovie expands on this by giving you the option to create clips that contain a solid color.

To insert a gap of black frames:

1. In the Timeline Viewer, select the clip that immediately follows the section where you want to add black frames.

2. Click and drag the clip to the right. A gap appears (**Figure 8.39**).

To change a gap's duration:

◆ When creating the gap, continue dragging the adjacent clip until the gap spans the duration you want.

Or

1. After the gap has been created, switch to the Clip Viewer (press Command-E). The gap is actually just a clip comprised of black frames (**Figure 8.40**).

2. Double-click the clip that appears in place of the gap to bring up the Clip Info dialog (**Figure 8.41**).

3. Change the time in the Duration field.

✔ Tips

- If a transition precedes the clip you want to move, you'll need to delete the transition first.

- Need a gap at both sides of a clip? In the Timeline Viewer, drag the clip to the right to create one clip, then Command-drag the clip back to the left.

Gap

Figure 8.39 Dragging a clip to the right in the Timeline Viewer creates a gap.

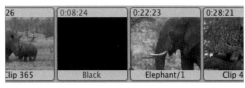

Figure 8.40 The same gap appears as a clip containing black frames in the Clip Viewer.

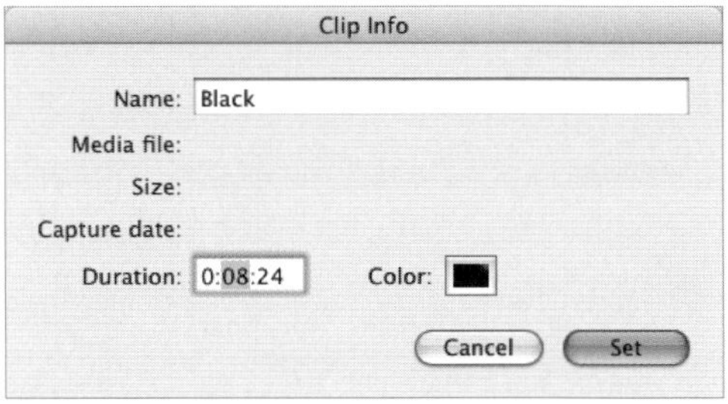

Figure 8.41 The Clip Info dialog for blank clips includes an option to change the clip's duration.

CREATING BLANK CLIPS

Figure 8.42 You can use the contextual menu to turn a gap into a blank clip.

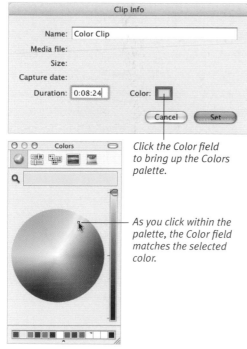

Click the Color field to bring up the Colors palette.

As you click within the palette, the Color field matches the selected color.

Figure 8.43 The Mac OS X Colors palette supplies a full range of colors to use for your clip.

To create a color clip:

1. Create a gap (see the previous page).

2. Position the Playhead within the gap, or switch to the Clip Viewer (where a gap becomes a clip containing black frames). If you're in the Clip Viewer, skip step 3.

3. From the contextual menu (Control-click), choose Convert Empty Space to Clip (**Figure 8.42**).

4. Bring up the Clip Info dialog by double-clicking the color clip, selecting it and choosing Show Info from the File menu or the contextual menu, or pressing Command-I.

5. Click the Color field to bring up the Colors palette.

6. Choose a color from the Colors palette (**Figure 8.43**).

7. Click the Set button to apply the color.

✔ Tips

- Be careful when selecting colors. Intense reds, for example, bleed on most television screens. This is a good reason to have an external video monitor connected to your editing system (see "Monitoring Your Movies" in Chapter 6).

- Blank clips don't need to be just place-holders. If you need some black footage longer than what's available using a transition such as Fade In or Fade Out, for example, insert a black clip. You can even paste the clip over footage to keep the audio playing while the screen is dark (see "Pasting Clips over Clips," earlier in this chapter).

CREATING BLANK CLIPS

105

Reverting Clips

It's not uncommon for me to chop up a single long clip into so many little pieces that I've lost track of where they are. Some thrown away, some trimmed and reversed, some in the Clips pane, and even a few in the movie itself. Direct Trimming lets you cobble pieces together, but what if you want to just start fresh?

Thanks to the way iMovie stores files, you can recover a pristine version of a clip. As I mentioned in Chapter 7, clips you create don't actually exist as new files on your hard disk. Instead, iMovie simply notes what changes have been applied to clips, and grabs the necessary information from the clip's original data file. Using the Revert Clip to Original command, iMovie can recover the clip as it was when you first imported it.

To revert a clip:

1. Select a clip in your movie or in the Clips pane that you want to restore.

2. Choose Revert Clip to Original from the Advanced menu. A dialog explains the amount of footage that will be restored if you proceed (**Figure 8.44**).

3. Click OK to restore, or Cancel to dismiss the dialog.

✔ Tips

- I like to make a copy of an altered clip before I revert it, just in case I need that edited snippet again.

- Say you take a clip and split it in half, then make edits to the second half. If you decide you want the entire clip back, revert the first half—the edits you made to the second half are retained.

Figure 8.44 No matter how many times you chop up a clip in iMovie, the Revert Clip to Original command is ready to pick up the pieces.

Rotating Clips

In Chapter 2, I mentioned that some people use a camcorder like a still camera and rotate it to take vertical shots. You'll need a paid version of QuickTime Pro Player to make the edit.

To rotate clips:

1. Export the footage from iMovie as a DV-formatted QuickTime file (see Chapter 16 for instructions).

2. Open the file in QuickTime Player Pro.

3. Choose Get Movie Properties from the Movie menu (or press Command-J).

4. Select Video Track from the left-hand popup menu.

5. Select Size from the right-hand popup menu.

6. Use one of the rotate buttons (the circular arrows) to rotate the clip.

7. Save the file, then import it back into iMovie.

EDITING STILL PICTURES

After purchasing a camcorder, I didn't immediately throw away my trusty digital still camera. In fact, on a day-to-day basis, I find myself taking more photos than shooting video footage, purely because my still camera is easier to carry around.

iMovie makes it easy to incorporate those stills into your movie projects, whether you're creating a slideshow, adding a series of pictures to accentuate video footage, or creating graphics or Photoshop-enhanced title screens. With iMovie, it's a snap to add any image from your iPhoto library.

This chapter also includes information about the highly touted Ken Burns Effect, a pan-and-zoom operation that adds motion to otherwise static images.

Importing Pictures from iPhoto

iMovie can easily import photos you've scanned or taken with a digital still camera. iMovie makes this process easier by giving you access to your iPhoto library of pictures.

To import pictures from iPhoto:

1. In the Media pane, click the Photos button to view the Photos list (**Figure 9.1**).

2. Your entire photo library is shown in the preview area. If you want to access a specific photo album, choose its name from the list. You can also type a name into the search field to locate pictures based on their titles (**Figure 9.2**).

3. Click a photo to select it for importing. A preview appears in the Monitor. Using the Preview controls, you can (**Figure 9.3**):

   ▲ Click the Play button to start or stop playback of the preview.

   ▲ Click the Loop button to start or stop continuous playback.

   ▲ Drag the Preview playhead in the preview's scrubber bar.

   ▲ Click the Hide Preview button (marked X) to cancel the photo.

   ▲ Click the Apply button (marked with a checkbox) to apply the photo, which adds it to the Timeline.

   The Photo Settings palette also appears (**Figure 9.4**). If the Ken Burns Effect is enabled, click the checkbox to turn it off for now. We'll cover Ken Burns later in this chapter.

4. When imported, the photo is treated as a video clip, so set the clip's length by using

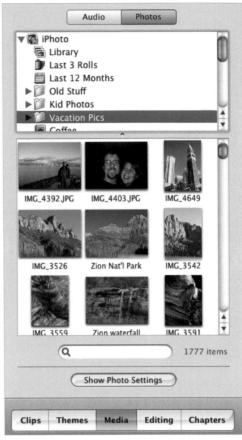

Figure 9.1 All the pictures in your iPhoto library are accessible from within the Photos pane.

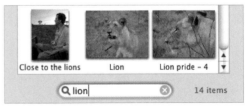

Figure 9.2 Use the search field to quickly locate photos using names you assigned to them in iPhoto.

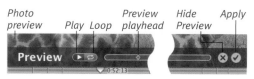

Figure 9.3 Use the Preview controls to see how the rendered photo will appear.

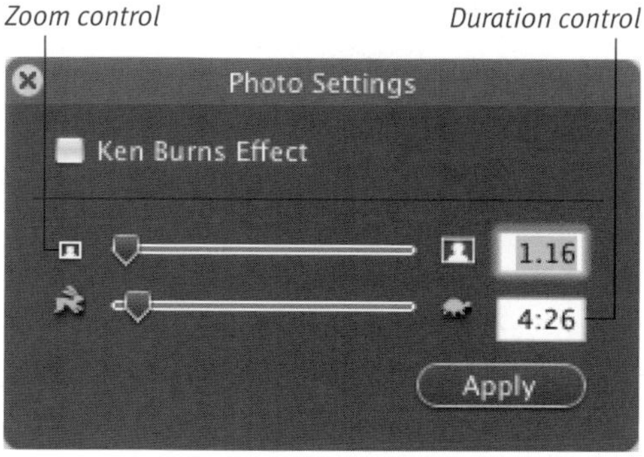

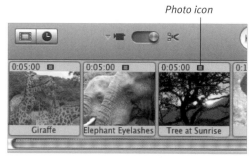

Figure 9.4 The floating Photo Settings palette appears when you select a photo or click the Show Photo Settings button.

Figure 9.5 Imported photos appear in the Timeline just like other video clips. The small square icon in the Clip Viewer indicates that a clip is a still picture.

the Duration slider, or type a value in the Duration field (in timecode's `seconds:frames` format).

5. For most photos, iMovie doesn't automatically scale the image to fit the screen. To compensate, use the Zoom slider or field to enlarge the picture slightly (see next page).

6. Drag the picture from the Photos pane to the Timeline, where it appears as a regular clip (**Figure 9.5**). Or, click the Apply button to add the picture to the end of the Timeline.

✔ Tips

■ Command-click to select multiple photos at once, then drag them to the Timeline.

■ The number to the right of the search field indicates the number of pictures in the selected photo album.

■ Do you shoot movies using the video capture feature on your digital still camera? If you use iPhoto to import you pictures to your Mac, those movies also show up in the Media pane's Photos list. As with photos, simply drag them to the Timeline to add them to your movie.

■ Double-click a movie file in the Photos list to preview it. The video plays only within the icon's thumbnail, but that's enough to get a sense of what the clip is (especially if it's named something like "MVI_0379.AVI").

■ One more tip on working with movies in iPhoto: I created a Movies smart album in iPhoto (set up a few "Filename contains" selectors to match common video file extensions such as .mov and .avi). That way I can display all my movie clips without hunting for them.

Dealing with black borders

DV video resolution isn't as cut and dried as it may seem. For example, although your movie may appear to be 640 by 480 pixels, video pixels are actually rectangular, not square, so the actual resolution is closer to 720 by 480 pixels. iMovie HD uses a new scaling algorithm that takes discrepancies like this into account, but it leads to the imposed black borders as shown in **Figure 9.6**. It's easy enough to change the Zoom setting to compensate, but I'd rather not tweak it for every picture. Instead, prepare your pictures in iPhoto to make them fill iMovie's screen. (Also see "Importing Pictures from Other Sources," later in this chapter.)

To prepare pictures in iPhoto 6:

1. In iPhoto 5, double-click a photo you want to import into iMovie to edit it.

2. From the Constrain popup menu, choose Custom and enter the following values, depending on the format of your project (**Figure 9.7**):
   ▲ **DV, MPEG-4, and iSight:** 4.09 x 3
   ▲ **DV Widescreen:** 1.818 x 1
   ▲ **HDV 1080i and 720p:** 16 x 9

3. Drag the selected area to position which area of the photo is to remain visible (**Figure 9.8**).

4. Click the Crop button.

5. Click Done.

6. Import the photo according to the directions on the previous page.

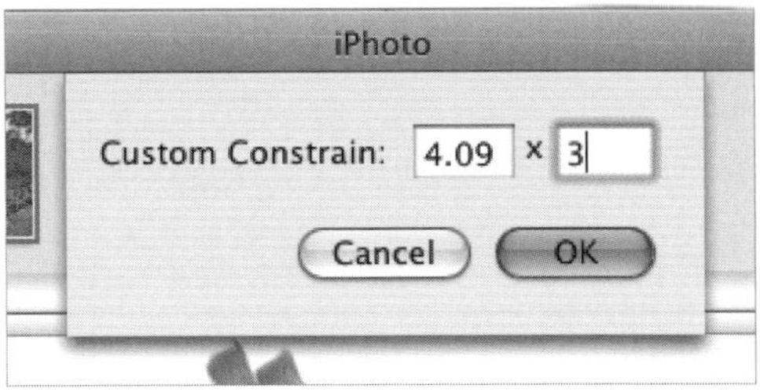

✔ Tip

■ By default, the Ken Burns Effect is applied to any imported image. To add the photo without any motion applied, uncheck the Ken Burns Effect checkbox before you import.

Figure 9.6 Importing a photo with no zoom applied results in black borders on the sides. Eww.

Figure 9.7 Set a custom constraint in iPhoto to crop your images before importing them into iMovie.

Area to be cropped out   Crop button

Figure 9.8 After setting the constrain values in iPhoto, position the visible area and then crop the image.

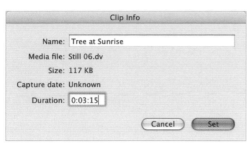

Figure 9.9 Double-click a still clip to access the Clip Info screen, where you can change the duration value.

Changing the Duration of a Still Clip

Now that your picture has been added to iMovie, it can be edited like any other clip (see Chapter 8). However, if you haven't applied the Ken Burns Effect (see the next page), the change you're most likely to make is to the clip's duration. Instead of trimming the clip, simply tell iMovie how long the clip should be.

To change a picture's duration:

1. Double-click the still clip, or choose Show Info from the File menu (or, press Command-I).

2. In the Clip Info dialog, enter a new value into the Duration field (**Figure 9.9**). The field uses timecode format (`seconds:frames`, though you could also enter a full `hours:minutes:seconds:frames` value such as `01:34:25:19` if you wanted).

✔ Tips

■ Use the Duration field in the Photo Settings palette to change the duration of multiple selected photos.

■ Other video clips do not have an editable Duration field in the Clip Info dialog.

Adding Motion with the Ken Burns Effect

Who says still photos must remain still? A common effect used by documentary film-makers is *pan and zoom*, where the camera moves across a still image, zooms in on (or out of) a portion of the image, or performs a combination of the two.

To apply the Ken Burns Effect:

1. Select an image in the Photos list.

2. In the Photo Settings palette, click the Ken Burns Effect checkbox to enable the feature (if it's not already checked).

3. Set a duration for the effect using the Duration slider or field.

4. Click the Start button to set the appearance at the first frame of the sequence.

5. Specify a zoom setting using the Zoom slider or field (**Figure 9.10**). A setting of 1.0 displays the entire image on screen.

6. Click the image in the preview window and drag it to define the portion of the picture that initially appears. (If you're not zoomed-in at all, you probably don't need to do this.)

7. Click the End radio button, then perform steps 5 and 6 to set the appearance of the last frame in the sequence (**Figure 9.11**).

8. When the effect is set up to your liking, do one of the following to add it to your movie:

   ▲ Click the Apply button; iMovie adds the clip to the end of your movie.

   ▲ Drag the photo from the iPhoto preview area to the Timeline.

   Figure 9.12 approximates the effect as it appears when played back.

Figure 9.10 Click the Start button and set up the opening frame of the effect. Here, we're starting off with a shot of a warthog family.

Figure 9.11 Now we're setting up the last frame of the effect—zoomed in and shifted to the right by dragging in the preview window.

Start

End

Figure 9.12 The completed Ken Burns Effect zooms in and pans over to the baby warthog.

Figure 9.13 Click the Reverse button to quickly swap the Start and Finish settings.

Ken Who?

Ever one to capitalize on name recognition, Apple named this feature after Ken Burns, a documentary filmmaker who frequently employs the effect in his popular documentaries. Examples include *The Civil War, JAZZ,* and *Baseball.* For more information, see www.pbs.org/kenburns/.

✔ Tips

- iMovie automatically plays the effect in the Monitor; if the End button is highlighted, it means the preview has finished. Clicking the Start or the End buttons interrupts the preview.

- If you decide you want your effect to run backwards from the way you set it, click the Reverse button to swap the Start and End settings (**Figure 9.13**).

- If you want to change how the effect appears, make your changes and click the Update button.

- You can use the Ken Burns Effect's controls to crop photos. With the Ken Burns Effect button unchecked, specify a zoom amount. When you click the Apply button, the photo is added to the Timeline as a regular still photo, not a Ken Burns clip.

- Option-click the Start button to apply its settings to the End frame, and vice-versa.

- Higher-resolution photos generally display better than lower-resolution ones. Although iMovie does a good job of interpolating the image, zooming way in can cause blurry images. To ensure higher quality, create your images in multiples of the sizes found in "Importing Pictures from Other Sources," later in this chapter. For example, in a DV Widescreen project, start with an image that is 1,748 by 960 pixels (twice the recommended resolution) to get better quality when zooming.

- To apply these settings to multiple photos, drag the photos to the Timeline.

- With multiple photos selected and Ken Burns settings applied, Option-click the Apply button: the effect is reversed on every-other photo (zoom in, then zoom out, then zoom in again, etc.).

To apply the Ken Burns Effect to a non-iPhoto still picture clip:

1. Move the clip to the Timeline, if it's not already there, and make sure it's selected.

2. Switch to the Photos list in the Media pane; the picture appears in the Monitor and the Photo Settings palette appears.

3. Set the Start and End values (detailed on the previous pages) to define the pan and zoom effect.

4. Use the Preview controls to view a rough version of the effect .

5. Click the Update button (which was formerly the Apply button) to render the settings and turn the picture clip into a video clip (**Figure 9.14**).

Figure 9.14 Click the Update button to apply changed settings and re-render the Ken Burns Effect clip.

✔ Tips

- For a different effect, drag the image out of the preview window entirely at the starting point, then drag it out of the opposite side of the frame for the finish point—the image glides across the screen as if it were in motion.

- Unfortunately, you can't create a still frame from a video clip and apply the Ken Burns Effect to it. As a workaround, export the frame as a still image using the File menu's Save Frame As command, then re-import that file back into iMovie.

- For far more control over pan-and-zoom effects, look to third-party iMovie plug-in vendors. In particular, I like Still Life (www.grantedsw.com/still-life) or Photo to Movie (lqgraphics.com/software/), which gives you the capability to rotate the camera, and add other photos and audio (**Figure 9.15**). You can then export the clip as a video file to be imported into iMovie (see Appendix B).

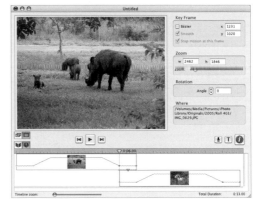

Figure 9.15 Photo to Movie offers more control over pan-and-zoom effects.

Figure 9.16 Crop images before importing them into iMovie to ensure that they appear without black bars at the edges (Photoshop shown here).

Figure 9.17 Using the Import command, you can see a preview of your image before you import it.

Figure 9.18 Come on, did you honestly think I could write an iMovie book and not include a kid's picture?

Importing Pictures from Other Sources

iMovie can easily import photos you've scanned or taken with a digital still camera—or better, images that you've modified in an image-editing program such as Adobe Photoshop (www.adobe.com/products/photoshop/) or GraphicConverter (www.lemkesoft.com). But first, make sure the image is ready to be imported.

To prepare a still picture for import:

1. Open the picture in your favorite image-editing application.

2. Size the image so that its dimensions match the format you're working in (**Figure 9.16**):

   ▲ **DV, MPEG-4, and iSight:** 655 by 480 pixels

   ▲ **DV Widescreen:** 874 by 480 pixels

   ▲ **HDV 1080i:** 1,920 by 1,080 pixels

   ▲ **HDV 720p:** 1,280 by 720 pixels

3. Save the image as a JPEG file.

To import a still picture:

◆ Drag an image file from the Desktop to iMovie's Clips pane or Timeline.

Or

1. In iMovie, choose Import from the File menu (or press Command-Shift-I).

2. In the Import File dialog, select the still image you want (**Figure 9.17**) and click the Open button. The image appears as a clip on the Clips pane, which can be added to your movie like any other clip (**Figure 9.18**).

Creating a Still Clip from a Video Clip

Thousands of still images flicker by as we're watching video—sometimes too quickly. Perhaps you'd like to linger on a sunset or highlight the one short moment when everyone in your family was looking at the camera. You can create a still clip from a single frame of video. You can also save a frame as an image file on your hard disk.

To create a still clip:

1. Position the Playhead at the frame you wish to use.

2. Choose Create Still Frame from the Edit menu, or press Command-Shift-S. A new five-second clip appears on the Clips pane, named "Still 11.dv" or similar—iMovie sets the number in the title (**Figure 9.19**).

To save a frame as an image:

1. Position the Playhead at the frame you wish to use.

2. Choose Save Frame from the File menu, or press Command-F. iMovie asks you to specify a file name and a location on your hard disk (**Figure 9.20**).

   Images are saved as JPEG files by default, but you can also choose to save them in PICT format.

✔ Tips

- Remember that you're still working in video resolution, so your still clip won't be the same higher-quality that you'd get by taking a photo using a digital still camera.

- When I import a still photo, iMovie scales it to match the video resolution. So if you bring a picture in from iPhoto and then save a frame of it to disk out of iMovie, the new file will have less resolution than the original photo.

Figure 9.19 A new five-second clip appears on the Clips pane when you choose Create Still Frame.

Figure 9.20 Use the Save Frame command to export a single frame as a still image to your hard disk.

EDITING AUDIO

How important is audio in a movie? If you ever get the chance to attend an advance test screening of a Hollywood movie, the answer may be painfully clear. I've been to screenings where the audio in some scenes consisted of just what was recorded on set—no background music, no sound mixing to balance actors' voices and dampen background noise, no re-recorded dialogue to enhance enunciation. Although quite a bit of work goes into editing audio, people tend not to notice it unless something is wrong.

I covered some methods for capturing quality audio in Chapter 5, which is the first step. But audio can be much more than just video's underappreciated sibling. In this chapter, you'll see how editing audio tracks can give depth to your movie by working independently of the video, and by adding music, narration, and sound effects.

Changing a Clip's Volume

When you import footage, the video and audio are combined in the Timeline Viewer's video track (**Figure 10.1**). So, as you're editing video clips, you're also editing the audio—splitting, trimming, and cropping it with the visuals. You can control how loud an individual clip plays, or change the volume level within the clip.

To set a clip's volume evenly:

1. In the Timeline Viewer, select one or more clips you want to edit.

2. Use the volume control slider, or enter a percent value in the field, to set the clip's volume (**Figure 10.2**).

To change volume within a clip:

1. In the Timeline Viewer, select the clip you want to edit.

2. Choose Show Clip Volume Levels from the View menu (**Figure 10.3**), or press Command-Shift-L; a purple volume level bar appears within the clip.

3. In the Timeline Viewer, click on the volume level bar to set a marker where you want the volume change to occur (**Figure 10.4**). iMovie creates the marker (a yellow circle) and a beginning point for the marker (a small square).

4. Drag the marker up or down to increase or decrease the volume. All audio following the marker in that clip is affected.

5. Drag the marker's beginning point to the right or left to determine how quickly the volume change occurs.

To remove a volume marker:

1. Click a marker to select it.

2. Press the Delete key.

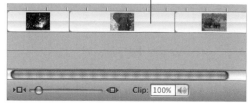

Video and audio data combined

Figure 10.1 Although the top track is usually referred to as the video track, it also contains the clip's audio.

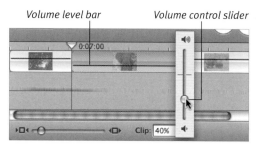

Volume level bar   *Volume control slider*

Figure 10.2 With a clip selected, drag the volume control slider to adjust the clip's volume uniformly. The volume level bars appear while you drag.

View	Markers	Share	Advanced
Switch to Clip Viewer			⌘E
Scroll to Playhead			⌥⌘P
Scroll to Selection			⌥⌘S
Zoom to Selection			⌥⌘Z
Show Clip Volume Levels			⇧⌘L
Show Audio Waveforms			⇧⌘W

Figure 10.3 When you're editing the audio for multiple clips, you may want to keep this option on.

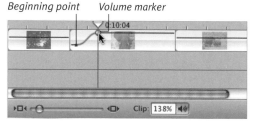

Beginning point   *Volume marker*

Figure 10.4 iMovie can edit volume levels within a clip. The audio between the beginning point and the volume marker is automatically incremented smoothly to a louder or softer level.

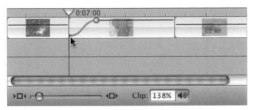

Figure 10.5 To fade in, move the beginning point to the bottom-left corner of the clip.

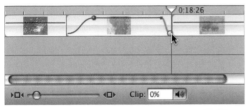

Figure 10.6 To fade out, move the volume marker to the bottom-right corner of the clip.

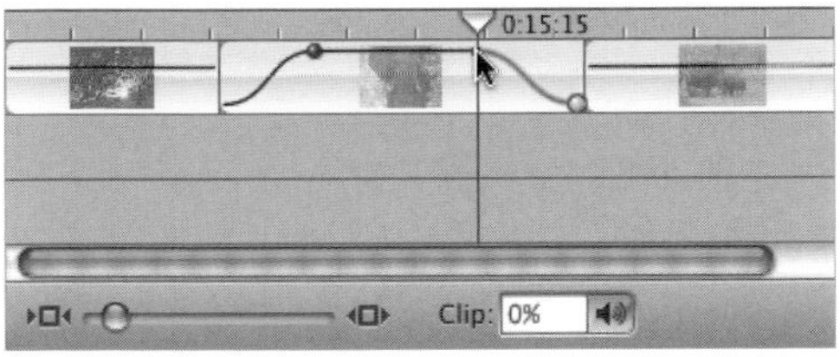

Figure 10.7 Move the beginning point left or right to determine the duration of the fade.

Fading Audio In or Out

One of the more common audio effects is to fade the sound in from silence at the beginning of a scene, or fade it out at the end. Follow these steps to create and customize your audio fades.

To fade audio completely in or out:

1. If the volume levels aren't already visible, choose Show Clip Volume Levels from the View menu.

2. Select a clip in the Timeline Viewer.

3. Click the volume level bar to create a new marker at the beginning or end of the clip, depending on which fade you want.

4. If you want a fade in, drag the beginning point (the square box) to the bottom-left corner of the clip (**Figure 10.5**).

   If you're looking to fade out, drag the volume marker (yellow circle) to the lower-right corner of the clip (**Figure 10.6**).

To change the fade duration:

◆ Drag the beginning point left or right to dictate the fade's length (**Figure 10.7**). You may need to first move the volume marker—which drags the beginning point behind it—then adjust the beginning point to extend the fade duration.

✔ Tips

■ If you drag a marker so that it lines up with an existing volume level, a dotted line appears and the marker is automatically deleted.

■ When you apply a Fade In or Fade Out transition (see the next chapter), the audio automatically fades to accompany the visual effect. But you can edit the volume levels in the transition, too (if you want the video to fade to black, but bring the volume down only halfway, for example).

Extracting Audio

So far, I haven't mentioned the two obvious audio tracks that appear in the Timeline Viewer. These are typically where you would work with sound effects or imported audio files, but they're also the sandboxes for playing with audio that comes with your video footage. Before we can play, however, we need to extract the audio from the video clip.

To extract audio:

1. Select the clip in the video track.

2. Choose Extract Audio from the Advanced menu, or press Command-J. An audio clip, represented as a purple bar, appears in the audio track beneath the video clip (**Figure 10.8**).

✔ Tips

■ If you later delete an extracted audio clip, it's not gone forever. The original sound is still embedded in the video track, but its volume is turned down to zero so it does not interfere with the audio tracks. If you can't undo the deletion, select the clip and increase its volume to restore the sound. You can then extract the audio again, which places a new copy in the audio track.

■ Extracting audio clips makes it possible to start playing audio before the visuals begin (or after they're done). For example, when editing the video of a recent camping trip, I wanted to portray how it felt to wake up one morning to rain (**Figure 10.9**). I opened on a few seconds of black frames with the sound of the rain pattering on a tarp, then faded in on the image of the wet tarp. The audio and visuals weren't synchronized, but that didn't matter because the clip was an establishing shot with background sounds.

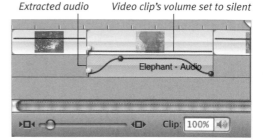

Extracted audio   *Video clip's volume set to silent*

Figure 10.8 Extracted audio clips appear on the first audio track. The video clip's audio becomes silent.

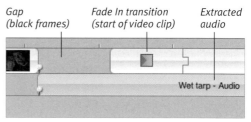

Gap (black frames)   *Fade In transition (start of video clip)*   *Extracted audio*

Figure 10.9 Extracting the audio from the "Wet tarp" clip allowed me to begin playing the sound of the rain during a few seconds of black frames, then fade in on the visual of the tarp itself (top). You can view this clip at www.jeffcarlson.com/imovievqs/.

Figure 10.10 Once unlocked, you can position an audio clip anywhere in the movie. Here, the clip on the right is shifted out of sync with its video.

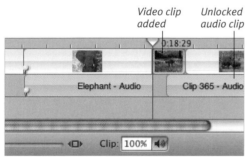

Figure 10.11 The unlocked audio clip gets pushed further out of sync when a new video clip is added.

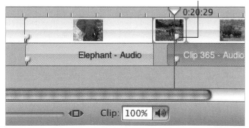

Figure 10.12 Choosing Lock Audio Clip at Playhead anchors the audio clip at a specific location.

Locking and Unlocking Audio Clips

After you extract an audio clip, it appears with a pushpin icon at its far left. This icon indicates that the video and audio tracks are synchronized, or locked, at that point. But you can unlock the clip, then drag it elsewhere on the Timeline.

To unlock an audio clip:

1. Select the audio clip (not the video clip) in the Timeline Viewer. If you've just extracted the audio clip, it should be already selected.

2. Choose Lock Audio Clip at Playhead from the Advanced menu, or press Command-L. (If you don't see this command, it means the audio clip isn't selected.) The pushpin icon disappears (**Figure 10.10**).

Similarly, you can lock an extracted audio clip to any video clip in your movie. Locking it ensures that the sound remains synchronized, even if you add video clips later (**Figure 10.11**).

To lock an audio clip:

1. Position the audio clip where you want it to appear on the Timeline.

2. Move the Playhead to a spot where the audio and video clips overlap (it doesn't have to be at the beginning).

3. Choose Lock Audio Clip at Playhead from the Advanced menu, or hit Command-L. A new pushpin icon appears at the Playhead location (**Figure 10.12**).

✔ Tip

- Position the playhead in the middle of the clips you want to lock. Then you can trim the start and end points of the clips without disrupting the synchronization.

Waveforms and Audio Scrubbing

Rather than relying solely on your ears to pick up audio cues, you can use visible audio track waveforms to see a clip's sound levels. This makes it possible to edit audio clips with more precision.

To view audio clip waveforms:

◆ Choose Show Audio Waveforms from the View menu (**Figure 10.13**), or press Command-Shift-W. The waveforms appear as vertical lines on audio clips (**Figure 10.14**).

To scrub audio:

◆ Hold down the Option key while dragging the Playhead in the Timeline Viewer. The audio plays back at the speed that you drag the Playhead, so it's likely to be sped-up or slowed-down. This lets you quickly locate an audio cue without playing your clips back in real time.

✔ Tips

■ Zoom in on the Timeline to display more waveform detail.

■ Press the up and down arrow keys in a selected audio clip to temporarily raise or lower waveforms to see them better (**Figure 10.15**). (This has no effect on the volume of the clip.)

■ The Timeline snapping feature works within audio clips, too. When the Playhead comes within three frames of audio silence, the yellow snap line appears.

■ Displaying waveforms is fairly processor-intensive, so if iMovie is bogging down, turn them off.

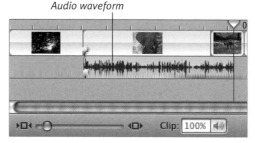

Figure 10.13 Turn on the display of audio track waveforms from the View menu.

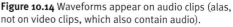

Audio waveform

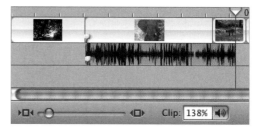

Figure 10.14 Waveforms appear on audio clips (alas, not on video clips, which also contain audio).

Figure 10.15 Press the up arrow key to make the waveform appear bigger in a selected clip.

Sound level indicator   Record button

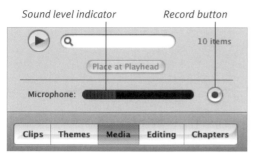

Figure 10.16 Press the Record button to record a voice-over directly into the Timeline.

Voice-over recording

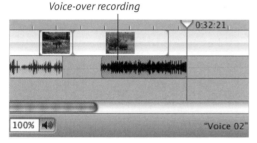

Figure 10.17 The recorded voice-over appears in the Timeline Viewer as a regular audio clip, named "Voice 02" (or whichever number applies).

Recording Voice-overs

I read that while shooting *Crouching Tiger, Hidden Dragon*, actor Chow Yun Fat (who doesn't speak Mandarin Chinese natively) didn't put much work into pronouncing his dialogue correctly during filming. Instead, he fine-tuned his accent when re-recording the dialogue in post production. Most likely you won't be doing much re-recording (also called *looping*), but iMovie's narration capability lets you add voice-overs or other sounds directly to your movie.

To record a voice-over:

1. Connect a microphone to your Mac, if necessary.

2. Click the Media button to display the Media pane, and then click the Audio button.

3. Position the Playhead in the Timeline where you want to begin recording.

4. Click the round Record button to begin recording (**Figure 10.16**). The indicator beside the button lights up according to the sound level.

5. Click the Record button again to end. A new audio clip, which can be edited just like other audio clips, is now in the Timeline (**Figure 10.17**).

✔ Tips

■ You can record multiple takes, then delete the ones you don't end up using.

■ Some Mac models do not include an audio-in port or a built-in microphone, unfortunately. Instead, consider buying an inexpensive USB audio device such as the iMic, from Griffin Technology (www.griffintechnology.com). Or, an iSight works quite well, too.

Editing Audio Clips

When you extract audio, it becomes its own clip that you can edit independently of its original video clip. As with video, you can use Direct Trimming to edit audio clips easily (see Chapter 8 for a complete explanation of Direct Trimming).

To split an audio clip:

1. Select the audio clip. Unlike video clips, which are split at the Playhead even if they're not selected, audio clips must be selected with the Playhead in place.

2. Choose Split Selected Audio Clip at Playhead from the Edit menu, or press Command-T (**Figure 10.18**).

To edit an audio clip using Direct Trimming:

1. Position the mouse pointer at the left or right edge of the audio clip.

2. Click and drag to reveal or hide the audio frames you choose (**Figure 10.19**).

To rename an audio clip:

1. Double-click the audio clip to display the Clip Info dialog.

2. Type in a new name in the Name field, then click OK.

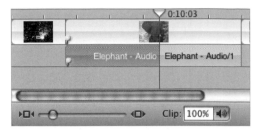

Figure 10.18 You can split an extracted audio clip without splitting the video clip to which it's attached.

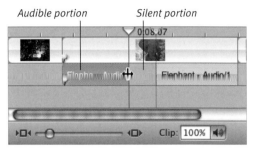

Figure 10.19 Drag an audio clip's edges to set which portion will be audible during playback.

Last video clip in Timeline

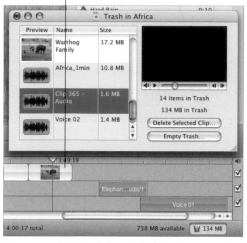

Figure 10.20 The Trash (surprisingly) or the end of your movie are convenient locations to temporarily store unused audio clips.

✔ Tips

- Clips can go into either audio track in the Timeline Viewer, though iMovie tends to use the second track for imported audio.

- You don't have to select an audio clip before you edit it using Direct Trimming. When you click and drag a clip's edge, it's automatically selected for you.

- Hold Option while dragging to create a copy of the selected audio clip.

- Editing audio is one area where the Timeline Viewer's Zoom control is especially useful. Zoom in to make precise changes.

- Although audio clips act like video clips in most respects, you can only edit them in the Timeline Viewer; there's no audio equivalent to the Clips pane. However, you can temporarily store audio clips you aren't yet using: simply drag them beyond the end of the last video track or into the Trash (as long as you don't empty it) (**Figure 10.20**).

- Unlike video clips, audio clips can overlap (though this can create audible gibberish, but that may be what you're going for).

- Experiment with overlapping clips that contain fades. This is an easy way to blend dialogue, (one quickie method for playing voices in a character's head), or even tighten scenes by reducing the amount of lag between speakers.

Adding Music from iTunes and GarageBand

When the first version of iMovie appeared, the idea of storing one's music as MP3 files on a hard disk hadn't yet caught on. Now, however, iTunes can rip and store thousands of songs, all of which are ready to be added to your iMovie project. You can also import compositions directly from GarageBand.

To locate songs in your iTunes or GarageBand libraries:

1. Switch to the Media pane and click the Audio button to display the Audio list.

2. Click iTunes or GarageBand in the list. Your library appears in the main window (**Figure 10.21** and **Figure 10.22**); click the triangle beside either name to view your playlists.

3. Scroll through the list to find the song you want to use.

   Or, type a word in the Search field if you're looking for a particular song or artist name. The list updates as you type (**Figure 10.23**). Click the Cancel button (with the white X on it) to clear the field and return to the full list.

To listen to a song:

1. Select a song in the list.

2. Click the round Play Audio button to play the track from the beginning.

   Click the button again to stop playing.

✔ Tips

- Set up a custom iMovie playlist in iTunes that contains the music you want to use for a particular project to help you find songs faster.

- The Search field only looks for song titles and artist names.

Figure 10.21 You don't have to leave iMovie to import your digital music—everything in iTunes is available.

Figure 10.22 When viewing the GarageBand list, the songs with a full guitar icon can be previewed. The songs with document icons must be saved again in GarageBand with an iLife preview before you can play or import them in iMovie.

Play Audio   Search field   Cancel

Q pink martini   ⊗   27 items

Place at Playhead

Figure 10.23 Type the name of a song or artist into the Search field to display only the matches in the list.

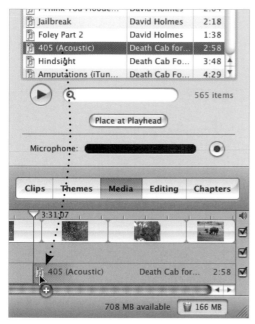

I Think You Hood...	David Holmes	2:04
Jailbreak	David Holmes	2:18
Foley Part 2	David Holmes	1:38
405 (Acoustic)	Death Cab for...	2:58
Hindsight	Death Cab Fo...	3:48
Amputations (iTun...	Death Cab Fo...	4:29

Q   565 items

Place at Playhead

Microphone: ⊙

Clips   Themes   Media   Editing   Chapters

3:31:07

405 (Acoustic)   Death Cab for...   2:58

+

708 MB available   166 MB

Figure 10.24 Drag songs directly from the Audio pane to the Timeline Viewer to add them to the movie.

Name	Artist	Time ▲
Dig Your Grave	Modest Mouse	0:12
Ostriches & Chirping	Elliott Smith	0:33
Interlude (Milo)	Modest Mouse	0:58
We've Got a File On...	Blur	1:02
Fewer Words	Badly Drawn ...	1:13
Life's Incredible Ag...	Michael Giacc...	1:24
30 Century Man	Scott Walker	1:26
Lava In the Afterno...	Michael Giacc...	1:29
The Chase	Stephen Trask	1:31
The Way I Feel Inside	The Zombies	1:34
Mr. Huph Will See ...	Michael Giacc...	1:35
Don't Ask Me I'm O...	Badly Drawn ...	1:36
Let Me Tell You Ab...	Mark Mothers...	1:38

Figure 10.25 Sorting the iTunes library by time makes it easy to find music that matches the length of your video clips or sequences.

To add music from the Media pane:

◆ Drag one or more songs from the Audio list to either audio track in the Timeline Viewer (**Figure 10.24**).

Or

1. Position the Playhead in the Timeline Viewer where you want the song to begin.

2. Click the Place at Playhead button, or drag the song to the Monitor; the audio clip is imported and appears on the Timeline's lower audio track.

✔ Tips

■ Click the column headings to sort the list. For example, I often click the Time column to find songs that fit within a given section of a movie (**Figure 10.25**).

■ iMovie can import any file format that iTunes can play, so you're not limited to just MP3 files.

■ You can make any folder of songs appear in the Audio list: simply drag the folder from the Finder to the top portion of the Media pane.

■ Music encoded in MP3 or AAC format in iTunes is compressed, meaning that some audio data have been removed to make the file size smaller. Most people probably won't notice the difference, but some audiophiles can tell. If you need to use the highest-quality music in your movie, import the songs in AIFF format within iTunes.

■ It's worth pointing out that most songs you import from iTunes are probably copyrighted material. For most people this is no problem, since only friends and family are likely to see their edited movies. But if you're planning to distribute the movie or play it for a lot of people, you need to get permission to use the music.

ADDING MUSIC FROM ITUNES AND GARAGEBAND

Adding Sound Effects

You can't capture *every* sound when you're shooting—the laser blasts in *Star Wars* weren't real, for example (they were actually recordings of wrenches striking power cables). Sometimes you need ready-made sound effects (many are included with iMovie), or you can even create your own.

To add a sound effect to your movie:

1. Switch to the Media pane and click the Audio button.

2. At the top of the pane, choose a sound effects collection (**Figure 10.26**).

3. Double-click an effect's name to preview it, or select an effect and click the Play button.

4. Drag the effect you want to the Timeline Viewer and drop it into one of the audio tracks (**Figure 10.27**).

    You can edit sound effects just as you can any other audio clip in iMovie.

To add new sound effects to iMovie:

1. Quit iMovie.

2. Make sure the sound file is in the AIFF or MP3 format.

3. Copy the sound file to [Home]/Library/iMovie/Sound Effects.

4. Launch iMovie. The sound is now listed in the iMovie Sound Effects list.

✔ Tips

■ Kudos to Apple's engineers: iMovie automatically displays the Timeline Viewer when you start dragging a sound effect.

■ Don't go overboard with adding sound effects to iMovie's library: the more items, the longer it takes iMovie to launch.

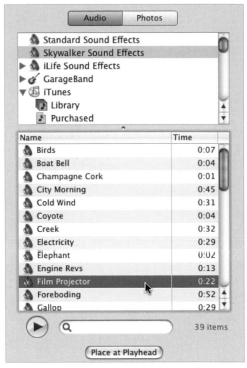

Figure 10.26 iMovie includes a number of common sound effects that you can add to your movie.

Figure 10.27 A sound effect appears in the Timeline like any other audio clip.

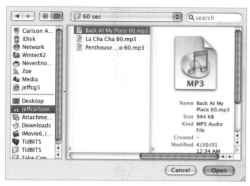

Figure 10.28 Locate an audio file. iMovie reads any format supported by QuickTime.

AIFF file added at Playhead

Figure 10.29 iMovie automatically places imported audio files into track 2 in the Timeline Viewer.

Importing Audio Files

Many companies provide royalty-free music and audio clips. iMovie can import any audio files that are supported by QuickTime.

To import an audio file:

1. Position the Playhead in the Timeline Viewer where you want the imported file to begin.

2. Choose Import from the File menu, or press Command-Shift-I.

3. In the dialog that appears, navigate to the audio file (**Figure 10.28**). Click Open.

4. Wait several seconds for the file to be imported, then be amazed when it shows up as an editable audio clip in the Timeline Viewer's track 2 (**Figure 10.29**).

11

TRANSITIONS

Transitions can be equally wonderful and terrible things. They can move you from one scene to another without the abruptness of a straightforward cut, or help define a movie's pace by easing you gently into or out of a scene.

But transitions can also become a distraction, because you're introducing motion or visuals that weren't recorded by the camera. Too many transitions can be like using too many fonts in a word processing application: pretty soon, all you see is the style, not the content.

My best advice is to let the content determine the transition, if one is even needed: most of the time, a jump cut (moving from one clip to another without a transition) is all that's required. I'm not saying you should skip this chapter—rather, using fewer, *better* transitions is almost always the better route.

Experiment with different transitions, all the while knowing that iMovie creates professional transitions without breaking a sweat, enabling you to concentrate on how your movie plays instead of trying to jump over technical hurdles.

Editing Transition Settings

Configure a transition's behavior before you add it to your movie.

To choose a transition:

1. Click the Editing button and then click the Transitions button to view the list of available transitions (**Figure 11.1**).

2. Click a transition name. The Monitor automatically plays a preview version of the transition. Using the Preview controls, you can (**Figure 11.2**):

   ▲ Click the Play button to start or stop playback of the preview.

   ▲ Click the Loop button to start or stop continuous playback.

   ▲ Drag the Preview playhead in the preview's scrubber bar.

   ▲ Click the Hide Preview button (marked X) to cancel the transition.

   ▲ Click the Apply button (marked with a checkbox) to apply the transition, which adds it to the Timeline.

To change a transition's duration:

1. Select a transition, either in the Transitions list or one that you've already added to the movie.

2. Drag the Speed slider or type a value into the Speed field. Transitions can be as short as 1 frame or as long as 10 seconds.

✔ Tip

■ iMovie creates a preview based on the location of the Playhead. If it's near the beginning of the clip, iMovie transitions the previous clip into the current one; if the Playhead is near the end of a clip, it transitions the current clip to the next one.

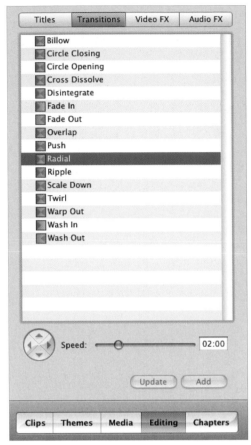

Figure 11.1 Choose a transition type from the Transitions list in the Editing pane.

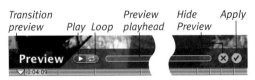

Figure 11.2 Use the Preview controls in the Monitor to see how the rendered transition will appear.

Direction of Push transition

Directional control

Figure 11.3 Push is one transition that features a directional control.

Figure 11.4 Use Overlap to slowly dissolve from a clip to a modified still image.

To set an effect's direction:

1. Select the Push transition for an example of this type of setting. Billow also uses a directional control.

2. Click a button on the directional controller to specify how the effect plays (**Figure 11.3**). Using Push, the control indicates where the old clip exits the frame and the new clip enters (by default, the new clip "pushes" the old clip from left to right).

✔ Tips

- If you click the *name* of the Push transition, it reverts back to the default left-to-right push, even if you specified a different direction.

- Transitions can also blend between movie footage and still clips. For example, you're editing an interview and you want to dissolve to an embarrassing high school photo of the interviewee. You can also achieve some low-tech special effects: suppose you want to end your video with a still image overlaid with styled text. Save one frame as a still image (explained in Chapter 9), and add the text in Photoshop or a similar program. Then, import the changed still image, and add a Cross Dissolve or Overlap transition before it (**Figure 11.4**).

- iMovie includes the most commonly used types of transitions, but you may be looking for a different kind of effect. If so, check out transitions and plug-ins offered by third-party developers. Although I can't honestly say I'll ever use a transition that draws video within a heart shape, for example, other transitions range from the beautifully subtle to truly psychedelic. See Appendix B for a list of iMovie plug-in developers.

Adding Transitions

Adding a transition to your movie is as easy as dragging and dropping an icon. The trickery (and I use the term loosely) is in configuring how it appears in the movie. Don't worry about nailing it the first time: you can always change a transition's settings, even after you've added it to your movie.

To add a transition:

◆ Drag the transition to the intersection of two clips in the Clip Viewer or Timeline Viewer. (Transitions can be added to the beginning and end of the movie as well.) A transition icon appears with a red line moving from left to right (**Figure 11.5**).

That line indicates iMovie's progress of rendering the transitions. To build a transition, iMovie recreates the affected frames of the clip with the transition applied. For example, if we add a Fade In transition that's one second (30 frames) in duration, iMovie redraws each frame with a different brightness setting (**Figure 11.6**). This ensures that in the final movie, the transition appears at its best resolution and plays smoothly.

✔ Tips

■ Leave enough padding in your clips to accommodate transitions. Otherwise, iMovie displays an error that one or both of the clips is too short (**Figure 11.7**).

■ To cancel a transition while it's rendering, choose Undo from the Edit menu or press Command-period (.).

■ Go ahead and continue working while a transition is rendering, or even add other transitions, which are rendered concurrently. You can also play your movie before the rendering finishes, though the unrendered clips will appear jumpy and rough until they're fully rendered.

Render progress bar ⌐ ⌐ *Transition icon*

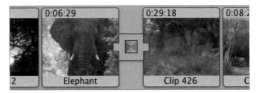

Figure 11.5 Transitions need to render before they can play back smoothly in the Monitor (top). The transition icon is similar in the Clip Viewer (bottom).

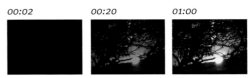

Figure 11.6 An iMovie transition recreates your footage with the transition's effect applied. Here are three frames from a Fade In transition.

This clip needs more footage if you want to add a transition after it (and avoid the error below).

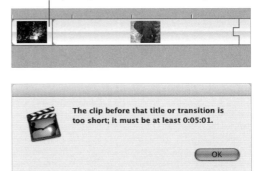

Figure 11.7 iMovie needs a certain amount of source material to work with. It will tell you how much footage is needed, based on your Speed slider setting.

Figure 11.8 Select multiple contiguous clips to easily add transitions between them.

Figure 11.9 After clicking the Add button, the same type of transition is added between each clip.

Most Valuable Transitions

In most situations, you'll find yourself using only a handful of transitions: Fade In, Fade Out, Cross Dissolve, and Overlap. I'm also partial to Wash In and Wash Out, in the right context. The others, to me, are usually too flashy for regular use.

One of the best uses of the subtle Fade In and Fade Out transitions is to pair them back to back to intercut a series of short scenes or still images: the picture goes from black to full strength (Fade In), runs for a second or two (or even shorter), then dissolves to black again (Fade Out), only to start again with a different scene. I've created an example and posted it at www. jeffcarlson.com/imovievqs/.

Adding Multiple Transitions

One great feature in iMovie is the capability to add several transitions to your movie at once. If you want the same type of transition to appear in multiple places, this approach will save you a lot of dragging.

To add multiple transitions:

1. Select two or more adjoining clips (**Figure 11.8**).

2. Select a transition and configure its settings.

3. Click the Add button. The transition is added between each clip (**Figure 11.9**).

✔ Tips

- If you perform these steps on a range of clips that already includes a transition, that transition remains unaffected.

- If one of the clips you selected does not have enough frames available for the transition, a dialog appears with the option of having iMovie calculate a new duration for the transition.

- Even if you don't want all of your transitions to be the same, this is an easy way to add placeholder transitions that you can go back and edit later (see the next page for details).

- I like to use a combination of Fade Out and Fade In transitions sometimes. The Add feature works well here, too: simply apply Fade Out, then apply Fade In with the same clips selected.

Editing Transitions

You can easily edit the attributes or even change the transition type for one or more transitions at once.

To modify existing transitions:

1. Select the transition in the Clip Viewer or Timeline Viewer.

2. Adjust the transition's settings in the Transitions pane.

3. Click the Update button to re-render the transition (**Figure 11.10**).

To modify multiple transitions:

1. Select two or more transitions in the Clip Viewer or Timeline Viewer by Command-clicking them.

2. Adjust the transitions' properties in the Transitions pane.

3. Click Update to apply the changes.

✔ Tips

■ Since transitions become their own clips, you can edit their volume levels, including fading sound in and out. The Fade In and Fade Out transitions apply audio fades automatically, which you can edit (see Chapter 10).

■ If you've selected multiple types of transitions in the Timeline and then change the settings in the Transitions pane, they will all become the one type that's highlighted in the Transitions pane's list.

■ You can't move transitions the way you can rearrange other clips. In fact, if you try to grab one and move it in the Timeline Viewer, the clips connected to it can get shifted to the right, creating a gap (**Figure 11.11**). It's better to delete the transition and place another in the new location.

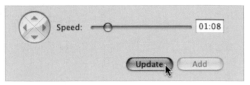

Figure 11.10 If you change a transition's settings, click the Update button to re-render it in the Timeline.

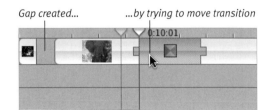

Gap created...   *...by trying to move transition*

Figure 11.11 Attempting to move a transition can cause the clips attached to it to shift within the Timeline Viewer.

iMovie's Habit of Stealing Time

As you add transitions, you may notice something odd happening: your movie is getting *shorter*. Is it possible to add things to a movie and still end up with less than when you started? (And if so, does it apply to eating ice cream?)

Yes. (But no to the ice cream.) Here's how iMovie steals time using transitions (**Figure 11.12**):

1. For the sake of not straining my math abilities, let's assume we want to add a Cross Dissolve transition between two 10-second clips. In order to maintain a comfortable pace, we decide to make our transition 2 seconds long.

2. We drag the transition into place between the clips, and notice that each clip has become 8 seconds in length, not 9 seconds (to split a 2-second transition between two clips leaves 1 second for each clip: 10 − 1 = 9).

3. The mystery is solved when we look at how iMovie is building the transition. It needs to start dissolving one clip into the other clip at the very beginning of the transition, so iMovie merges 2 seconds of each clip, removing 4 seconds total. The transition is still 2 seconds in duration, but required 4 seconds to perform the blends. Think of it as tightening a belt: you still have the same amount of material, but the overlap where the buckle rests allows you to encompass a smaller area.

Watching iMovie grab and modify clips is also the best motivation for locking any audio clips you've extracted (see Chapter 10). It only takes one transition to throw the rest of your movie out of sync.

Total movie time before transition: 20 seconds

Clips before adding transition

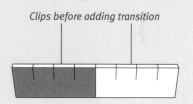

Total movie time decreased to 18 seconds after adding transition

Two-second transition steals a total of four seconds from the affected clips.

Overlap at point of transition

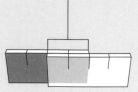

Figure 11.12 Some transitions, such as Cross Dissolve, need to overlap two clips in order to merge the number of frames needed for the effect. This creates a shorter overall movie.

Removing Transitions

Think of transitions as clips that are placed on top of the video track, rather than wedged between the other clips. This enables you to delete them without worrying that you're destroying any underlying footage.

To delete a transition:

1. Select the transition in the Clip Viewer or Timeline Viewer.

2. Press the Delete key, or choose Cut or Clear from the Edit menu. The sections of clips that were used by the transition are restored (**Figure 11.13**).

Before

After

Figure 11.13 A transition acts like a regular clip most of the time, but when you delete it, the pieces of footage it used are returned to the nearby clips.

TITLES

In Hollywood, movie titles aren't mere words that flash up on the screen. Actors, agents, and studio executives negotiate for the length of time a person's name appears, how large or small the typeface is, whether the name comes before or after the movie title, and all sorts of other conditions that inflame my natural aversion to fine print. Hopefully, you won't deal with any of that, because the other aspects of movie titles—i.e., actually *creating* them—are made extraordinarily easy in iMovie.

As with a lot of iMovie capabilities, you're creating elements quickly and cheaply that used to cost a fortune for studios and film-makers.

Editing the Text

iMovie offers three types of text fields, depending on the type of title used. To begin editing titles, click the Editing button and then the Titles button (**Figure 12.1**).

Text fields

Most of the title options use a set of two text fields. The top field typically acts as the primary title and appears larger in some titles than the bottom field.

To add text to title fields:

1. Choose a title from the list. A preview appears in the Monitor. Using the Preview controls, you can (**Figure 12.2**):

   ▲ Click the Play button to start or stop playback of the preview.

   ▲ Click the Loop button to start or stop continuous playback.

   ▲ Drag the Preview playhead in the preview's scrubber bar.

   ▲ Click the Hide Preview button (marked X) to cancel the title.

   ▲ Click the Apply button (marked with a checkbox) to apply the title; see "Adding Titles," later in this chapter.

2. Click within a field to position the pointer.

3. Type new title text, then press Return or click outside the field.

To insert special characters:

1. Click within a field to position the pointer.

2. Choose Special Characters from the Edit menu, or press Command-Option-T.

3. Select a character from the Character Palette.

4. Click the Insert button. The character appears in the text field (**Figure 12.3**).

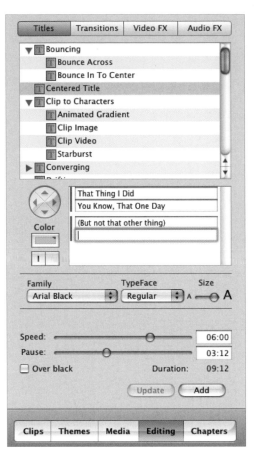

Figure 12.1 Choose from several animated text options in the Titles list.

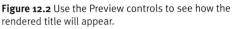

Figure 12.2 Use the Preview controls to see how the rendered title will appear.

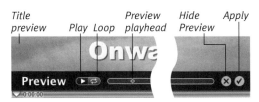

Figure 12.3 It's easy to use special characters (also known as "dingbats") in titles.

Figure 12.4 Multiple text fields enable you to create titles with opposing elements, such as Rolling Credits.

A Subliminal Production by
Someone Else

Color

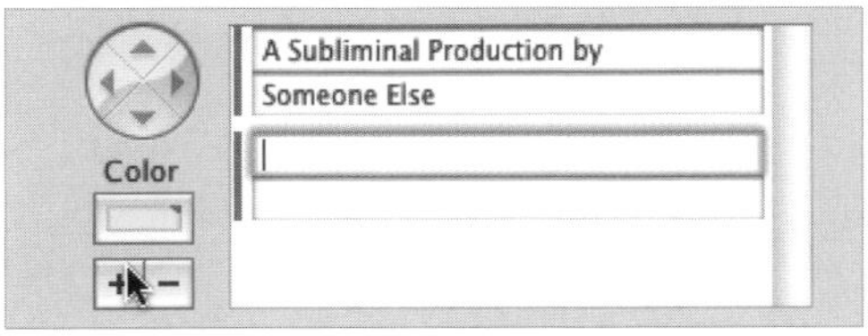

Figure 12.5 In title styles with multiple text fields, use the plus-sign button to add more fields.

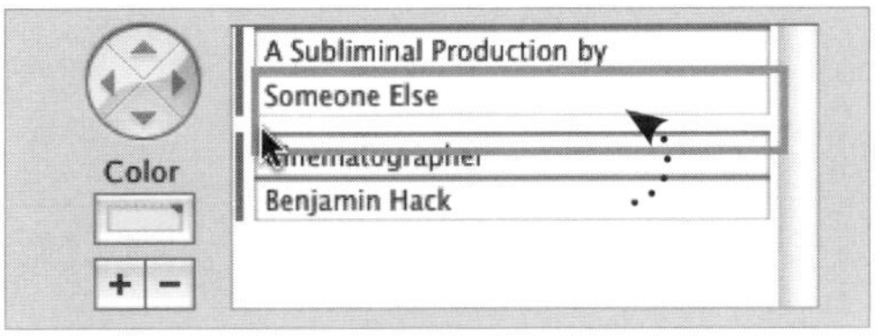

A Subliminal Production by
Someone Else

Cinematographer
Benjamin Hack

Color

Figure 12.6 Think your name needs to appear sooner in the credits? Click and drag the text field into place.

Titles Don't Look Good Onscreen

One of the most common questions I get from readers is, "Why don't my titles look good when I play them in iMovie?" Text appears jagged, or sometimes there's a lot of visual noise surrounding the letters.

Don't worry, this is actually normal. The picture you're viewing in the Monitor has been optimized to fit into a normal television aspect ratio—in reality, the video dimensions are wider than what appears in iMovie. To view your titles properly, export your movie to tape and play it back on a television (see Chapter 15), or connect a monitor to your computer (see Chapter 6).

Multiple text fields

If a two-line title isn't long enough, some titles offer multiple text fields, which are one or more field pairs. Usually, the extra fields are used for animating the text—for example, Centered Title displays the first field pair, clears the title, then displays the next field pair. Multiple fields are also used to set up titles, such as Rolling Credits, which face each other across the screen (**Figure 12.4**). You can add more text pairs and change their order, if you like.

To add text fields:

1. With a title selected that offers multiple text field pairs, click the plus-sign button. A new pair is created (**Figure 12.5**).

2. Type your text into the fields and press Return or click outside the field.

To remove text fields:

1. Click a text pair to select it.

2. Click the minus-sign button. The pair is deleted.

To rearrange text fields:

1. Click a text pair to select it.

2. Drag the selection up or down the list to change its position, then drop it in place (**Figure 12.6**).

✔ Tips

- You can select (and therefore delete or move) only one text pair at a time.

- iMovie remembers the last text you entered, so you don't need to type it again if you click another title effect—or even if you create a new project.

EDITING THE TEXT

Text blocks

If you still need more text in your title, use a style with a text block field, such as Music Video. It accommodates more text and can wrap your words (i.e., move them to the next line) as space allows.

To add text to block fields:

1. Type your text into the field.

   or

   Paste some text you've copied elsewhere, such as from a word processing application (**Figure 12.7**).

2. Click the name of the text style to apply the text. (Unlike the other text fields in iMovie, pressing the Return or Enter key in a text block creates a line break instead of applying the edit.)

Text style

Now that you've entered some text, it's time to give it style: select a color and a typeface, change the type size, and optionally view the title on a black background.

To select text color:

1. Click the rectangular Color field below the Titles list. The Colors palette appears (**Figure 12.8**).

2. Click within the color wheel to select a color, or click one of the buttons at the top to change selectors (such as sliders or even Crayon colors). You can try as many colors as you like while the palette is visible, and see them applied to text in the Monitor's preview.

3. Click the close button in the upper-left corner of the palette to accept the last color you applied.

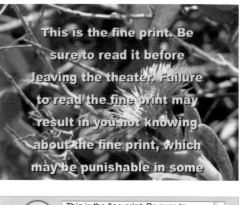

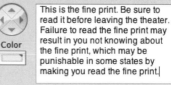

Figure 12.7 Text blocks let you enter more text than is allowed in other text fields.

Color field

Figure 12.8 Click the Color field to bring up the Colors palette, which gives you a full range of hues.

Figure 12.9 Choose a font family, typeface, and size for your title.

Over black enabled   Next clip remains intact

Over black disabled   Title uses part of next clip

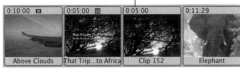

Figure 12.10 When the Over black option is enabled (top), the text clip that's created doesn't incorporate the next clip's footage (middle). When Over black is turned off, the text clip uses the next clip's footage (bottom) as background for the title.

Figure 12.11 Both titles were made using the same font at the largest setting.

Typography in iMovie HD 6

iMovie HD 6 is supposed to let you use the Mac OS X Fonts palette to define numeric text sizes and other attributes—a feature I've wanted forever. However, as of version 6.0.2, it doesn't work, so I'm still waiting.

To specify font and size:

1. Choose a font and style from the Family and TypeFace popup menus.

2. Drag the Size slider to increase or decrease the type size (**Figure 12.9**).

To display text against a black background:

◆ Click the Over black checkbox. When you apply this style to your movie, it pushes aside the clip that follows the title and displays the text on a black background, rather than overlaying it on clip footage (**Figure 12.10**). Make sure any extracted audio clips are locked in place before you add a title with Over black enabled.

✔ Tips

■ Instead of running a title over video footage or a black background, consider importing abstract images that can be used as backdrops for your titles.

■ The text style settings apply to every title effect listed in the Titles pane. When I'm creating a title, I'll play with five or six options before settling on one, so it's nice that I don't need to enter the settings each time I click a title.

■ To ensure that fonts appear smooth in titles, use Adobe PostScript, TrueType, or OpenType fonts. These include the fonts included with the Mac OS.

■ The longer your title, the smaller it appears, regardless of the font size you've specified (**Figure 12.11**). iMovie adjusts the proportions of the text to fit.

■ The color control affects the color of the text itself, except in the case of Stripe Subtitle, where the color setting applies to the text's background stripe. A few of the Clip to Characters titles also use color as a background element.

EDITING THE TEXT

143

Setting Title Duration

If we were dealing with still images, our work here would be done. But video is about movement, so don't expect titles to just flash onscreen and then disappear. Almost every iMovie title is animated in some way, which means you need to control how it moves. iMovie has two methods of doing this: the speed of the effect, and the length of the pause following the effect.

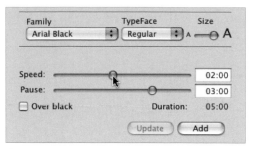

Figure 12.12 The Speed slider dictates the duration of a title effect's animation.

To set a title's duration:

1. Drag the Speed slider (or enter a value in the field) to specify how long the title's effect takes to complete (**Figure 12.12**). The time includes animation before and after the text fully appears; for example, a speed of 2:00 provides animation for 1 second at the beginning and 1 second at the end of the entire title sequence.

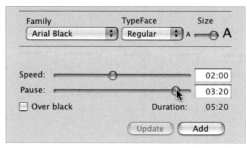

Figure 12.13 The Pause slider controls how long the title remains onscreen once the effect is finished. Dragging the slider updates the total time of the effect, as shown in the Duration indicator.

2. Drag the Pause slider (or enter a value in the field) to specify how long the titles remain onscreen after the title animation has finished (**Figure 12.13**). Some effects, such as Subtitle, don't offer a pause option.

   The Duration value combines the times and indicates the total time of the title.

✔ Tips

- Some titles' speeds vary depending on what you've typed into the text fields. The Flying Letters title, for example, needs more time if there are more letters, which is why the maximum Speed setting changes for long titles (after typing your title, click another title style, then click Flying Letters again to see the difference).

- Remember that not everyone may be able to read as fast as you. Give your viewers plenty of time to read your title—without boring them, of course.

Figure 12.14 The directional controller on some title effects determines which way the words move onto the screen.

Figure 12.15 A few titles let you set vertical position by clicking within the preview window. A crosshair icon with a yellow dot indicates that a title supports this capability.

Figure 12.16 Music Video gives you a little more control over text positioning because it's a block title.

Setting Title Position

Some effects, such as Bounce In To Center, feature a control for specifying the direction in which the text animates. Others, such as Centered Title, let you place text on the screen.

To set title direction:

1. Click the title you wish to use.

2. Click an arrow on the directional controller next to the title fields (**Figure 12.14**).

To set vertical title position:

1. Click the title you wish to use.

2. Click within the Monitor's preview to set the position from top to bottom of the text (**Figure 12.15**). (This feature applies to a few titles only, such as Typewriter.)

✔ Tips

- Clicking the preview using the Starburst title sets the origin of the starburst lines.

- The Music Video title gives you the option of running text along the left or right side of the screen. But it's also a text block title, so you can type line breaks (using Return or Enter). If you put the two features together, you can position text in the upper-left or upper-right corners of the screen (**Figure 12.16**).

- All sorts of controls can appear in the Titles pane, as you'll discover if you install third-party plug-ins. The Bounce Across title adds a control for setting the amount of "waviness" applied to the text.

Adding Titles

Once you've decided how your title will look, you're ready to add it to your movie.

To add a title:

◆ Drag and drop the title's name or icon to the left of the clip onto which it will appear in the Timeline (**Figure 12.17**). iMovie begins rendering the title in a new clip.

◆ Position the Playhead at the point where you want the title to begin and click the Add button.

Title clip rendering

When a title is rendered, iMovie actually writes the pixels to your footage, rather than generating them on the fly (such as when you preview a title). And like transitions and effects, titles render as their own clips. You can continue to work or play your movie while the title is rendering, though playback won't be as smooth.

If a title clip is longer than the clip it's being applied to, the title clip runs on into the next clip (**Figure 12.18**).

✔ Tips

■ Hold down the Command or Control key to prevent Clip Viewer icons from sliding around before you drop the clip.

■ Add multiple titles to the same section of footage by applying titles to a section of footage that already contains a title. For example, I've used Centered Title to gradually display a scene's name, and added a Music Video title within the clip that shows the time (**Figure 12.19**).

■ iMovie creates a new file in your project file called "Subtitle 01" (or similar) that contains the rendered footage; the original clip remains still intact.

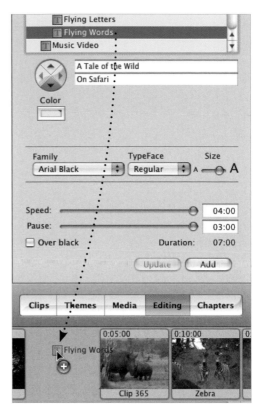

Figure 12.17 Once you've specified how your title will appear, drag and drop it onto the Clip Viewer or Timeline Viewer.

Before

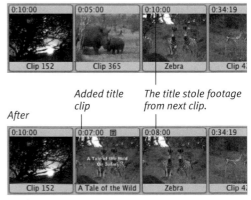

Added title clip   *The title stole footage from next clip.*

After

Figure 12.18 The title is 0:07:00 in length, so putting it in front of a clip that's 0:05:00 ("Clip 365") causes the title to render over all of "Clip 365" and grab footage from the next clip ("Zebra").

Figure 12.19 Combine multiple titles by applying a new title effect to an existing one.

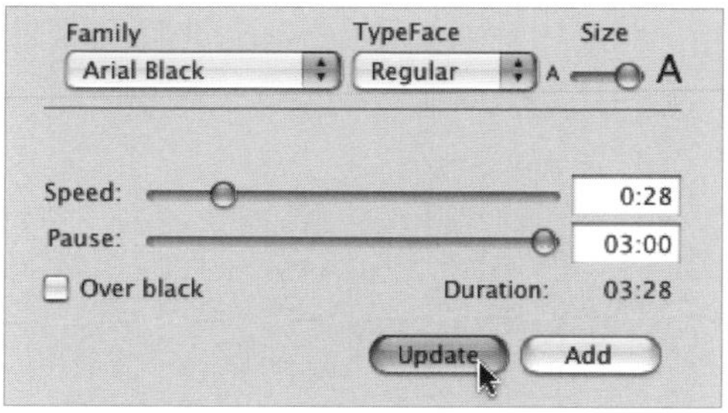

Figure 12.20 The Update button becomes active if you select a clip with a title applied. Change its settings and click Update to re-render the clip.

Modifying and Deleting Existing Titles

When you add a title clip, it actually exists on top of your footage. If you don't like the way it turned out, you can easily change its properties, or get rid of it altogether.

To modify an existing title:

1. Select the title clip.

2. Make any changes you wish in the Titles pane.

3. Click the Update button to apply your changes (**Figure 12.20**).

To delete a title:

1. Select the offending title clip.

2. Press the Delete key, which removes the title from the Timeline and sends it to the Trash. You can also drag the clip to the Trash if you're in the Clip Viewer. Or, you can choose Cut or Clear from the Edit menu.

✔ Tip

- You can always pull a title clip out of iMovie's trash if you need to. However, deleting a title breaks any connection to your original footage, so if you move a title from the trash to the timeline, it won't be superimposed over your footage; instead, it will be a new, separate clip. You're better off just re-creating the title.

EFFECTS

By now, you're probably sold on the notion of working with digital footage, but just in case there are any lingering doubts, consider iMovie's effects capabilities. Because you're manipulating pixels instead of strips of film, you can apply several types of changes to your footage, ranging from rudimentary color correction to special effects.

When I first heard that iMovie offered effects, I admit I feared the worst. What better way to destroy footage you worked so hard to shoot than to apply a bunch of filters to mangle those pixels?

I'm happy that my fears were unfounded. Instead of garish methods of swirling video into a toilet bowl of colors, iMovie gives you genuinely useful and powerful tools to adjust color, sharpen blurry images, and easily turn your multi-hued images into classic-looking black-and-white footage.

iMovie HD 6 also adds something long anticipated: audio effects. Not only can you make your voice sound like a chipmunk, you can apply basic noise filtering and other effects.

The area of effects is also where third-party iMovie plug-in developers have focused their attentions. If you're looking for an effect that iMovie can't accomplish on its own, be sure to check the companies listed in Appendix B.

Editing Effect Settings

Like transitions and titles (see the previous two chapters), iMovie's visual effects are accessed from the Editing pane; click the Video FX button to view video effects and the Audio FX button for audio effects (**Figure 13.1**).

To preview an effect:

◆ Click an effect's name to display it in the Monitor. Using the Preview controls, you can (**Figure 13.2**):

  ▲ Click the Play button to start or stop playback of the preview.

  ▲ Click the Loop button to start or stop continuous playback.

  ▲ Drag the Preview playhead in the preview's scrubber bar.

  ▲ Click the Hide Preview button (marked X) to cancel the effect.

  ▲ Click the Apply button (marked with a checkbox) to set the effect; see "Applying Effects," in this chapter.

To control how an effect begins and ends:

1. Select an effect's name in the list.

2. Move the Effect In and Effect Out sliders (or enter values in their text fields) to control the time it takes for the effect to start and end (**Figure 13.3**). You can, of course, leave them set at 00:00 to apply the effect throughout the entire clip, but changing these values lets you ease into and out of the effect. For example, suppose you want someone's flashback to appear in black and white, then blend back into color as the flashback merges into the present day.

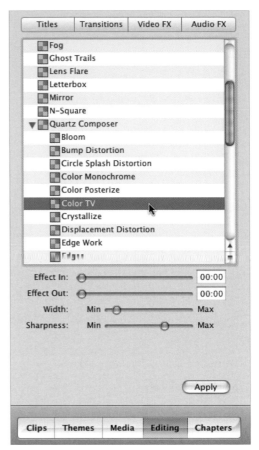

Figure 13.1 The Video Effects pane is a similar layout to the Transitions and Titles panes.

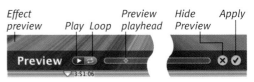

Figure 13.2 Use the Preview controls to see how the rendered effect will appear.

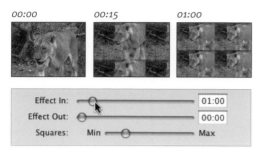

00:00 00:15 01:00

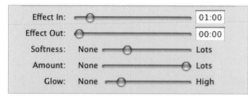

Effect In: | 01:00
Effect Out: | 00:00
Squares: Min | Max

Figure 13.3 Setting Effect In to 01:00 causes the effect to gradually apply, instead of starting at the beginning of the clip. In this case, the N-Square effect pushes the mirror image into the scene from the left. If we kept the Effect In slider set to 00:00, the first frame would look like the 01:00 frame, above.

Effect In: | 01:00
Effect Out: | 00:00
Softness: None | Lots
Amount: None | Lots
Glow: None | High

Figure 13.4 Effect-specific controls appear below the list of effects. Changing them updates the preview dynamically.

Figure 13.5 Some effects feature controls within the Monitor's preview. For example, clicking in the Monitor with Circle Splash Distortion sets the center of the distortion.

To adjust an effect's settings:

1. Select an effect's name in the list. If it features additional controls, they appear below the list (**Figure 13.4**).

2. Move the sliders to adjust the effect's settings. The preview shows your changes immediately, so feel free to experiment.

To adjust an effect's settings in the preview:

◆ If an effect includes controls in the preview window, click within the window to specify a focus point (**Figure 13.5**). A yellow crosshair indicates that such a control is available for that effect.

✔ Tip

■ Third-party iMovie plug-in developers have gone wild with effects. In addition to adding "painterly" looks, you can create picture-within-picture effects (as seen on TV newscasts), and even perform some rudimentary greenscreen matting effects (for when you want to make your cat look like she's rampaging through downtown Tokyo!). See Appendix B for a list of plug-in vendors.

EDITING EFFECT SETTINGS

151

Applying Effects

Unlike with transitions and titles, you do not drag effects to the Timeline. Instead, use the Apply button located at the bottom-right corner of the pane.

To apply an effect:

1. Select the clip you want to modify.

2. Select the effect you want to apply, and adjust its settings to your liking (see the previous two pages).

3. Click the Apply button. The clip begins rendering with the effect applied. In the Clip Viewer, clips with effects are marked with a checkerboard icon (**Figure 13.6**).

✔ Tips

- You can reverse steps 1 and 2. Sometimes I select a clip first, sometimes I tinker with effects settings without any clip selected. For its preview, iMovie uses whatever clip is under the playhead.

- Effects cannot be applied to clips on the Clips pane. However, you can add an effect to a clip in the Timeline and then drag it to the Clips pane for use later.

- To cancel rendering, press Command-period (.) or choose Undo from the Edit menu.

- If you apply some types of effects to a still image, the image needs to be converted to a regular clip. Don't worry, iMovie warns you if this is the case, and gives you the option to cancel (**Figure 13.7**). (See Chapter 9 for more on using still images.)

- After you've applied an effect, you can still add transitions or titles to that clip.

- If you apply multiple effects to a clip, a number next to the effects icon tells you how many there are (**Figure 13.8**).

Effect icon

Figure 13.6 Clips with effects applied show up in the Clip Viewer with a checkerboard icon.

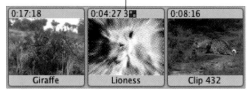

Figure 13.7 Some effects require that still images be converted to regular clips.

Multiple effects applied

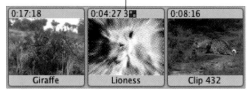

Figure 13.8 The number next to the effects icon indicates how many effects have been applied to the clip.

Effect applied   *Effect deleted*

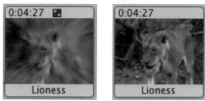

Figure 13.9 Deleting an effect doesn't delete the entire clip.

Before

After   *Effect 4 is deleted.*

Figure 13.10 Deleting multiple effects from a clip is like peeling paint in an old house—sooner or later you get to the original.

Removing Effects

On the off chance that you applied several effects in your sleep, waking up in horror to discover that everyone on your spouse's side of the family has been mirrored, there's an easy way to restore those clips: simply delete the effect, as you would with a title or transition.

To remove an effect:

1. Select the clip in your movie to which the effect has been applied.

2. Press the Delete key or choose Clear from the Edit menu. The effect is deleted, leaving the original clip intact (**Figure 13.9**).

✔ Tips

- When multiple effects are applied to a clip, you must remove each one in turn (**Figure 13.10**). To save time, you *could* use the Revert Clip to Original command (from the Advanced menu), but then you get the clip's entire original footage—overkill.

- Unfortunately, if you decide that you want to keep effect number 3, but not effects 1 and 2, you need to delete all three and then re-apply the effect you want.

Modifying Existing Effects

Way back in iMovie 2, you could tweak an effect's settings after you had applied it to a clip, then click the Update button to apply the new settings. However, if you wanted to use multiple effects, you first needed to *commit* the clip, rendering it so that iMovie no longer recognized it as an effects-laden clip. iMovie 3 and later no longer require the commit step, but you cannot modify settings in effects that have already been applied. You must delete the effect and start over. I recommend making a copy of the clip before deleting its effect (Option-drag it to the Clips pane) so you have a backup of the first version of the effect.

Reversing Clip Direction

Playing a clip backwards can be good for more than just comic value or special effects. This feature comes in handy more often than I ever thought: a clip played in reverse can sometimes blend better into the next scene (for example, zooming out of a landscape). Then again, I find it hard to resist tweaking reality by making a spilled glass of milk clean itself, or coaxing waterfalls to rush upwards.

To reverse clip direction:

1. Select a clip.

2. Select the Fast/Slow/Reverse effect.

3. Enable the Reverse Direction checkbox (**Figure 13.11**).

4. Click the Apply button.

✔ Tips

■ Reversed clips feature backwards audio as well as visuals. You'll probably want to make the clip silent and play some other audio track in its place.

■ When you apply the Fast/Slow/Reverse effect to a clip that you've edited using Direct Trimming, you lose any hidden footage as long as the effect is active—it becomes its own self-contained clip. However, if you remove the effect, you can still access your hidden footage to the original clip.

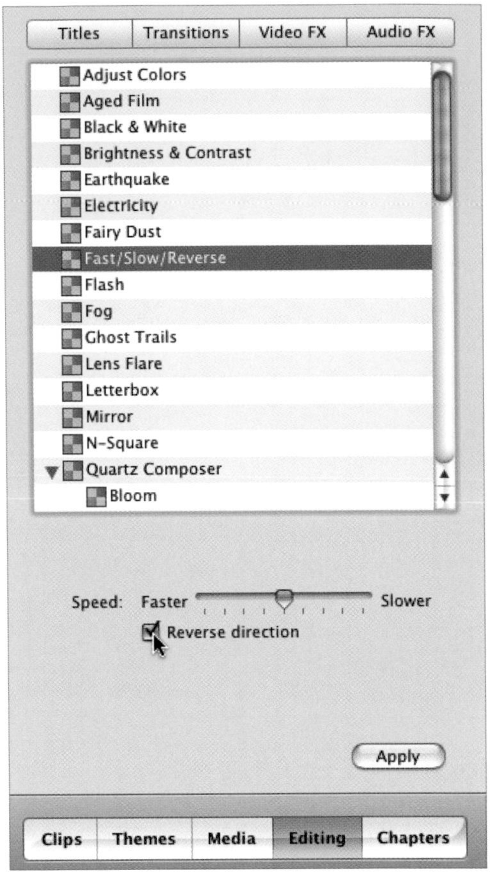

Figure 13.11 Use the Fast/Slow/Reverse effect to make a clip play backward.

Normal speed

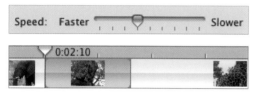

Twice as fast

Maximum speed

Speed comparison in Clip Viewer

Figure 13.12 I've used the Fast/Slow/Reverse effect to speed up the original clip up to five times faster.

Changing Playback Speed

Creating sped-up or slow-motion imagery previously involved changing a camera's shutter speed (the faster the film moved, the more individual pictures could be shot, creating slow motion, for example). In iMovie, all you have to do is move a slider.

To speed up or slow down video:

1. Select the clip you wish to alter.

2. Select the Fast/Slow/Reverse effect.

3. Move the Speed slider toward Faster or Slower to change the speed (**Figure 13.12**).

4. Click the Apply button.

iMovie's Speed slider can make a clip five times faster or five times slower than the original speed. If you need a clip that's faster or slower than that, follow these steps.

To make clips super fast or super slow:

1. Speed up or slow down the footage in your movie as described above.

2. Export the footage to a DV-formatted QuickTime file (see Chapter 16).

3. Re-import that footage into iMovie. Since it's regular footage now, iMovie considers its speed to be normal.

4. Apply the Fast/Slow/Reverse effect to change the speed of the imported clip.

✔ Tips

■ You can also simply click a portion of the slider's scale to adjust the speed, instead of moving the slider knob.

■ Changing clip speed is especially helpful on clips of scenery or backgrounds. Draw out scenes you shot too quickly, or speed up long pans to improve pacing.

Audio Effects

One frequent drawback to amateur movies is poor sound quality. Even if you use the advice in Chapter 5 when recording audio, you may want to sweeten the sound during editing. iMovie HD 6 adds a number of new audio effects that can help. Note that audio effects are tools for manipulating audio, and are different from sound effects, which are recordings of specific sounds (see Chapter 10).

To apply an audio effect:

1. In the Editing pane, click the Audio FX button to view the list of audio effects (**Figure 13.13**).

2. Cilck a video or audio clip in the Timeline that will have the effect applied.

3. Choose an audio effect from the list; controls specific to each effect appear below the list.

4. Edit the effect settings and click the Preview button to hear how it will sound.

5. Click the Apply button to apply the effect. For video clips, iMovie renders the audio and extracts it to one of the audio tracks (**Figure 13.14**). If you applied the effect to an audio-only clip, the effect operates on top of the clip in the same way video effects work (**Figure 13.15**).

To edit an audio effect:

◆ Like video effects, you can't edit an audio effect once you've applied it. Instead, delete the last effect and apply a new one.

To remove an audio effect:

1. Select the extracted audio clip and press the Delete key.

2. If you're working with a video clip, restore the clip's audio using the Clip volume slider.

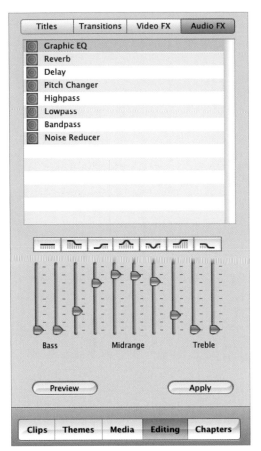

Figure 13.13 The Audio FX list in the Editing pane provides options for tweaking your movie's sound.

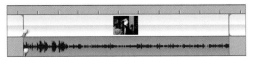

Figure 13.14 iMovie extracts an audio effect as a separate (but linked) extracted audio clip.

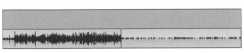

Figure 13.15 I've split this music clip into two pieces and applied effects to the clip on the right. When you apply audio effects to a clip in an audio track, iMovie layers the clips on top of each other.

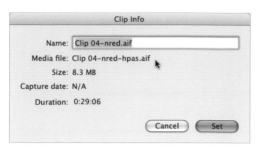

Figure 13.16 The name of the media file indicates which audio effects have been applied (ignore the clip name). In this case, Clip 04 is augmented with Noise Reducer (nred) and Highpass (hpas).

✔ Tips

■ After clicking the Preview button, you can dynamically change the settings to hear how they affect the audio.

■ Like video effects, you can overlay multiple audio effects onto the same clip. To see how many layers are applied, choose Show Info from the File menu and look at the name of the media file (**Figure 13.16**).

■ No one is going to confuse iMovie with professional audio editing software, but it does a good job of fixing common problems. For example, the Noise Reducer is a blunt tool, but it helps me minimize camera noise. If you find yourself wanting more audio control, consider Audacity (`audacity.sourceforge.net`), SoundStudio3 (`www.freeverse.com/soundstudio/`), or Apple's Soundtrack (included with Final Cut Express HD).

iMovie's Audio Effects

Highpass? Bandpass? What is this stuff?

◆ **Graphic EQ:** Use the 10 sliders to equalize different frequencies, or click the button presets.

◆ **Reverb:** Simulates an acoustic environment by changing the amount of reverberation introduced into the sound. iMovie offers six environments: Room, Club, Cathedral, Atrium, Arena, and Plate.

◆ **Delay:** Control the amount of echo added to a clip.

◆ **Pitch Changer:** Perhaps my favorite slider in iMovie, the Pitch Changer can make voices deeper or higher (**Figure 13.17**).

◆ **Highpass, Lowpass, and Bandpass:** These effects allow some frequencies and block others. Highpass keeps high frequencies, Lowpass keeps low ones, and Bandpass sets a range from high to low and rejects frequencies outside that bandwidth.

◆ **Noise Reducer:** This effect minimizes white noise, and is great for dealing with camera noise, crowd noise, and that pervasive hum inside airplanes, for example.

Figure 13.17 Even if you never use the Pitch Changer effect, you gotta admit it's the best...slider...ever.

AUDIO EFFECTS

Part 3
Sharing from iMovie HD

SCORING YOUR MOVIE IN GARAGEBAND

A movie's soundtrack doesn't need to consist of popular music—in fact, most films are scored instrumentally, according to the needs of each scene. If you have musical leanings, you may want to do your own scoring. With the inclusion of GarageBand in Apple's iLife suite, you can (even if you're not particularly musical, like me).

With a musical instrument and some hardware to get the audio into your Mac, you can perform your own music. Personally, I like GarageBand because I can choose from hundreds of existing background loops and create segments that are just as long as I need them to be. Those loops are also copyright- and royalty-free, so I don't need to worry about securing rights if I decide to release the movie in public.

Sharing to GarageBand

Send your entire movie to GarageBand, where you can build music with the video as reference. This option is great for timing music cues with your movie.

To share your movie to GarageBand:

1. To export only a few clips, select them in the Timeline (or the Clips pane). To export the entire movie, skip to step 2.

2. Choose GarageBand from the Share menu, or press Command-Shift-E and click the GarageBand icon (**Figure 14.1**).

3. Click the box labeled Share selected clips only to export the range you selected in step 1. Otherwise, ignore this step.

4. Click the Share button. iMovie exports your movie and launches GarageBand, where the movie appears in a new video track (**Figure 14.2**).

✔ Tips

■ All audio from your movie appears on one track in GarageBand, even if you had multiple tracks set up in iMovie. You may want to mute the Video Sound track while working on your score (**Figure 14.3**).

■ Having your video appear within Garage-Band is an enormous help, but it comes at a cost: even on fast machines, playback can be stuttery. GarageBand is simply a resource hog. You can regain some performance by locking audio tracks (click the padlock icon below the track name); this tells GarageBand to create a temporary "mixdown" of the locked tracks, which requires less processing power.

■ I'm just scratching the surface of Garage-Band in these few pages. Be sure to read the program's online help, or pick up a good book (such as Peachpit's *Apple Training Series: GarageBand 3*).

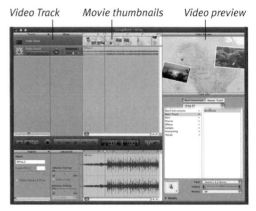

Figure 14.1 Share your movie to GarageBand to start the scoring process.

Video Track *Movie thumbnails* *Video preview*

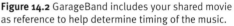

Figure 14.2 GarageBand includes your shared movie as reference to help determine timing of the music.

Mute Track button

Figure 14.3 Make the Video Sound track silent so you can focus on building the score in other tracks.

Loop Browser button   *Loop Browser*

Figure 14.4 The Loop Browser categorizes Garage-Band's loops according to instrument and genre.

Loop list

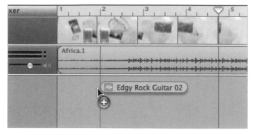

Figure 14.5 As you make instrument selections, the loop list displays loops that match your criteria.

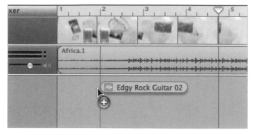

Figure 14.6 Drag a loop from the Loop Browser to GarageBand's Timeline to create a new track.

Making Music Using GarageBand

With a MIDI keyboard or guitar and amp you can start recording your own tunes. For simplicity's sake, however, I'm going to concentrate on using GarageBand's built-in loops to create a song.

To create a music loop in GarageBand:

1. Display the Loop Browser by clicking the Loop Browser button, choosing Show Loop Browser from the Control menu, or pressing Command-L (**Figure 14.4**).

2. From the first three columns of the Loop Browser, click an instrument name. You can also choose multiple musical styles (from the next three columns) to refine the list of loops. The list of available loops matching your selections appears in the right-hand column (**Figure 14.5**).

3. Click a loop to hear it. The loop will continue to play until you click it again or click another loop.

4. Choose a loop and drag it to Garage-Band's Timeline to add it to your song (**Figure 14.6**).

5. Press the Play button or the spacebar to preview your song. I recommend also clicking the Cycle button (which has a picture of circled arrows) so that the song repeats as you're working. You can always hit spacebar again to stop playback.

continues on next page

163

6. The Time display shows measures, beats, and ticks. Click the small "unlit" clock icon in the left corner of the display to switch to absolute time (hours, minutes, seconds, fractions) (**Figure 14.7**).

7. Position your mouse pointer at the right edge of the loop you added, which Garage-Band calls a *region*, so that the cursor changes to a rounded circle, called the *loop pointer* (**Figure 14.8**).

8. Drag the loop pointer to the right to extend the region for as long as you want it to continue playing within your song. Rounded-corner breaks within the region indicate where the loop starts and ends (**Figure 14.9**).

9. Repeat steps 2 through 4 to select another loop and add it to the Timeline as a new track. Add as many combinations as you like (guitar, drums, etc.) until the song sounds good to you.

✔ Tips

■ If the GarageBand window is too narrow, the Loop Browser and Video Preview won't appear at the same time. Extend the width of the window to see both.

■ You don't need to create a brand new track for each loop you add—they can coexist in the same tracks. But separating out the tracks makes it easier to edit.

■ When you save the project, GarageBand asks if you want to save an iLife preview (**Figure 14.10**). If you click Yes, iMovie will be able to preview the song in the Media pane.

Absolute time button

Figure 14.7 I'm much more familiar with absolute time than with measures, beats, and ticks. Changing the Time display helps to define the song's length.

Region (selected)   *Loop pointer*

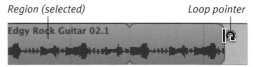

Figure 14.8 The region is the track's audio clip. Drag the edge of the region with the loop pointer to extend the duration of the loop.

Rounded corners indicate a loop within a region.

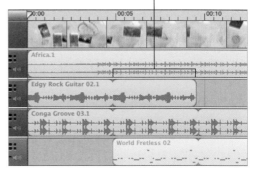

Figure 14.9 Loops are created so that they play cleanly from start to finish without breaks.

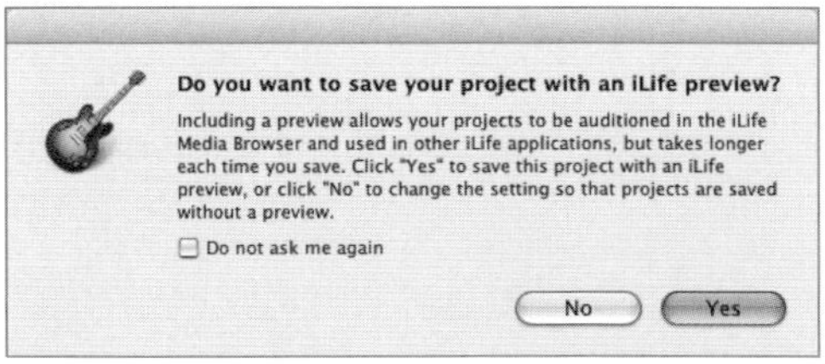

Do you want to save your project with an iLife preview?

Including a preview allows your projects to be auditioned in the iLife Media Browser and used in other iLife applications, but takes longer each time you save. Click "Yes" to save this project with an iLife preview, or click "No" to change the setting so that projects are saved without a preview.

☐ Do not ask me again

No   Yes

Figure 14.10 If you don't save your GarageBand project with an iLife preview, you won't be able to import the song into iMovie later.

Figure 14.11 When you import a GarageBand song, even if it includes video footage in GarageBand, iMovie brings in only the audio.

Getting the Score Back into iMovie

When you share your movie to GarageBand, iMovie assumes that you've finished editing and are ready to hand it off. But what if you want to go back and do more editing? There's no round-trip method to automatically pass the soundtrack back to iMovie. However, it is possible to import the song manually.

To import your song into iMovie:

1. In iMovie, switch to the Media pane and click the Audio button (if it's not already selected).

2. From the Audio list, choose GarageBand to display a list of your GarageBand files.

3. Drag the song you created to the Timeline Viewer or click the Place at Playhead button to add the song to your movie (**Figure 14.11**). Only songs saved with an iLife preview (indicated by a guitar icon) can be added in this way.

✔ Tips

- If you change the song in GarageBand, it won't automatically be updated in iMovie. You'll need to import the GarageBand file again.

- You may need to quit and restart iMovie for it to recognize new GarageBand songs you've created.

- A tune in GarageBand always ends nicely because the program fades out the lingering sound of the instruments after the song itself has ended. But when you bring it into iMovie, it often ends abruptly. Although you could set the volume to fade out in GarageBand, I prefer to set the fade using iMovie's audio controls; that way, I can change the duration of the fade without having to redo the song in GarageBand and re-export it for iMovie.

RECORDING BACK TO TAPE

Your movie is finished! Now what?

While it's feasible that you could transport your Mac (especially if it's a laptop) to every location where someone might see your movie, that plan runs into a few snags when you want to share your masterpiece with grandparents in Humboldt or your sister in South Africa. Fortunately, getting completed footage out of iMovie is almost as simple as bringing raw footage in.

One method is to export the movie back to a MiniDV tape in your camcorder. The best reason for this approach is that you maintain the same high quality that came from the camera in the first place—exporting to the Web or iDVD compresses the footage and degrades the image, even if it's not easily perceived (one exception to this is HDV video, which is compressed back into the MPEG-2 based HDV format, but the quality is still pretty darn good).

The camera also stores the footage in digital format, so you'll have a copy saved off your computer that retains the same level of quality as what you edited. This is handy in case you need to make a backup of your work so far, or for when you want to hook your camcorder up to a television to show the movie.

Exporting to the Camera

The FireWire connection between your Mac and your camcorder runs both ways, enabling you to write data back to the tape.

To export to the camera:

1. Switch your camcorder to Play/VCR/VTR mode and make sure you're not recording over existing footage on the tape.

2. If you want to export only a few clips from your movie, select them in the Timeline (but also see the first tip, below).

3. Choose Video Camera from the Share menu, or press Command Shift E and click the Videocamera icon at the top of the dialog (**Figure 15.1**).

4. If you want some black frames before or after your movie, enter numbers in the two Add fields. This gives you some extra time on the tape and tends to look more professional than just launching into the movie from the beginning.

5. Click the box labeled Share selected clips only to export the range you selected in step 2. Otherwise, ignore this step.

6. Click the Share button to begin exporting (**Figure 15.2**). When it's finished, iMovie automatically stops the camera.

✔ Tips

- Unfortunately, a bug in iMovie 6.0.2 currently prohibits exporting selected clips. Hopefully it will be fixed soon.

- To ensure that you get a smooth export to tape, quit all other running applications. iMovie hogs the processor when exporting, which can lead to stuttered playback (and therefore recording) to the tape.

- When sharing selected clips, you must select a contiguous set (all connected and in order on the Timeline).

Figure 15.1 The Videocamera tab of the Share dialog includes controls for setting up the camcorder and adding black frames.

Figure 15.2 Exporting to camera requires the same amount of time as your movie's length.

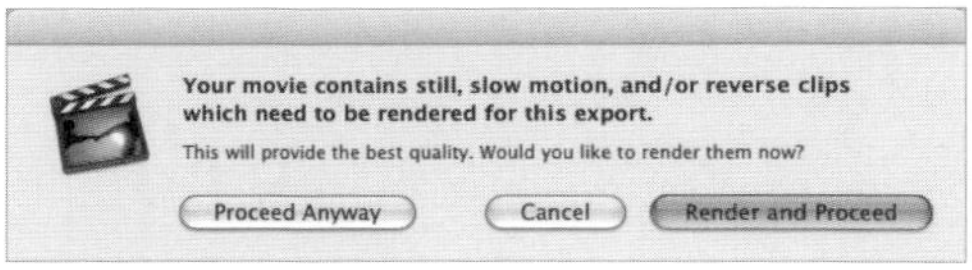

Figure 15.3 iMovie alerts you if any of your clips need to be rendered before exporting the movie to tape.

- If your movie contains clips that are slow motion, reversed, or still photos, iMovie must render them before exporting to the tape—a dialog appears asking if you want to render those clips. Rendering significantly improves their display. However, if you're just looking for some test footage, click the Proceed Anyway button to export the movie without rendering (**Figure 15.3**).

- The rendered clips above can get de-interlaced, resulting in poor image quality when viewed on a television. Try proceeding without rendering and testing the results. For some suggested workarounds, go to www.jeffcarlson.com/imovievqs/im6/rendering.html.

- When you export HDV footage from iMovie to the camera, be prepared for quite a wait. As I explained in Chapter 7, iMovie transcodes the HDV format to Apple Intermediate Codec (AIC) during the import process, which is why you'll see a lag between what's playing on the camera's LCD screen and what appears in iMovie's Monitor. To go back to the camera, iMovie transcodes from AIC to HDV, and then writes the video to tape. This iMovie-to-camera lag is much longer than importing, because the Mac is doing all the MPEG-2 video compression, not the dedicated chip built into the camera. In my testing, for example, a 1-minute movie took 6 to 8 minutes to export to the camera on a dual-2.5 GHz Power Mac G5, and over 20 minutes on a 1.25 GHz PowerBook G4.

Tape Backup

Exporting your footage to tape serves another important function: providing a backup of your work. Even a modest iMovie project will swamp many backup capacities (such as DAT tape systems) due to the sheer number of gigabytes needing to be backed up. Instead, export your movie to DV tape. In the event that you suffer a hard disk crash (trust me, it's not a fun experience), you won't have your iMovie project, but you'll be able to re-import the edited footage and not lose all of your work.

Transferring to Videotape

Not everyone owns a DVD player or a Mac equipped with a SuperDrive. If burning a DVD isn't an option, record to a VHS tape from your camcorder or directly from iMovie.

To transfer from your camcorder:

1. Export your movie from iMovie to your camcorder's tape as discussed on the previous pages.

2. Connect your camcorder to a VCR using the AV cable that came with the camcorder (**Figure 15.4**).

3. Switch the camcorder to Play/VCR/VTR mode if it's not already on.

4. Put a blank videotape in the VCR, and rewind the camcorder's tape to the beginning of your movie.

5. Push Record on the VCR.

6. Push Play on the camcorder.

7. When the movie is finished, push Stop on both machines.

To transfer directly from iMovie:

1. Connect your camcorder and VCR as described above.

2. Connect the camcorder to your Mac via FireWire, if it's not already connected.

3. In iMovie's preferences, enable the option labeled Play DV project video through to DV camera (**Figure 15.5**).

4. Remove the tape from the camcorder, then choose Export from the File menu. A dialog notifies you that there's no tape (**Figure 15.6**). Click Continue.

5. Press Record on your VCR, and click the Export button in iMovie.

6. When the movie is finished, push Stop on the VCR.

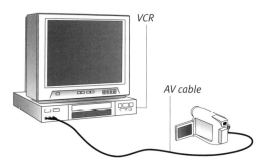

Figure 15.4 Connect your camcorder to a VCR using the AV cable included with the camcorder.

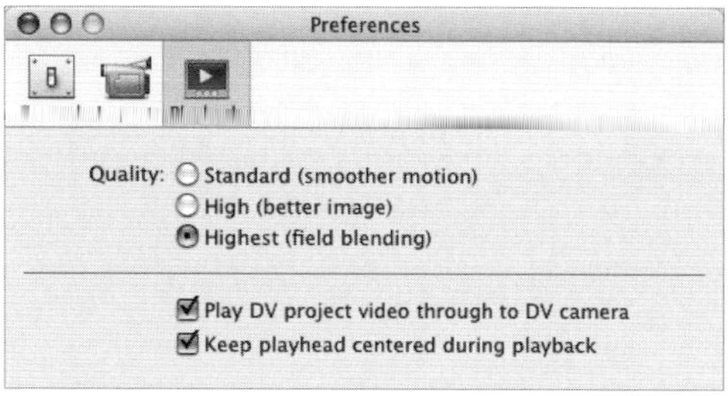

Figure 15.5 Be sure this option is selected before attempting to record to the VCR.

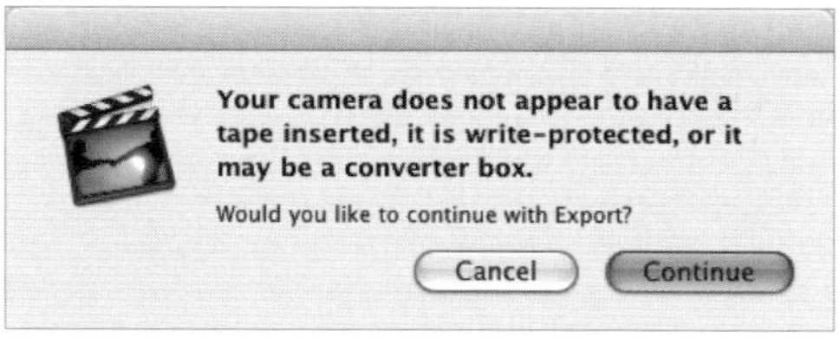

Figure 15.6 iMovie displays this error if you try to export a movie with no tape in the camcorder.

16

QuickTime

On the surface, QuickTime is a great little utility for playing movies on your Mac. I often visit www.*apple*.com/*trailers*/ to see which new movie trailer is ready for download—I click a link, and in a couple of minutes the clip is playing. (It's amazing what you can learn about filmmaking from trailers, by the way; they're some of the best sources for how to present ideas and images in a short time span.) Sometimes the movie appears in a window in your Web browser, while other times the QuickTime Player plays the movie.

iMovie gives you the opportunity to export your movies to the QuickTime format. In so doing, you gain a number of advantages: your file sizes become much smaller (a 1-minute clip can easily shrink from around 200 MB to 2 MB without destroying its quality); your movies can be played on any Macintosh sold within the last several years; and you can upload them to the Web, where anyone with a Web browser and the QuickTime software (that includes Windows users, too) can download and view the movie.

Choose one of iMovie's recommended settings or configure the details yourself to tweak performance.

Exporting to QuickTime

Exporting your movie to QuickTime can be as straightforward or as complicated as you want it to be. Understanding that most users won't wade into the complexities of what the QuickTime format can offer, iMovie gives you five pre-configured settings. Following are the basic steps for creating a QuickTime movie from your footage.

To export as a QuickTime movie:

1. To export only a few clips, select them in the Timeline or Clips pane. To export the entire movie, skip to the next step.

2. Choose QuickTime from the Share menu, or press Command-Shift-E.

3. In the Share dialog, click the QuickTime icon if it's not already selected.

4. Select a format from the popup menu labeled Compress movie for (**Figure 16.1**). These are common settings for various types of distribution (such as Web versus CD-ROM). See "Choosing a QuickTime format" below for explanations and examples of each.

5. Click the box labeled Share selected clips only to export the range you selected in step 1. Otherwise, ignore this step.

6. Click the Share button to begin creating the QuickTime movie.

Choosing a QuickTime format

When you're exporting to QuickTime, remember to keep your audience in mind. If your cinematic masterpiece is several hundred megabytes in size, it won't be downloaded online or fit onto a CD-ROM easily. iMovie offers five preset export configurations (**Figures 16.2** and **16.3**); the DV specifications for each are shown in **Table 16.1**.

Figure 16.1 iMovie includes five presets for exporting movies into the QuickTime format.

Email

*Web,
Streaming Web,
CD-ROM*

Full Quality

Figure 16.2 This should give you an idea of how the QuickTime export settings compare in iMovie. These images are roughly 25 percent of actual size.

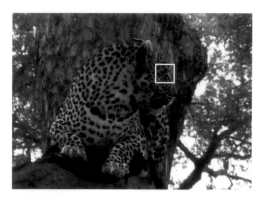

 Email

CD-ROM

Web

Full Quality

Figure 16.3 The different QuickTime export formats vary in visual quality, too, based on how much compression is applied.

◆ **Email.** This is the smallest format available from the presets, and represents quite a sacrifice of quality in favor of small file sizes. Don't expect titles to be read easily (or at all), but do expect speed: this movie can be half the size of a Web movie.

◆ **Web.** Web is a good compromise between file size and video quality. Its compression favors dial-up and low-speed broadband users in an attempt to appeal to the largest audience.

◆ **Web Streaming.** A movie that's streamed is played as it downloads, so you don't have to wait for the entire movie to arrive before viewing it. Slightly larger in file size than the Web movie above, this format includes data that enables the movie to be streamed from a dedicated streaming server (versus downloaded as a file, then played back).

◆ **CD-ROM.** The CD-ROM format increases the file size quite a bit from the Web movie, but the quality differences are immediately apparent. Note that the "CD-ROM" designation refers to file size, not a requirement that it can only be used on CD-ROMs.

continues on next page

Table 16.1

iMovie's Stock Compression Settings for a DV Project							
iMovie Format	**Video Compression**	**Size (pixels)**	**Frame Rate**	**Audio Compression**	**Stereo/ Mono**	**Sample Rate**	**Sample File Size***
Email	H.264	160 x 120	10.00 fps	AAC	Mono	32.000 kHz	1.1 MB
Web	H.264	320 x 240	12.00 fps	AAC	Stereo	32.000 kHz	1.4 MB
Web Streaming	H.264	320 x 240	12.00 fps	AAC	Stereo	32.000 kHz	1.6 MB
CD-ROM	H.264	320 x 240	15.00 fps	AAC	Stereo	32.000 kHz	5.0 MB
Full Quality DV	DV - NTSC	720 x 480	29.97 fps	DV	Stereo	48.000 kHz	215.8 MB

* File size is based on exporting the sample one-minute movie found on the previous page.

EXPORTING TO QUICKTIME

◆ **Full Quality.** This format should be titled "Full Quality HUGE" due to its massive file size. What makes it so big? It's the same format as what your camera produces, so essentially you're looking at uncompressed footage. It's big and beautiful, but you take a serious hard disk hit (about 200 MB per minute of video for DV footage).

✔ Tips

■ In the Share dialog, iMovie offers a handy estimate of how much space the exported movie will occupy on disk (**Figure 16.4**).

■ If you want to export your movie for later import into another editing program, such as Final Cut Pro or Final Cut Express, use Full Quality to create a new file saved in your project's native format. For example, when exporting HDV footage using the Full Quality option, the file is saved in the Apple Intermediate Codec (AIC) format, not QuickTime or DV. Make sure you have plenty of disk space, though!

■ Why is the video size for DV footage at Full Quality set to 720 x 480, instead of the Monitor's size of 640 x 480? You know that each frame is composed of pixels, but what's not obvious is that the pixels in digital video are rectangular (taller than they are wide, as shown in **Figure 16.5**). Similarly, the NTSC frame rate of 29.97 fps isn't rounded up to 30 fps. Way back when the first color televisions were introduced, the frame rate needed to be adjusted slightly to avoid audio distortion—and the setting stuck.

> Your movie will be compressed to 15 frames per second, approximately 320 x 240, with full-quality stereo sound. Estimated size: 5.8 MB to 8.2 MB.

Figure 16.4 The Share dialog summarizes your current export settings and estimates the movie's size on disk.

Full Quality (720 x 480 pixels)

Full Quality (640 x 480 pixels)

Figure 16.5 The Full Quality option exports video measuring 720 x 480 pixels in DV format, compared to the 640 x 480 pixel size you're accustomed to. If you were to import it into another video-editing application, it would appear as 640 x 480 (just like in iMovie).

Video Compression Terms You Should Know

Codec: Short for compression/decompression; another name for a compressor.

Compression: The method used to reduce the size of the movie file while still retaining image quality. Video and audio compression make for a tricky business: you have to weigh the benefits of smaller file sizes (and therefore potentially faster downloads) against the desire to have the best-looking movies possible. Many methods of compression are available, each with its own strengths. **Table 16.2** (later in this chapter) provides an overview of the compressors available when exporting from iMovie. More are available if you export files from QuickTime Player Pro, and still more offered by professional editing packages such as Apple's Compressor (part of Final Cut Studio) or Cleaner (`www.autodesk.com/cleaner/`).

Data Rate: The amount of data sent from one point to another during a given time, such as the number of kilobytes delivered during a Web download.

Frame Rate: The number of frames displayed during 1 second. As more frames are included, the movie will play smoother—but adding frames increases the size of the file. Uncompressed DV video runs at 30 frames per second (fps) for NTSC, or 25 fps for PAL; a typical QuickTime movie contains 15 or 12 frames per second.

Key Frame: A complete movie frame that acts as the image base for successive frames. Unlike film, which displays 24 full frames per second on a reel of celluloid, QuickTime compares most of the frames in a movie with its key frames and notes the differences. Although this sounds like more work than just displaying each frame in its entirety, it actually means the movie player is drawing less data.

For example, consider a clip where the camera is stationary, filming a person talking. Every pixel of the first frame, the key frame, is drawn; in the next frame, the only change is that the person's lips have moved. Instead of redrawing the background and everything else, Quick-Time holds onto the first frame and only changes the pixels around the person's mouth. So, the second frame (and third, fourth, and so on) contain only a few pixels' worth of information, dramatically reducing the total amount of data required and creating a smaller file. Of course, the entire movie likely won't be composed of just the person talking, so QuickTime creates several key frames along the way, allowing the player to regroup and start over. The more key frames that appear in your movie, the larger the file size will be.

Sample Rate: The quality of audio, measured in kilohertz (kHz). The higher the number, the more audio data is present, and therefore the better the quality of sound.

Exporting to QuickTime Using Expert Settings

iMovie's stock QuickTime format settings are good for most situations, but you can also use other compression formats and options by way of QuickTime's Expert Settings.

To change image settings:

1. To export only a few clips, select them in the Timeline or Clips pane.

2. Choose QuickTime from the Share menu, or press Command-Shift-E.

3. In the Share dialog, click the QuickTime icon if it's not already selected.

4. Click the box labeled Share selected clips only to export the range you selected in step 1. Otherwise, ignore this step.

5. Choose Expert Settings from the Compress movie for popup menu (**Figure 16.6**).

6. Click the Share button.

7. In the Save Exported File As dialog, make sure Movie to QuickTime Movie is selected in the Export popup menu, and click the Options button (**Figure 16.7**).

8. The Movie Settings dialog displays the current video and sound settings (**Figure 16.8**). To fine-tune the type and amount of video compression applied, click the Settings button under Video.

9. In the top area of the Compression Settings dialog, choose a compression method from the first popup menu (**Figure 16.9**). (Note that this dialog may look different depending on the compression type you're using. The option shown here is H.264.)

10. Move the Quality slider to the lowest level you can that maintains good image

Figure 16.6 QuickTime's Expert Settings provide many more options for controlling the compression.

Figure 16.7 Click the Options button in the Save dialog to access specific custom settings.

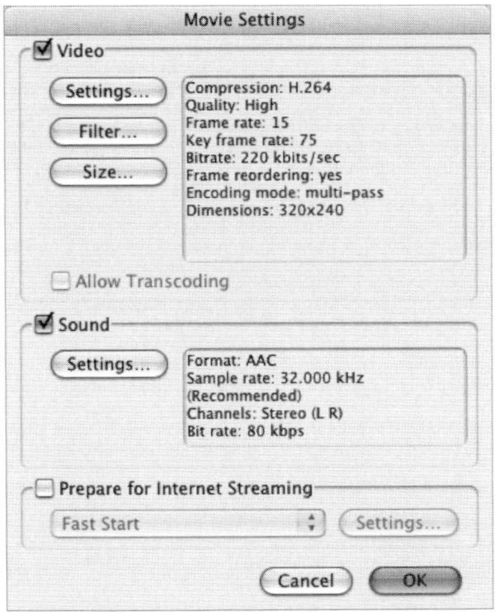

Figure 16.8 The Movie Settings dialog presents an overview of the current export settings.

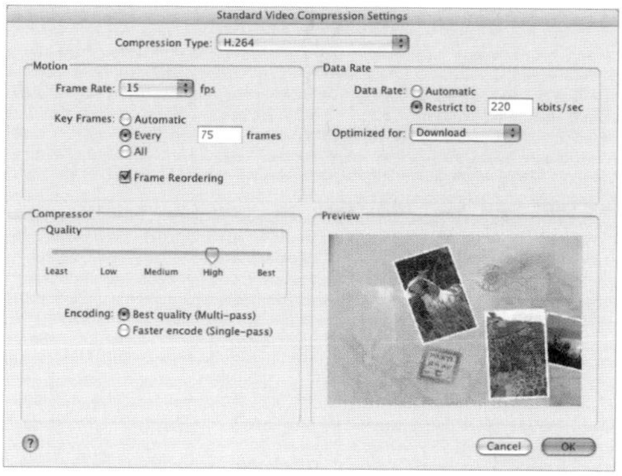

Figure 16.9 After that long progression of dialogs, you finally reach Compression Settings, where you can adjust the type and amount of compression used for exporting.

quality; the thumbnail shows you how much compression is being applied.

11. In the Motion area, select the number of frames per second from the Frame Rate popup menu.

12. Enter a number in the Key Frames Every [number] frames field to set how often a key frame is generated. Compression works by removing areas of a frame that have not changed since the preceding frame; to create a key frame, iMovie draws an entirely new frame.

13. To target a specific data rate, enter a value in the field labeled Restrict to [number] kbits/sec.

14. Click OK to return to Movie Settings.

15. Click OK to get back to the Save dialog, and then click the Save button to create the file.

✔ Tips

- To get a sense for how the compressors compare, create a short movie (30 seconds or so) that's representative of your footage. Then, export it using the various formats and compare the results.

- The Sorenson Video codecs are highly regarded for having high video quality with good compression.

- When you select clips in the Clips pane to export, iMovie exports them in the order they were imported, regardless of their positions in the Clips pane.

- See **Table 16.2** on the next page for a summary of the video compressors included with QuickTime.

- The H.264 codec is mighty impressive, but it's also a resource hog, especially if you opt to use Multi-pass compression. It may take a while to export the file.

QuickTime versus QuickTime Pro

Every Mac comes with QuickTime, including the free QuickTime Player, which allows you to play back QuickTime movies and a host of other file formats (ranging from MPEG-formatted movies to MP3 audio files). If you're serious about optimizing your QuickTime movies for the Web, however, consider paying the $30 for a QuickTime Pro license, which turns QuickTime Player into a sophisticated movie editor. Not only does it give you an easy way to resize or recompress QuickTime movies, it also lets you save your movies into other formats, such as AVI, which Windows users can view if they don't have QuickTime installed.

Table 16.2

Video Compressors Included with QuickTime*

COMPRESSOR NAME	COMMENTS
Animation	Works best on computer-generated animations with broad areas of flat color. Doesn't work well for scenes with lots of color changes.
Apple H.263, VC.263	Originally designed for videoconferencing. Very high compression ratios. Sometimes good for Web video.
Apple Pixlet Video	A low file size format developed by Apple and Pixar for desktop editing of high-resolution footage.
BMP	Used for still images to be exported in BMP format. Does minimal compression. Inappropriate for video-based movie playback.
Cinepak	Commonly used for video movies that require CD-ROM playback. Compresses very slowly.
Component Video	High-quality compressor. Good for capture on Macs with built-in video capture capabilities and for use as an intermediate storage format. Low compression ratios (larger files).
DV-PAL, DV/DVCPRO-NTSC, DVCPRO-PAL	Used with digital video cameras.
Graphics	Good for 8-bit graphics files. Usually better than the Animation compressor in 8 bits. Slower to decompress than Animation.
H.261	Originally designed for videoconferencing. Extremely high compression ratios.
H.264	A high-quality, scalable video format included with QuickTime 7 (and available under Mac OS X 10.4 Tiger or later). H.264 is designed to run on devices as varied as cellular phones and high-definition televisions, and is the backbone of upcoming HD DVD formats.
JPEG 2000	High image quality and resolution for still images, using wavelet compression.
Motion JPEG A, Motion JPEG B	Used to decompress files made with certain Motion JPEG cards when the card isn't available or to compress in a format that can be played by certain hardware Motion JPEG cards.
MPEG-4 Video	High quality compressed video based on QuickTime.
None	Good for capture only. Does almost no compression.
Photo-JPEG	Ideal for high-quality compressed still images. Also useful as an intermediate storage format for movies and QuickTime VR panoramas. Decompresses too slowly for video-based playback.
Planar RGB	For images with an alpha channel.
PNG	Typically used for still-image compression. Can get high compression ratios.
Sorenson Video 2	Very high compression ratios and high quality. Excellent for Web and CD-ROM.
Sorenson Video 3	Very high compression ratios and very high quality (better than Sorenson Video 2). Currently the best choice for Web and CD-ROM.
TIFF	Typically used for still-image compression. Does minimal compression.
Video	Very fast video compression and decompression. Decent compression ratios. Good for real-time capture of video, particularly when hard disk space is at a premium. Good for testing clips. OK for hard disk playback. Image quality is poor when compressing enough for CD-ROM playback.

Note: The Minimum Install of QuickTime (which many users will choose) doesn't install all these compressors. If the computer being used to play a movie that requires one of these compressors has an Internet connection, QuickTime downloads the necessary compressor when it is needed for decompression.

* This table has been adapted from one that originally appeared in *QuickTime 5 for Macintosh and Windows: Visual QuickStart Guide*, by Judith Stern and Robert Lettieri, and is used here with their permission. (www.judyandrobert.com/)

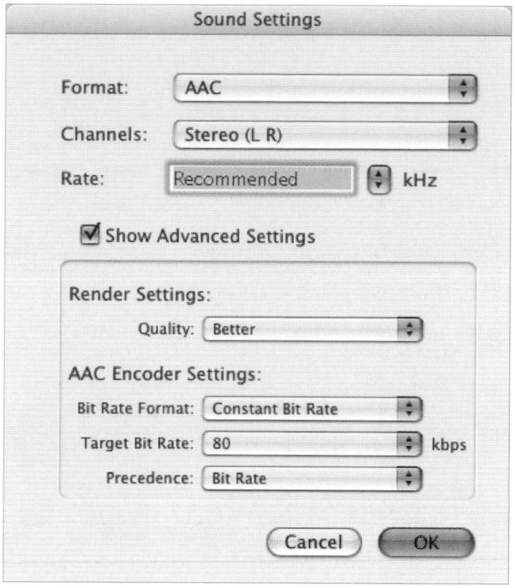

Sound Settings

Format: AAC

Channels: Stereo (L R)

Rate: Recommended kHz

☑ Show Advanced Settings

Render Settings:

Quality: Better

AAC Encoder Settings:

Bit Rate Format: Constant Bit Rate

Target Bit Rate: 80 kbps

Precedence: Bit Rate

Cancel   OK

Figure 16.10 Choose an audio compressor to fine-tune how your movie's audio sounds after exporting.

To change audio settings:

1. Share your movie as described in the previous steps.

2. In the Sound portion of the Movie Settings dialog, click the Settings button to display sound-specific settings (**Figure 16.10**).

3. Choose a format from the Format popup menu. Some compressors include further settings, which are accessed by clicking the Show Advanced Settings checkbox. These usually determine how the data is encoded, or specify a data rate (or bit rate).

4. Decide whether the audio will play back in stereo or mono by choosing an option from the Channels popup menu. Stereo sounds better, but Mono offers a smaller file size.

5. In the Rate field, type a kHz value or select one from the popup menu to the right. Lower kHz settings will degrade the sound quality.

6. Click OK to exit the sound settings portion of the dialog.

✔ Tip

■ If you want to export only the audio portion of your movie, choose Sound to AIFF from the Export popup menu in the Save Exported File As dialog. Or, when you're in the Movie Settings dialog, deselect the Video checkbox before exporting.

To prepare a movie for Internet streaming:

1. Share your movie as described in the previous steps.

2. In the Movie Settings dialog, click the Prepare for Internet Streaming box in the lower-left corner (**Figure 16.11**).

3. From the popup menu, select a streaming method:

   ▲ **Fast Start.** The movie file is downloaded like any other media file, and begins playing once enough data has been transferred.

   ▲ **Fast Start - Compressed Header.** Like Fast Start, the movie is downloaded as one file, but the header information is compressed to save disk space.

   ▲ **Hinted Streaming.** Use this option if the movie will be hosted by a QuickTime Streaming Server. Hinting the data breaks it up into more manageable chunks for streaming. With Hinted Streaming selected, you can click the Settings button to further tweak the settings (**Figure 16.12**). For more information, see Apple's article: `http://docs.info.apple.com/article.html?artnum=301355`.

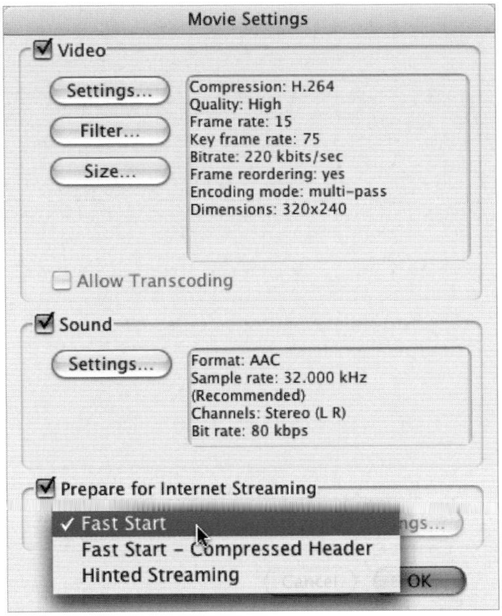

Figure 16.11 To enable Web streaming, click the Prepare for Internet Streaming box and choose a streaming method.

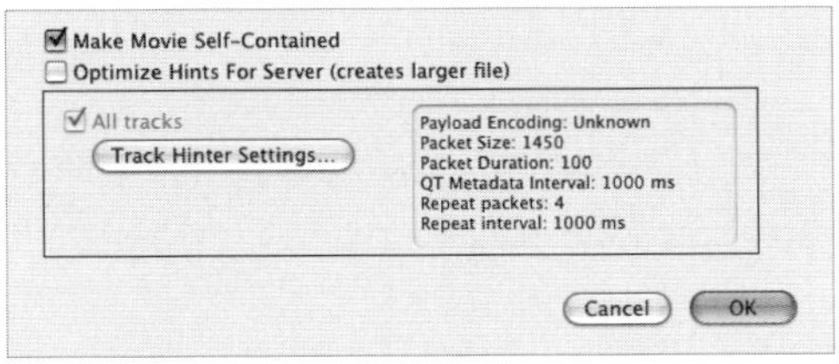

Figure 16.12 Preparing a QuickTime movie for streaming can get into a lot of geeky detail, but if you know what you're doing, you can improve streaming quality.

QuickTime Geekery

Trust me: everything described so far in this chapter is really just the tip of a very large iceberg. If you're willing to shell out the bucks, software such as AutoDesk's Cleaner can encode and compress your movies into nearly any possible movie format, with more control than can be found in iMovie's or QuickTime Player's export features.

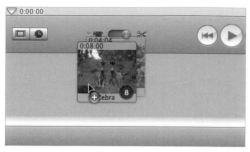

Figure 16.13 iMovie HD 6 lets you open multiple projects at a time and copy clips between them.

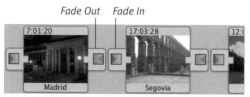

Figure 16.14 Combining Fade Out and Fade In transitions elegantly bridges these long segments.

Combining Movie Segments

It's often a good idea to break up a longer movie into smaller segments, working on 10- or 20-minute chunks at a time. Use the following steps when it's time to put the pieces back together.

To combine movie segments:

◆ Open two (or more) projects at the same time, and drag clips (even transitions on the Timeline) directly from one project to another (**Figure 16.13**). However, it doesn't include content on audio tracks: you can copy those over, but you'll have to do it separately.

Or

1. Export each segment using the Full Quality option shown on the previous pages. Make sure you have enough hard disk space to accommodate the segments you wish to combine.

2. Create a new iMovie project by choosing New Project from the File menu.

3. Import the segments from your hard disk. Depending on how you've split the segments, you may only have to add a simple transition between them to create a unified whole (**Figure 16.14**).

✔ Tips

■ You can also export your movie back to the camcorder, and then re-import it into your new iMovie project (see Chapter 15 and Chapter 7).

■ The downside to the second approach is that you need to make sure your movie segments are finished (or close enough to being done), because when you re-import them into iMovie, you won't have the clips of unused footage from the individual projects at your disposal.

Exporting to a Palm OS Handheld

A friend recently bought a Palm OS handheld with a color screen so she could show off digital photos of her grandchildren. Now, she can also store movies by exporting them in QuickTime format and running them through Kinoma Producer (www.kinoma.com).

To export movies to a Palm OS handheld:

1. Make sure you've installed Kinoma Producer and Kinoma Player on the handheld.

2. In iMovie, export your movie using the QuickTime options. Kinoma recommends using the highest resolution possible, so start with iMovie's Full Quality export option.

3. Launch Kinoma Producer and choose your handheld model from the Brand and Model popup menus (**Figure 16.15**).

4. Drag your exported QuickTime movie to the Files area in Kinoma Producer, or click the Add Files button and locate the movie (**Figure 16.16**).

5. Click the Convert Files button.

6. After the conversion is finished, copy the new file to your handheld. Depending on the size of the movie file, you'll probably need to store it on a memory card instead of the handheld's built-in memory; I use a USB card reader to quickly transfer the file to the memory card. Be sure to copy it to PALM > PROGRAMS > KINOMA folder.

7. Launch Kinoma Player and play the movie on your handheld (**Figure 16.17**).

Figure 16.15 In Kinoma Producer, choose your handheld's brand and model to begin.

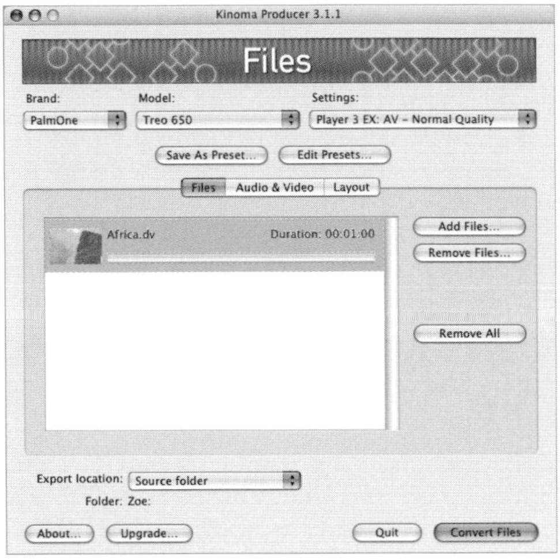

Figure 16.16 Add QuickTime movies you exported from iMovie to Kinoma's Files pane.

Figure 16.17 Play back the movie on the handheld using Kinoma Player, and impress your friends with your tech savvy.

EMAIL, iWEB, AND BLUETOOTH

You may be creating movies that will live only on your hard disk, for your eyes only, never to be seen by anyone. More likely, though, your movies are meant to be viewed. As I've covered already, you can export the movie to a DVD or videotape and mail it to your relatives—if you don't mind purchasing the media, filling it with movies (or just using a few minutes of it for one movie), then paying to mail it across the country or around the world. Where's the instant gratification in that?

Instead (or in addition), send your movie to the grandparents by email or post it to the Web. Previous versions of the software let you upload movies to a .Mac HomePage, but iMovie HD 6 jettisoned that option in favor of using iLife's newest member, iWeb.

Yet another option is to transfer the movie to a Bluetooth-enabled cellular phone or handheld organizer. As these devices become more sophisticated, it's likely that soon you'll be able to show off your entire film library to your friends over lunch or coffee.

Exporting to Email

iMovie can compress your video in an email-friendly size and pass it off to your email client as a file attachment.

To export to email:

1. To export only a few clips from your movie, select them in the Timeline or the Clips pane. Otherwise, skip to the next step.

2. Choose Email from the Share menu, or press Command-Shift-E.

3. In the Share dialog, click the Email icon, if it's not already selected (**Figure 17.1**).

4. Click the box labeled Share selected clips only to export the range you selected in step 1. Otherwise, ignore this step.

5. Choose your email program from the Send email using popup menu (**Figure 17.2**). Unless you alternate between several email clients, you'll likely need to perform this step only once.

6. Give your movie a name if you want to change it from the project name.

7. Click the Share button. iMovie compresses the movie using its default Email settings (see Chapter 16), then hands it off to your selected email program.

8. In the new outgoing message that is created, enter the name or email address of the person you want to send the message to (**Figure 17.3**).

9. Click the Send button (or equivalent in your email program) to send the message.

Figure 17.1 The Email tab of the Share dialog makes it easy to compress and send a movie to your friends via email.

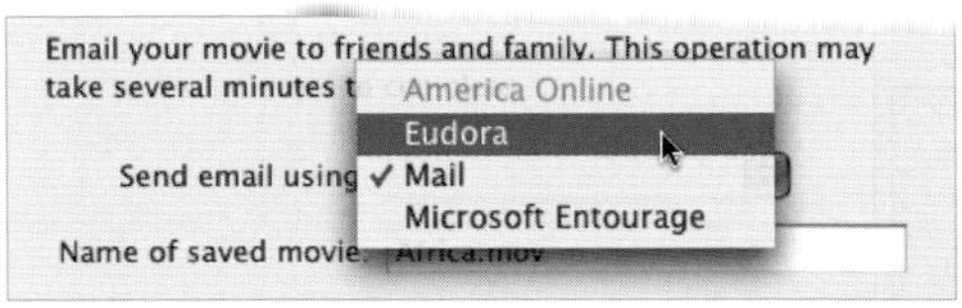

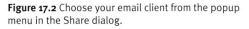

Figure 17.2 Choose your email client from the popup menu in the Share dialog.

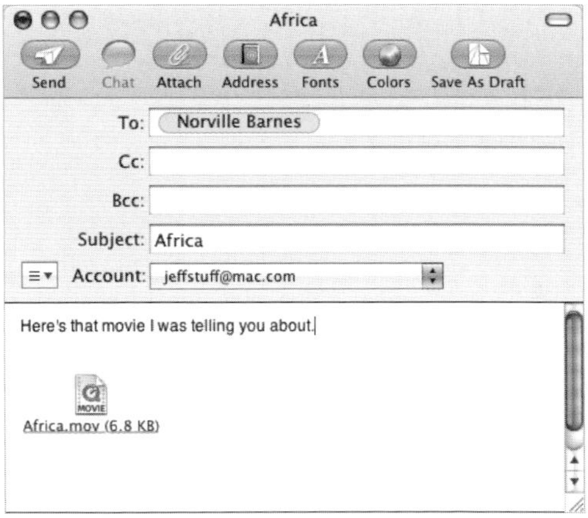

Figure 17.3 When iMovie sends the movie to your email software, a new message is created that includes the attachment and Subject line (Apple's Mail program shown here).

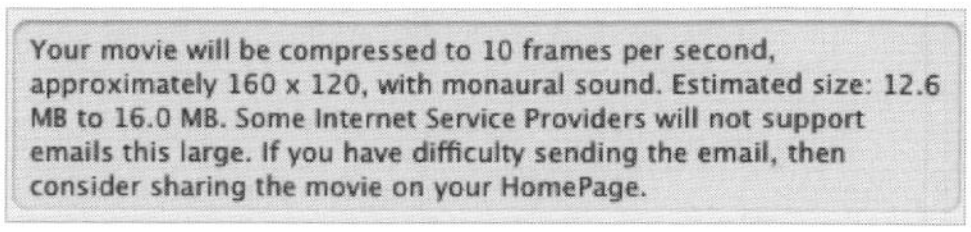

> Your movie will be compressed to 10 frames per second, approximately 160 x 120, with monaural sound. Estimated size: 12.6 MB to 16.0 MB. Some Internet Service Providers will not support emails this large. If you have difficulty sending the email, then consider sharing the movie on your HomePage.

Figure 17.4 iMovie will tell you when it thinks a movie might be too big to send via email.

Emailing Large Movies

iMovie warns you in the summary area if it thinks a movie might be too large to send via email (**Figure 17.4**). Try to send the smallest files possible, for two reasons.

Many Internet service providers limit the size of messages, so the file may not get through. The large number of viruses that arrive via email (mostly to Windows users) has prompted ISPs to crack down on file attachments.

Also, because the Internet is already so overloaded with those attachments and spam, every large file you send through email gateways contributes to the overall slowing down of the Internet.

Today's public service announcement is: Be a responsible Internet citizen. Consider posting your movie to the Web, or burning it to a CD or DVD and sending it through the old-fashioned postal system.

✔ Tips

■ Another way to send movies to a particular person is by using Apple's iChat AV. First, export the movie as a QuickTime file (detailed in Chapter 16). Then, assuming your friend is online, drag the file to her name in iChat's Buddy List. When she accepts the connection, the file is transferred (usually faster than it would have taken to send it through email).

■ If you're not fond of iMovie's defaut email compression settings, you can always export the movie to a QuickTime file and send it in your email program manually. That's what we were forced to do way back before iMovie 4, after walking to and from school in our bare feet uphill both ways....

■ The movie files that iMovie exports are saved in your iMovie project file. If you share movies often, that could make the file balloon in size even more. To go in and delete those files when you're done with them, first Control-click the project file in the Finder and choose Show Package Contents from the contextual menu that appears. Open the Shared Movies folder, then open the Email (or iWeb, etc.) folder to locate the file. You can then move, copy, or delete the files as you see fit.

Publishing to the Web Using iWeb

One of the easiest methods for putting your movies on the Web is to use Apple's .Mac service (www.mac.com). When you sign up for a $100 yearly membership, one of the benefits is using iWeb to build and maintain your own Web site.

To publish to the Web using iWeb:

1. To export only a few clips from your movie, select them in the Timeline or the Clips pane.

2. Choose iWeb from the Share menu, or press Command-Shift-E.

3. In the Share dialog, click the iWeb icon if it's not already selected (**Figure 17.5**).

4. Click the box labeled Share selected clips only to export the range you selected in step 1. Otherwise, ignore this step.

5. To create a single Web page that contains your movie, select the Share for web option.

6. Click the Share button. iMovie compresses the movie and launches iWeb.

7. In iWeb, choose a theme from the column at the left (**Figure 17.6**); each theme contains only one movie template, so that page is automatically selected in the right column.

8. Click the Choose button. iWeb creates a new page that contains your movie (**Figure 17.7**).

9. Type the page title, movie title, and page description text in the fields provided (**Figure 17.8**).

10. Click the Publish button to create and upload the new page to your site.

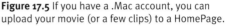

Figure 17.5 If you have a .Mac account, you can upload your movie (or a few clips) to a HomePage.

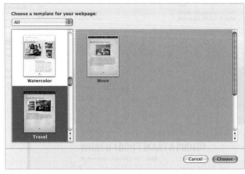

Figure 17.6 Depending on the length of your movie and the speed of your Internet connection, this step could take a while.

Figure 17.7 Edit your movie's Web page directly in iWeb and get a feel for how the end result will look.

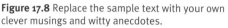

Kim and I went to South Africa last year and had a fabulous time. And if it weren't for those pesky lions, I would have returned with all of my fingers! I

Figure 17.8 Replace the sample text with your own clever musings and witty anecdotes.

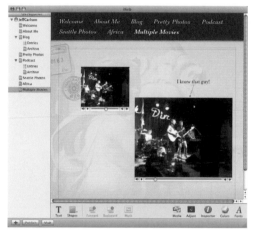

Figure 17.9 iWeb's Movie page template accommodates only one movie. Use the Blank template instead to include multiple movies on the same page.

Don't Worry, They'll Make More

If your allotted 1 GB is filling up, you may need to delete some files from your iDisk's Movies folder. Or, of course, Apple will happily sell you more! Simply go to your .Mac account page and click the Buy More button. You can purchase up to 4 GB of storage (at $100 per year).

To make changes to your page:

1. In iWeb, load the page by clicking its page icon in the left column.

2. Make any changes you want on the page. The page icon turns red to indicate that it's been edited but not published.

3. Click the Publish button.

To add multiple movies to one page:

1. Export your movies from iMovie as separate QuickTime files (see Chapter 16).

2. In iWeb, choose New Page from the File menu, and choose the Blank template.

3. Drag the movie files from the Finder or iWeb's Media palette (**Figure 17.9**).

4. Publish the page.

✔ Tips

■ iMovie exports iWeb movies with the same settings as the Web Streaming QuickTime format (see Chapter 16).

■ You can also publish movies to a .Mac HomePage without doing it from within iMovie (such as if you've exported your movie using QuickTime's Expert Settings; see Chapter 16). In that case, mount your iDisk and copy the movie file to the Movies folder. Sign in to .Mac on the Web, click HomePage in the navigation bar, and create a page from there.

■ iMovie gets your .Mac information from the .Mac preference pane in Mac OS X's System Preferences.

■ iMovie reads your .Mac member name when it launches; if you need to publish to a different .Mac account, you must quit iMovie and change the information in System Preferences, then launch iMovie.

Publishing a Video Podcast Using iWeb

If you're not familiar with podcasting, imagine a radio show where each episode is automatically downloaded to your computer for you to listen to whenever you please. Now, imagine the same thing with video that you produce.

It's long been possible to upload videos to the Web. What makes podcasting different is that people can subscribe to the audio or video stream, relieving them of the hassle of going out to find it on the Web. iMovie, GarageBand, and iWeb enable you to set up your own video podcasting studio, letting the software take care of the publishing details while you focus on the content.

To publish a video podcast from iMovie:

1. To export only a few clips from your movie, select them in the Timeline or the Clips pane.

2. Choose iWeb from the Share menu, or press Command-Shift-E.

3. In the Share dialog, click the iWeb icon if it's not already selected.

4. Click the box labeled Share selected clips only to export the range you selected in step 1. Otherwise, ignore this step.

5. Select the Share for video podcast option (**Figure 17.10**).

6. Click the Share button. iMovie compresses the movie and launches iWeb.

7. Choose whether to send the video to a blog ("weblog") page or a podcast page and click OK (**Figure 17.11**). The difference between the two is organizational; iWeb assumes that you probably want your blog separate from your podcast.

Figure 17.10 In the iWeb Share dialog, start by choosing Share for video podcast.

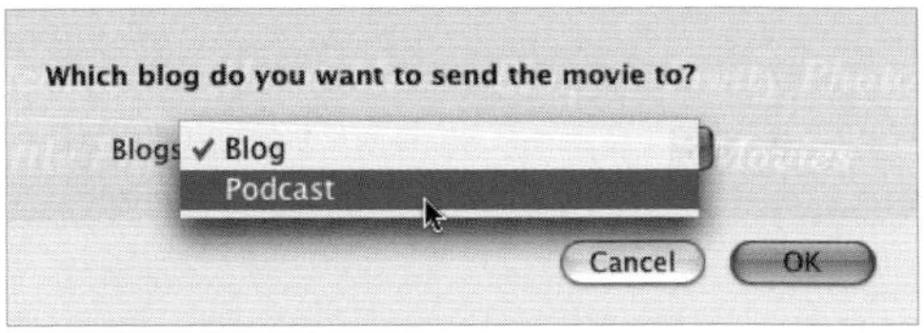

Figure 17.11 The video can be published on either a blog or a podcast in iWeb—your choice.

Sharing to an iPod

iMovie HD 6 offers one more exporting option: Share to iPod. If you own a video-enabled iPod, choose iPod from the Share menu. iMovie compresses the movie, formats it for the iPod, and then moves it to iTunes. The next time you connect your iPod, the movie is copied over.

Figure 17.12 Podcast entries appear at the top of the screen, with the actual page below them for editing.

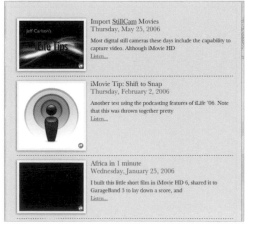

Figure 17.13 I created a one-frame image for the podcast episode at the top to avoid a black screen like the episode at the bottom.

8. Type the page title, movie title, and page description text in the fields provided (**Figure 17.12**).

9. Click the Publish button to create and upload the new page to your site.

To publish a video podcast from GarageBand:

1. If you want to add music and audio to your movie in GarageBand before creating a video podcast, follow the instructions in Chapter 14 for sharing the movie from iMovie to GarageBand.

2. When the movie is complete, choose Send Podcast to iWeb from the Share menu.

3. Follow steps 7 through 9 above to publish the podcast.

✔ Tips

■ Frustratingly, iWeb uses the first frame of your movie for its icon (also known as a poster movie; see "Creating a Poster Movie" later in this chapter). If your movie starts with a fade-in from black, viewers see a big black rectangle indicating the movie. To get around this, use iMovie's Create Still Frame command to make a one-frame image and position it as the first frame of your movie before bringing it into iWeb (**Figure 17.13**).

■ You can add movies to a blog or podcast page without coming from iMovie or GarageBand. But if you do, make sure you drop the movie into the page's movie placeholder; otherwise, the page may not appear in your subscription feed.

■ When narrating a video podcast, I find it helpful to type up a script of what I'm going to say and then read it while recording.

Writing HTML

iWeb makes it extremely easy to publish movies to the Web, but you may already have a site set up, you aren't a .Mac member, or you just like to dig into the code out of pure textual geeky joy.

This, of course, isn't a book about HTML, so I'm going to assume that you know the basics about coding Web pages, and that you have an application (such as Bare Bones Software's BBEdit, or even TextEdit) that you use to build pages. If that's not the case, check out Elizabeth Castro's book *HTML for the World Wide Web with XHTML and CSS: Visual QuickStart Guide*, which remains the best HTML guide I've read.

That said, there are two ways of going about it: you can copy the file to your Web directory (provided by your Internet service provider) then link directly to it; or you can embed the movie on a Web page so that it's part of the page's layout.

To link to a QuickTime movie file:

1. In your HTML editing application, enter the following code where you want your movie link to appear. The user will see only the linked text; clicking it will download the movie.

   ```
   <a href="http://www.youraddress.com/
   sample.mov">Click here</a>
   ```

2. Insert the real names of your Web address and movie filename in place of *youraddress.com* and *sample.mov* (**Figure 17.14**). For example, a movie on my Web site would look like this (go ahead and put the URL below into your Web browser to view the movie).

   ```
   <a href="http://www.necoffee.com/
   imovievqs/secretmovie.mov">Is it
   really a secret?</a>
   ```

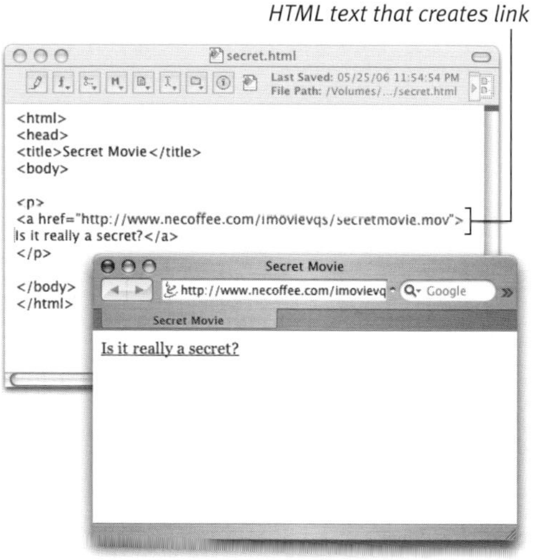

HTML text that creates link

Figure 17.14 Add a simple Web link that points to your QuickTime movie file. The HTML text in the top window creates the Web page in the bottom window.

Embed a Headache

If you know how to embed an object already, you may be wondering why the example on the next page contains so much other information. In late 2001, Microsoft stopped supporting the plug-in architecture used by Web browsers since long before Microsoft even got into the browser business (when a QuickTime movie appears on a page, a QuickTime plug-in—not the browser by itself—is doing the work of playing it back correctly). Instead, Microsoft switched to its own ActiveX architecture—but only under Internet Explorer 5.5 and later for Windows. So although movies added using the regular method of embedding objects still work on your Mac, anyone with a recent version of Windows likely won't be able to see it. Find more information at developer.apple.com/quicktime/compatibility.html.

Deciphering HTML Attributes

So what is all that junk I threw in there? Here's a breakdown of the tag attributes:

OBJECT CLASSID: To work properly under Windows, a QuickTime movie must be defined as an object. The CLASSID value identifies the content as a Quick-Time movie.

WIDTH and **HEIGHT**: These values tell the browser the width and height of your movie in pixels.

CODEBASE: This URL gives Internet Explorer for Windows some necessary information about the QuickTime format.

PARAM: This is a parameter of the object, which consists of a name and a value. SRC is the URL that points to your movie file; AUTOPLAY tells the browser whether to automatically play the movie when it loads (in this case "true" means yes); CONTROLLER tells the browser whether to display the QuickTime controller beneath the movie (in this case "false" means no).

EMBED: This is the tag that actually puts your QuickTime movie on the page. It includes the same attributes as PARAM, though in a slightly more compact fashion. A Web page that contains only this tag will display the movie correctly in all Web browsers except Internet Explorer 5.5 and later for Windows.

PLUGINSPAGE: This tells the browser where to go in the event that the Quick-Time plug-in is not installed.

</EMBED> and **</OBJECT>**: These are closing tags, indicating the end of the commands.

To embed the movie on a page:

◆ In your HTML editing application, enter the following code where you want the movie to appear. Be sure to change the two instances of `sample.mov` to your actual filename, plus the two instances where the width and height are defined.

```
<OBJECT CLASSID="clsid:02BF25D5-8C17-
4B23-BC80-D3488ABDDC6B" WIDTH="160"
HEIGHT="144"
CODEBASE="http://www.apple.com/
qtactivex/qtplugin.cab">
<PARAM name="SRC" VALUE="sample.mov">
<PARAM name="AUTOPLAY" VALUE="true">
<PARAM name="CONTROLLER"
VALUE="false">
<EMBED SRC="sample.mov" WIDTH="160"
HEIGHT="144" AUTOPLAY="true"
CONTROLLER="false" PLUGINSPAGE=
"http://www.apple.com/quicktime/
download/">
</EMBED>
</OBJECT>
```

Note that the unintelligible gobbledy-gook following `CLASSID=` must be entered exactly as shown; it's required for viewing the page properly in Microsoft Internet Explorer 5.5 and later under Windows (see the sidebar on the opposite page).

WRITING HTML

Creating a Poster Movie

Accessing a QuickTime movie on the Web introduces one big problem: whether you link to it directly or embed it onto a page, the entire movie begins downloading. Depending on the size of the movie, this could slow your browser or other Internet applications while the movie is being fetched.

As an alternative, create a poster movie, which displays a one-frame movie that your visitors can click to initiate the download. (Sometimes this can be frustrating: I've clicked on links expecting the movie to load in the background while I'm working on something else, only to realize that I needed to then click the poster movie to get the download started. At least this route gives the visitor the option to start the movie at her convenience.) The poster movie has the added benefit of preloading the QuickTime plug-in before the movie starts.

Creating a poster movie involves two steps: creating the one-frame movie using Quick-Time Player (the Pro version), then adjusting the EMBED tag in the HTML to handle it properly.

To create the poster movie:

1. Open your movie in QuickTime Player.

2. Use the movie control buttons or the location indicator to find a frame you'd like to use as the poster movie's image (**Figure 17.15**).

3. Choose Copy from the Edit menu, or press Command-C. This copies the selected frame.

4. Create a new movie by choosing New (Command-N) from the File menu.

5. Choose Paste (Command-V) from the Edit menu. Your copied frame appears as its own one-frame movie.

Figure 17.15 Use the Playhead in QuickTime Player to locate the frame you'd like to use for the poster movie.

Figure 17.16 To make the poster movie work, your one frame needs to be saved as a QuickTime movie, not as an individual image format like TIFF or JPEG.

Figure 17.17 The end result is a single image that shows up in place of the movie, but one you can click to immediately begin playing the movie.

6. Save the movie with a distinctive name, such as "Africa_CD-ROM_poster.mov", to use my example (**Figure 17.16**).

To embed the poster movie:

1. In your HTML editor, type the code you used to embed the movie (shown two pages back).

2. In the EMBED tag, add the HREF and TARGET attributes (underlined):

```
<EMBED SRC="sample_poster.
mov" WIDTH="160" HEIGHT="144"
AUTOPLAY="true"
CONTROLLER="false" HREF="sample.mov"
TARGET="myself" PLUGINSPAGE=
"http://www.apple.com/quicktime/
download/">
```

The EMBED tag tells the browser to first load the poster movie; the HREF tag tells it to load the real movie when clicked; and the TARGET tag instructs it to play the real movie in the same space as the poster movie.

3. Save and upload your files. When you view them in a Web browser, the poster image shows up first (**Figure 17.17**).

✔ Tips

■ If you're seeing only half of the movie controller, add 15 to the height values in the OBJECT and EMBED tags.

■ Be sure the controller attributes are set to "false," or else you'll see a controller in the poster movie, which can be confusing. Viewers might click the controller to play the movie, which works—but only plays the one frame.

■ It's a good idea to include instructions near the poster movie that say something like, "Click to play movie."

Exporting via Bluetooth

Do you carry family photos in your purse or wallet? Do you also carry a cellular phone? If so, why show off still pictures of the kids when you can also play video? iMovie can export movies in 3GPP (Third Generation Partnership Program) format, which is used by cellular phone companies to play video on their devices. Once exported, iMovie can transfer the file to the phone using Bluetooth wireless networking.

To export via Bluetooth:

1. If you want to share specific clips, select them in the Timeline or the Clips pane. Otherwise, choose Share from the File menu, or press Command-Shift-E.

2. Click the Bluetooth icon. iMovie displays the estimated file size in the information area (**Figure 17.18**).

3. If you highlighted clips in step 1, click the option marked Share selected clips only. Otherwise, click the Share button. iMovie then compresses the movie.

4. After compression, choose a Bluetooth device in the dialog that appears, and click Select (**Figure 17.19**). iMovie transfers the movie file.

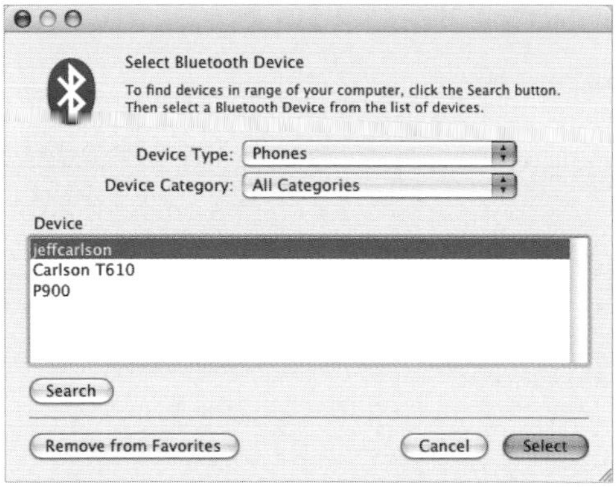

✔ Tips

- The default 3GPP compression settings favor small file size over video quality. If you want to create a higher-quality movie file, share the clips using QuickTime's expert settings (see Chapter 16). Set the Export popup menu to Movie to 3G. I've found that increasing the data rate and setting a lower key frame rate improves quality substantially (**Figure 17.20**).

- For more on the 3GPP format, see www.apple.com/mpeg4/3gpp/.

Figure 17.18 iMovie lets you share movies with Bluetooth-enabled devices such as some cellular phones.

Figure 17.19 The Bluetooth devices you've paired with your Mac appear in this dialog.

Default Bluetooth export   Custom 3GPP export

Figure 17.20 To improve video quality, I've set the movie at right to a data rate of 160 bits per second, and the key frame to every 5 frames.

MOVING FROM iMOVIE TO iDVD

18

My father had amassed a pretty large videotape collection over the past several years. So you can imagine that he did a fair bit of eye-rolling as DVD discs quickly gained in popularity, because now he needs to build a DVD collection, too.

DVD has several key advantages over VHS. The discs are smaller than videotapes, their image and sound quality are much better, and discs don't degrade over time (at least, not remotely as fast as tape, a fact you're no doubt aware of if you have an aging wedding or graduation video sitting on a Clips pane). And DVDs are interactive: jump to your favorite scene in a movie; play a director's commentary while watching a movie; or, in the case of making and playing iMovie videos, store several movies on one disc that can be accessed without fast-forwarding (and rewinding, then fast-forwarding again as you try to find selected clips on a tape).

This chapter explains how you can easily export your footage from iMovie and bring it into the equally easy-to-use iDVD software.

Creating Chapter Markers

When you watch a feature movie on DVD, you usually have the option of skipping to specific scenes, or chapters. You can set up chapter markers in iMovie that iDVD or video podcasts import as chapters.

To create a chapter marker:

1. Place the Playhead at the point that you'd like to set as a marker.

2. Switch to the Chapters pane.

3. Click the Add Marker button; a thumbnail of the current frame appears in the list (**Figure 18.1**), and a yellow diamond appears in the Timeline Viewer (**Figure 18.2**).

4. iMovie inserts the name of the current clip as the chapter name. If you want to call it something else, type a new name into the highlighted field.

5. If you want a clickable URL to appear in a podcast, double-click the Link URL text and add a Web address.

✔ Tips

■ You can't move a chapter marker to a new time location. Instead, simply create a new marker at the new location and delete the old marker.

■ Highlighting chapters in the Chapters pane is a fast way to reposition the Playhead in long movie projects. (Also see "Using Bookmarks" in Chapter 8.)

■ I love keyboard shortcuts. With a chapter highlighted in the Chapters pane, press the up or down arrow key to select the previous or next chapter. Press Return or Enter to make the chapter title editable. If the title is editable, you can press Tab to switch to the next chapter, or Shift-Tab to switch to the previous chapter.

#	Frame	Chapter Title
◇ 1	0:18:12	Elephants Link URL
◇ 2	0:31:07	Rhinos Link URL

Add Marker   Remove Marker

Clips Themes Media Editing **Chapters**

Figure 18.1 Click the Add Marker button to create a new iDVD chapter marker.

Chapter marker

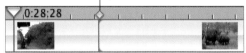
0:28;28

Figure 18.2 Chapter markers appear in the Timeline as yellow diamonds.

Podcast URLs Not Quite Ready

As of iMovie HD 6.0.2, using podcast URLs in chapters is problematic, either crashing iMovie when exporting or just not including the URL. Stay away for now.

Figure 18.3 Click the iDVD icon in the Share dialog to send your movie to iDVD.

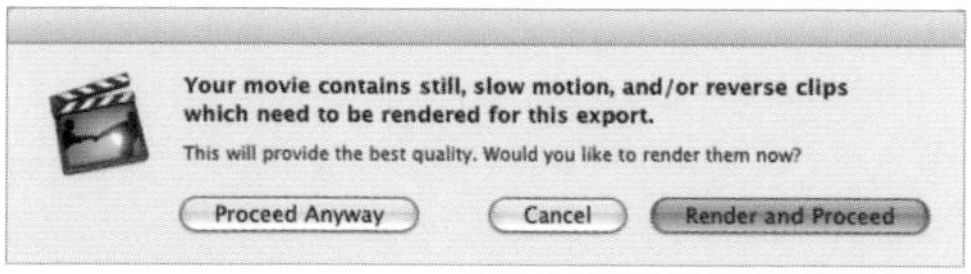

Figure 18.4 iMovie gives you the option of rendering clips that need to be rendered before sending the movie to iDVD.

Figure 18.5 The new iDVD project includes an option to play your entire movie (top), or you can access the chapters you created by double-clicking the Scene Selection option (result at bottom).

Creating an iDVD Project

One of the benefits of iLife integration is the capability to send your iMovie project directly to iDVD, which creates a new project that includes your movie.

To create an iDVD project:

1. Choose iDVD from the Share menu, or press Command-Shift-E and click the iDVD icon (**Figure 18.3**).

2. Click the Share button.

If any clips in your movie are sped up, slowed down, or reversed, iMovie displays a dialog with the option to render the clips (**Figure 18.4**), which redraws them at a higher quality than the preview you see during normal playback. If you choose the Proceed Anyway option, those clips may flicker or otherwise look bad when you play back the DVD.

When those steps are completed, iMovie launches iDVD (if it's not already running), and switches to it (**Figure 18.5**).

✔ Tips

■ iDVD automatically saves the new project in the Documents folder within your Home directory. To work on it somewhere else (such as a large external hard disk), quit iDVD, copy the project to the new location, and open it from there.

■ As with other methods of sharing, you can create an iDVD project that contains only clips that you choose. Select the clips in the Timeline or the Clips pane, then go to the Share dialog. Mark the checkbox labeled Share selected clips only before you click the Share button.

Exporting Movies for DVD

You don't need to rely on the share to iDVD feature to get your movies into iDVD. You can also export QuickTime files that can be added manually to an iDVD project.

To export for DVD:

1. Choose QuickTime from the Share menu, or press Command-Shift-E.

2. In the Share dialog, click the QuickTime icon if it's not already selected.

3. From the popup menu, choose Full Quality (**Figure 18.6**).

4. Click the Share button to export the movie.

5. Name the movie file and choose a location, then click the Save button. iMovie saves it as a QuickTime movie in the same format as your iMovie project.

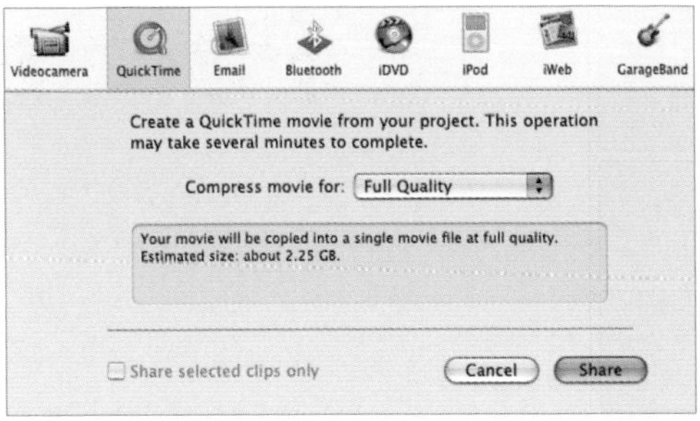

✔ Tips

■ These steps are necessary if you want to export your iMovie into another program such as DVD Studio Pro (www.apple.com/dvdstudiopro/).

■ The file created by this operation is a self-contained QuickTime file, which means all the video and audio is present in the single file. That's the best method to use if you need to transport the movie file to another computer. However, if you're using iDVD on your own machine, and you want to create a DVD containing your entire movie (versus selected clips), it's easier to just drag an iMovie project file into iDVD's main window. The movie is added as a new link (see the next Chapter for more information).

Figure 18.6 Choose the Full Quality option to export a movie that can be used with other programs such as DVD Studio Pro.

Part 4
iDVD

iDVD Overview

iMovie took a technology dominated by professionals—movie editing—and made it easy to use for normal people. In some ways, though, iDVD is even more impressive.

Quite a lot of highly technical work goes into creating a DVD—in the background. While you're focused on choosing which photo should appear on the title page of your DVD, iDVD handles the specifics of building the structure necessary for most consumer DVD players to play back your masterpiece. More importantly, it manages the MPEG-2 compression needed to cram multiple gigabytes' worth of data onto a shiny platter the size and shape of a regular audio CD.

iDVD also does something that no other program can do: it gives you style. Apple has clearly put a lot of thought into the DVD themes that ship with iDVD, making each one something you'd actually want to show off to people. An iDVD project, whether you like it or not, is *polished*, which goes a long way toward making people think, "Wow, I had no idea he was so talented."

This chapter offers a look at iDVD's interface and major functions in order to give you the foundation you'll need for the next chapters that deal with building projects and customizing them.

HD and iDVD

iMovie HD can create HD movies, but don't expect to create a high-definition DVD for now. No standard for high-def DVDs has been reached, despite two competing formats (Blu-ray and HD-DVD, which each have different corporate backers). So, even if iDVD could burn HD projects, no hardware exists to burn them to. As I write this, you can buy drives that read both formats, with disc writers due to appear around the corner. But an accepted standard is still on the horizon.

In the meantime, iDVD imports HD projects with ease and converts them into widescreen DV format. True, it's not the same as seeing the picture at high-definition quality, but it's a start.

About DVDs

The Digital Versatile Disc is quite the wonder: it's physically small, like a CD, but packs nearly seven times the data into the same space: a CD stores roughly 700 MB, while a DVD holds approximately 4.7 GB. In addition to storing all this data, DVDs can be set up so they automatically play movie files and include a menu system to give you control over how the content plays.

DVD physical formats

Before you rush out and buy a mega-pack of blank DVDs, take a few minutes to acquaint yourself with the different formats that are out there.

- **DVD-R.** DVD-Recordable discs can be burned once, and then played back in nearly any consumer DVD player and DVD-capable computer. When purchasing DVD-R media, be sure to get DVD-R (General); the other type, DVD-R (Authoring), is used in professional DVD writers and is not supported by iDVD. The discs Apple sells are DVD-R format.

- **DVD-RW.** DVD-Rewritable discs can be erased and burned hundreds of times, which make them great for testing purposes (you can burn iterations of your project onto one DVD-RW disc, instead of making lots of DVD-R coasters).

- **DVD+R, DVD+RW.** These two formats use a different method of recording data than DVD-R and DVD-RW. They don't offer more storage or features, and cost about the same as the -R and -RW discs.

- **DVD-ROM.** DVD-Read Only-Media discs cannot be burned because their data has already been written to disc. The iLife '06 installation disc is an example of DVD-ROM.

4x DVD Media Alert!

Before you burn any DVD disc, make sure your SuperDrive's firmware has been updated. All SuperDrives can burn 1x- and 2x-speed DVD-R media. When using 4x-speed media, however, some older mechanisms can not only fail to write the disc, but they can also be permanently damaged! Fixes are available—see http://docs.info.apple.com/article.html?artnum=86130 for more information.

DVD Logical Structure

A blank DVD disc contains no information or directory structure. The way a DVD's data is stored on the disc depends on how the disc will be used.

- **DVD-Video.** A DVD that contains just a movie (and its associated menus and extras) is in DVD-Video format. The folders and filenames are specific: a folder called VIDEO_TS stores all of the movie's video and audio files. iDVD typically creates DVD-Video discs.

- **DVD-ROM.** When you store just data on the disc, without the need to play back automatically in DVD players, the disc is in DVD-ROM format. This is just like using a CD-ROM, only with more storage capacity. The Finder can create DVD-ROM discs, such as when you're backing up data.

- **Hybrid DVD.** You can store a DVD-Video project on a disc that also contains DVD-ROM data, which makes the disc a Hybrid DVD. iDVD can create Hybrid DVDs.

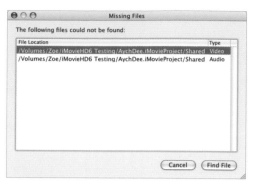

Figure 19.1 If iDVD cannot locate the media files used in your project, it displays this dialog.

Switch Between NTSC and PAL

Choose Project Info from the Project menu, and change the Video Mode setting at any time. Also, in iDVD's preferences you'll find a Video Mode setting in the Projects area that applies to new projects.

DVD Disc Speeds

DVD discs are marked as being 1x, 2x, 4x, or 8x speed. The SuperDrive that comes in the current iMac, for example, writes data at 8x speed, which means the laser that carves into the disc's surface is fast enough to keep up with a faster-spinning disc. The SuperDrive in the MacBook, on the other hand, writes data at 4x speed. All recent SuperDrives can write to higher-speed media, even if they're not 4x- or 8x-speed drives, at 1x or 2x speed.

Using iDVD on Non-SuperDrive Macs

You can run iDVD 6 on a Mac that does not include a SuperDrive, then archive your project or save it to a disc image for burning on another computer (see Chapter 23).

Working with iDVD Projects

If iDVD is currently running because you shared a movie from iMovie, you don't need to open, create, or save your project—it's all done for you. If you just launched iDVD independently, you can create a new project or open an existing project from the File menu; doing so closes the current project (only one project can be open at a time).

The iDVD project file

The iDVD project file by default appears in your Documents folder (within your Home folder), and ends in the extension ".dvdproj". Like iMovie, iDVD stores all of its related files in the project file itself, which is a *package*.

✔ Tips

- Many of the newest Mac models sport SuperDrives that burn dual-layer DVD media, which can store up to 8.5 GB of data and hold around three hours of video footage.

- Make sure you have plenty of free hard disk space available—at least 10 to 20 GB.

- Storing the project file in the Documents folder may be fine for casual use, but an iDVD project may not fit on your startup disk. While traveling, I move the project file to another partition of my PowerBook's hard disk, or offload everything to a speedy external FireWire drive.

- If you do move your iDVD project, make sure it can still locate your original iMovie project and its media files. If iDVD gets confused, it warns you with a dialog (**Figure 19.1**). Select a file from the list and click Find File if the file is actually available somewhere else, or click Cancel to proceed. You can still work on the project if you cancel, but you'll get a broken link warning if you play any of the footage.

Using OneStep DVD

Sometimes you may want to just burn some footage to a disc, without dealing with pretty graphics or navigation. Film productions frequently create DVD "dailies" of each day's footage for the director or producers to review; wedding videographers sometimes offer the raw footage to the married couple, handed over at the end of the day. iDVD's OneStep DVD feature simply grabs video from your camcorder and burns it to disc, with no menu navigation or frills. When you play it in a DVD player, the movie starts playing right away.

To create a OneStep DVD:

1. Connect your camcorder to your Mac and make sure it's loaded with the tape containing your footage.

2. Choose OneStep DVD from the File menu, or press the OneStep DVD button on iDVD's title screen (**Figure 19.2**).

3. Insert a recordable DVD disc into your computer.

4. Sit back and wait. iDVD rewinds the tape, imports the footage, encodes it, and burns it to the disc (**Figure 19.3**).

5. If you want another copy made after iDVD finishes, insert another disc. Otherwise, click Done.

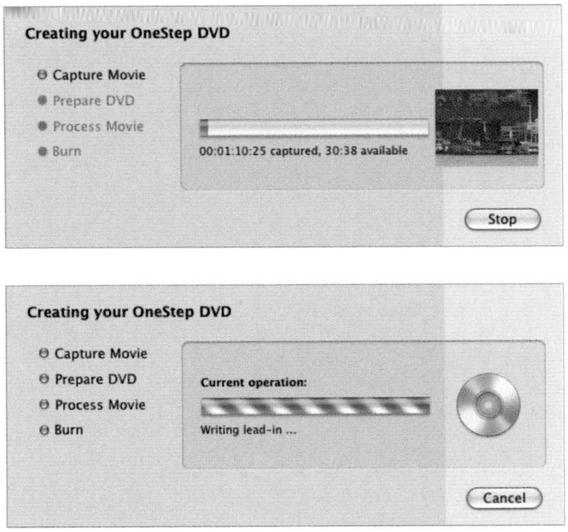

✔ Tips

- OneStep DVD imports footage until it reaches the end of the tape or the end of the footage. If you want just a portion of the tape recorded, press the Stop button in iDVD or on the camcorder.

- You can't start importing footage in the middle of a tape using OneStep DVD. If you want to burn just a portion of your video, import it into iMovie first.

Figure 19.2 If no iDVD project is currently open, start a OneStep DVD project from the title screen.

Figure 19.3 OneStep DVD automatically rewinds the camera's tape, imports the footage (top), and burns a DVD disc (bottom).

OneStep DVD Data Location

When you use the OneStep DVD feature, iDVD doesn't create a project that you can go edit later. All OneStep DVD files are stored in a temporary, invisible directory on your startup drive. But you can change the location: open iDVD's preferences, click the Advanced icon, and choose a new temporary folder location (say, a larger hard disk) at the bottom of the window.

USING ONESTEP DVD

Figure 19.4 Think of Magic iDVD as the parent who gave you a helpful push when you first learned to ride a bicycle (without crashing into the neighbor's tree, in my case).

Figure 19.5 After you choose Create Project, edit the project as described in the upcoming chapters.

Using Magic iDVD

To get more of iDVD's style without spending a lot of time building a full project, drag movies, music, and photos from your hard disk onto the Magic iDVD interface and let iDVD do the work. You can then burn it straight to disc, or use the project as the jumping-off point for your own customizing.

To create a Magic iDVD project:

1. Choose Magic iDVD from the File menu, or press the Magic iDVD button on iDVD's title screen.

2. In the Magic iDVD window, type a name for your DVD in the DVD Title field (**Figure 19.4**).

3. Choose a theme from the scrolling list.

4. Click the Movies button to view movies (including iMovie projects) on your computer, and drag the ones you want to the Drop Movies Here area.

5. To include slideshows, click the Photos button and drag photos from your iPhoto library to the Drop Photos Here area. Each slot represents a different slideshow that can include several photos.

6. If you want music with your slideshow, click the Audio button and drag songs from your iTunes library to a slideshow.

7. Click the Preview button at any time to see what the project looks like.

8. Click the Create Project button to create a new project (**Figure 19.5**), or click the Burn button to write directly to a DVD.

✔ Tips

- You can also drag media content from the Finder to the Magic iDVD areas.

- To preview a song or movie, double-click it, or select it and press the Play button.

iDVD's Interface

Some software is deep, with lots of hidden, out-of-the-way features. iDVD is not one of those programs. That's not to say it isn't deep in what it can do—rather, it's easy to find what you need, quickly.

Menu/main window

iDVD's main window, referred to as the *menu*, displays the first set of options that your viewers will encounter (**Figure 19.6**). Choose between standard or widescreen modes, depending on the aspect ratio of your movie.

To switch format modes:

◆ From the Project menu, choose Switch to Standard (4:3) or Switch to Widescreen (16:9), or press Command-Option-A (**Figure 19.7**).

✔ Tips

■ The term "menu" is confusing in iDVD. Normally, a menu is a list of commands that you access from the menu bar at the top of the screen. In DVD parlance, however, a menu is the screen you're looking at. Think of it like a restaurant menu: the main window is a space to list the items (movies, etc.) you can select.

■ The widescreen format is designed to play on widescreen televisions without letterboxing the picture. All themes can be made widescreen (even old ones).

■ Switch between standard and widescreen layout at any time; you're not locked into one or the other.

■ Motion-enabled menus are generally processor-intensive, so I rarely leave the Motion button enabled while I edit.

Preview window *Controls* *Themes pane*

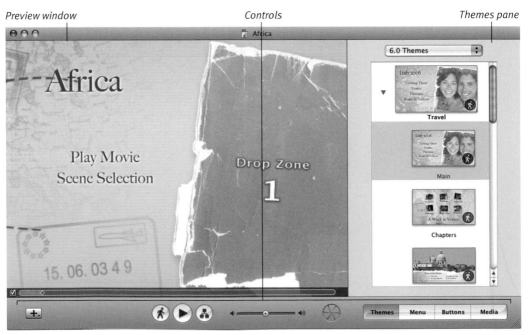

Figure 19.6 iDVD's main window contains all of the controls you need to build a professional-looking DVD.

Standard (4:3)

Widescreen (16:9)

Figure 19.7 Work in standard or widescreen mode.

Important iDVD Interface Terms

◆ **Button.** Any interactive element in the DVD workspace is a *button*, even if it doesn't always look like a button. New movies, slideshows, and chapters are all buttons, because they require some sort of action on the part of the user to activate them.

◆ **Submenu.** The exception to buttons are *submenus*, which are containers that hold more stuff. An example of a submenu would be the "Scene Selection" option that appears when you create an iDVD project from within iMovie. The item is a control that takes you to another menu screen, which includes buttons for each chapter that you've set up.

◆ **Theme.** A *theme* is the overall look of a menu screen, including the visual presentation (fonts, colors, etc.) as well as the way it interacts (with motion menus, etc.).

Controls

The program's main controls run below the preview window:

◆ **Add button.** Click this button to display a popup menu that lets you add a sub-menu, movie, or slideshow.

◆ **Motion button.** Click to toggle motion menus on and off. Many iDVD themes incorporate some type of animation; you can also set movie files to play within some themes. The Motion button turns them on or off while you're editing.

◆ **Preview button.** Switch into preview mode, which includes a virtual remote control, so that you can get a sense of how the DVD's menus and content will run. This helps you experience that genuine sinking-into-the-couch-and-too-tired-to-get-up feeling.

◆ **Map button.** Click to see the Map view, which displays the project's content structure. You can organize the project's structure, assign themes to menus, and specify media that will start playing when a disc is begun, even before the first menu screen.

◆ **Volume slider.** Set the volume of the theme elements (such as background music) while you're working; it doesn't affect the project's volume level.

◆ **Burn button.** Start the encoding and burning process to create a final disc.

◆ **Editing panes.** As with iMovie, clicking one of these buttons displays panes for editing the project's content.

✔ Tip

■ The iDVD window is finally resizable. Choose Actual Size from the Window menu to go back to the native resolution.

Creating a New Project

iMovie isn't the only entryway to iDVD. You can start by creating a new empty project.

To create a new project in iDVD:

1. Choose New Project from the File menu. The Save dialog appears.

2. Give the project a name and choose where to save it.

3. Choose an aspect ratio, and then click the Create button (**Figure 19.8**).

To import video footage:

1. From the File menu, go to the Import submenu and choose Video. Or, click the Media button and then the Movies button to display the Movies list.

2. Locate a video source, such as a Quick-Time movie, and click Import. A new button or submenu (depending on the movie) appears in the preview window for that video (**Figure 19.9**).

✔ Tips

■ You can also drag a QuickTime movie from the Finder to the iDVD window, but make sure you don't release it over a drop zone (see Chapter 20).

■ If you have an iMovie project that contains chapter markers, you can add it to an existing iDVD project and keep the chapters. Simply drag the iMovie project file to iDVD's main window, or drag it from the Movies section of the Media pane.

■ Movies that include chapter markers are split into two components when imported: a Play Movie button that plays the entire movie, and a submenu named Scene Selection. To change this behavior, choose an option in the Movies area of iDVD's preferences (**Figure 19.10**).

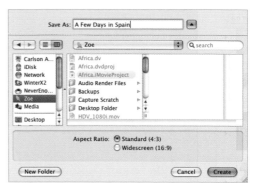

Figure 19.8 When you create a new project from scratch, choose a starting aspect ratio.

New movie added

Figure 19.9 When you import a video to an iDVD project, it appears as a new menu item.

Figure 19.10 Set the default behavior for importing movies in the Movies area of iDVD's preferences.

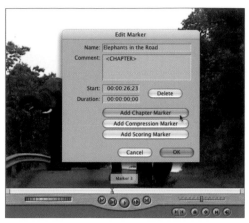

Figure 19.11 In Final Cut Express or Final Cut Pro, click the Add Chapter Marker button to ensure that iDVD will import the chapters correctly.

How to Add Chapters to an Existing iDVD Project

My wife and I worked on a vacation video using two different Macs, which meant that we had multiple iMovie projects—one for each day of the vacation. When it came time to create a DVD, I hit a stumbling block: once you've created an iDVD project, any new movies you import aren't included when you select the Play Movie option. So, our multi-part movie could only be accessed one day at a time. Ick.

The solution is to combine the separate iMovie projects into one, then use the combo movie as the basis for the iDVD project. Unfortunately, you'll have to redefine any chapter markers that were set up separately. (iDVD offers an intriguing option to Create Chapter Markers for Movie under the Advanced menu, but as of iDVD 6.0.2, it doesn't appear to work.)

Open a new iMovie project, then drag the clips from the other projects to the Timeline. Set up chapter markers, and then share the movie to iDVD.

Creating an iDVD Project from Final Cut

Video editors working in Final Cut Express or Final Cut Pro often bring their work into iDVD to create their DVD discs.

To export from Final Cut:

1. If you want to use Final Cut markers as iDVD chapter markers, be sure they're set up as such: locate a marker and press M to bring up the Edit Marker dialog.

2. Click the Add Chapter Marker button (**Figure 19.11**). The text <CHAPTER> appears in the Comment field. Click OK.

3. From the File menu, choose QuickTime Movie from the Export submenu.

4. In the Save dialog, make sure Audio and Video is chosen from the Include popup menu.

5. Choose Chapter Markers from the Markers popup menu.

6. Click Save to save the file.

7. In iDVD, import the file as described on the opposite page.

Creating a Submenu

If you used iMovie to set up chapter markers and create your iDVD project, your menu contains a Play Movie button that plays back the entire movie, and a button labeled Scene Selection. That second button is actually a *submenu* that branches off from the main menu. Double-clicking Scene Selection takes you to another menu screen that includes buttons to play chapters of your movie.

You can create new submenus that lead to other media—more movies or photos, for example.

To create a submenu:

1. Click the Add button and choose Add Submenu from the popup menu that appears. A new item named "My Submenu" appears (**Figure 19.12**).

2. Double-click the submenu name. The current theme is used for the new submenu, and includes a back arrow icon that, when clicked, leads to the main menu (**Figure 19.13**).

3. If you want, choose a different theme for the submenu.

To create a submenu in the Map view:

1. Click the Map button to switch to the Map view (**Figure 19.14**).

2. Select an icon for the menu where you want to add a submenu.

3. Click the Add button and choose Add Submenu. The new item appears in the project hierarchy attached to the menu (**Figure 19.15**).

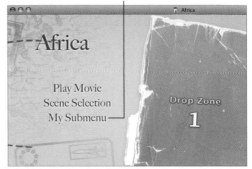

New submenu created

Figure 19.12 A new submenu looks like any other button in themes that use text buttons, but double-clicking it leads to a submenu.

Back button

Figure 19.13 The newly created submenu shares the previous menu's theme and is blank, except for a back arrow icon.

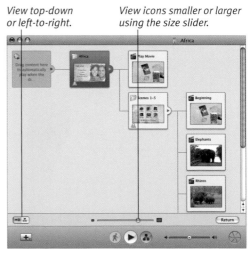

View top-down or left-to-right.   *View icons smaller or larger using the size slider.*

Figure 19.14 The Map view, once just a helpful snapshot, is now a useful tool in iDVD 6.

CREATING A SUBMENU

Submenu added to main menu   *Submenus hidden by clicking triangle*

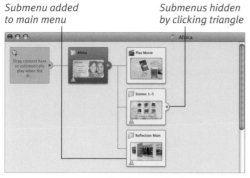

Figure 19.15 You can add submenus in the Map view.

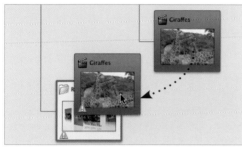

Figure 19.16 My favorite new feature in iDVD 6 is the ability to drag objects from page to page, or change the structure by dragging submenus to other menus.

To move objects to another submenu:

◆ Select an icon for a submenu, movie, or slideshow and drag it onto the icon for the submenu where the object will appear (**Figure 19.16**).

To delete a submenu:

1. Select a submenu's button (in the DVD menu) or icon (in the Map view).

2. Press the Delete key, or choose Delete from the Edit menu. The submenu disappears in a puff of smoke, as do any submenus, movies, or slideshows that it contained (but see the tip below).

✔ Tips

■ To delete a submenu but keep the objects that it contained, Control-click the submenu icon in the Map view and choose Smart Delete. Only the submenu is removed, leaving the other elements intact.

■ Want to move some menu items into their own submenu without creating the submenu separately? Select them and choose New Menu from Selection from the Project menu. A new submenu is created that contains the items. However, except for using Undo, note that you can't move them back to the main menu later if you decide they should have been there all along.

■ Click the small triangle to the right of a menu icon to hide or show lower-level items in the hierarchy (which is especially helpful when working on large, complicated projects).

■ Double-click an icon on the map to display the menu or play back the movie or slideshow. Clicking the movie or slideshow while it's playing takes you back to the Map view.

To use a transition between menus:

1. If you're currently within the submenu, click the back arrow icon to return to the previous menu. Transitions are applied to the menu that leads to the submenu.

2. Click the submenu's name or button to select it.

3. Click the Buttons button to display the Buttons pane. (By the way, now I can't stop saying "Buttons button." Thanks, Apple!)

4. Choose an effect from the Transition popup menu (**Figure 19.17**).

5. For transitions that move in more than one direction, such as Cube, click one of the directional arrows to the right of the popup menu.

6. Click the Preview button to see how your transition plays when you move between menus (**Figure 19.18**). (See "Previewing the DVD," later in this chapter.)

✔ Tips

■ Transitions can occur when switching between submenus, slideshows, and movies, but not when returning up through the hierarchy to the previous menu.

■ You can easily tell which menus include transitions by looking for a small blue circle to the left of their icons in the Map view.

■ Complex transitions can add to the time it takes to burn the disc.

Figure 19.17 Choose a type of transition to play when switching between menus.

Figure 19.18 Use the Preview mode to see how the transition plays (Mosaic Flip Small shown here).

CREATING A SUBMENU

Autoplay movie included

Figure 19.19 An icon in the upper-left corner of a theme's thumbnail image indicates an Autoplay movie.

Autoplay well

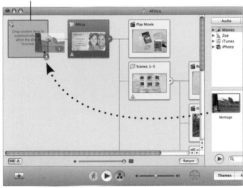

Figure 19.20 Drag a movie or photos to the Autoplay well to play them before the main menu appears.

Setting an Autoplay Movie

Nearly all of the commercial movie DVDs I've watched lately begin with either several screens of threatening information from various governmental agencies, or with some snazzy video animation or montage that plays before the main menu appears. In iDVD, this introductory material is known as an Autoplay movie, and is something you can create for your own projects. The Autoplay movie can be either a QuickTime movie or a slideshow. Themes with Autoplay movies include a special icon in their thumbnails (**Figure 19.19**).

To set an Autoplay movie:

1. Click the Map button to switch to the Map view. The icon in the upper-left corner is the Autoplay well.

2. Drag a movie file to the Autoplay well to set that as the Autoplay movie (**Figure 19.20**).

   You can also drag one or more photos, or an iPhoto album of photos, to the well, which turns them into a slideshow. To edit the contents of the slideshow, double-click the well (see Chapter 22).

To delete an Autoplay movie:

◆ Drag the contents of the Autoplay well outside the well. The media disappears with a poof.

✔ Tip

■ If you want to use an iMovie movie as the Autoplay movie, export it as Full Quality for the best image quality.

Previewing the DVD

The menu screen provides a good representation of what your viewers will see, but some aspects of a DVD—the way items are highlighted, for example—appear only when you preview the DVD. Obviously, you don't want to have to burn a new disc to see each iteration, which is why iDVD offers a preview mode.

To preview the DVD:

1. Click the Preview button to enter preview mode (**Figure 19.21**). The Customize panel retracts if it was visible, and a virtual DVD remote control appears.

   Using the remote, test the following features:

   ▲ Use the arrow keys, mouse pointer, or the arrow navigation buttons on the virtual remote control to move the button highlight between items (**Figure 19.22**).

   ▲ Use the forward and back buttons on the remote control to switch between chapters while watching the video.

   ▲ Click the Menu button to exit a movie and return to the movie's submenu, or click Title to return to the main menu.

2. Click the Exit button or the Stop button (with the square icon) to leave Preview mode.

✔ Tip

■ As you're previewing the project, pay attention to the order in which items are highlighted as you move the focus around the menu. Does it act the way a viewer would expect? Seeing the highlighting in action reminds me to re-arrange the order of my items. This is more important when your buttons don't align with the theme's invisible grid (see Chapter 21 for more on positioning items).

Button highlight   Remote control

Figure 19.21 Preview mode approximates what your viewer will see when the DVD is played.

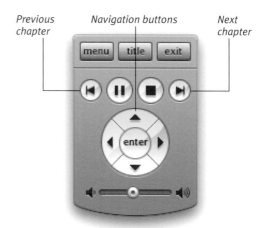

Previous chapter   Navigation buttons   Next chapter

Figure 19.22 Even Apple's *virtual* remote controls are designed better than most real-world remotes.

PREVIEWING THE DVD

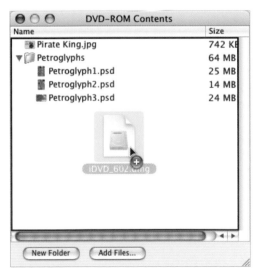

Figure 19.23 The DVD-ROM Contents window is a blank canvas where you can add files that can be accessed by people viewing your DVD on a computer.

Figure 19.24 I find it easiest to just drag files and folders from the Finder to the DVD-ROM Contents window.

Adding DVD-ROM Data

Earlier in this chapter I mentioned that it's possible to create a hybrid DVD, which contains a DVD project as well as DVD-ROM files that can be read and copied using a Mac or PC. iDVD provides a straightforward (though slightly tucked away) method of adding files and folders to the disc.

To add files and folders to the DVD-ROM:

1. From the Advanced menu, choose Edit DVD-ROM Contents. The DVD-ROM Contents window appears (**Figure 19.23**).

2. Choose from the following options:
   ▲ Click the New Folder button to create a new untitled folder.
   ▲ Click the Add Files button to bring up an Open dialog where you can choose files to add.
   ▲ From the File menu, go to the Import submenu and choose DVD-ROM Files. The Open dialog appears for you to locate files to add. This option is only available when the DVD-ROM Contents window is open.
   ▲ Drag files or folders from the Finder onto the DVD-ROM Contents window (**Figure 19.24**).

3. Close the window when you're finished adding files and folders.

To remove DVD-ROM files and folders:

1. In the DVD-ROM Contents window, select one or more files.

2. Press the Delete key, or choose Delete from the Edit menu.

✔ Tips

- When you create an iDVD slideshow, you can choose to store copies of those photos on the DVD-ROM portion of the disc. If this option is enabled, the files will appear in the DVD-ROM Contents window, but they will be grayed-out and inaccessible. You'll need to turn off the option labeled Add image files to DVD-ROM to remove the files. See Chapter 22 for more information.

- Click and drag the files and folders in the window to change their order in the list. You can also move files into different folders, nest folders, or move everything to the same hierarchy.

- iDVD creates links to the files you've added to the DVD-ROM Contents window; it doesn't copy the files themselves until it's time to burn your disc. If you add a file or folder and then move its location on your hard disk, the item's name appears in red and you get a "File not found" message when you burn the DVD. Either move the file back to its original location (if you know it), or delete the reference in the DVD-ROM Contents window and add the file again.

- Apple recommends that you not use the DVD-ROM feature in iDVD to create system backups of your hard disk, because saving "more than a few thousand files may not work." Instead, use the disc burning features in the Finder, or better yet, create a backup system using a dedicated backup application such as EMC's Retrospect (www.emcinsignia.com).

iDVD Themes

My wife is moderately addicted to several home decorating shows on TV, the ones where a designer takes over a room and the homeowners marvel at the transformation (okay, so maybe I've watched a few, too). It's amazing what a new window treatment and a fresh coat of paint can do to a room.

You might think that iDVD themes are nothing more than curtains to dress up your movies, but that would diminish the possibilities that a DVD theme offers. A theme gives your movie character, but more importantly, it provides a framework for the movie and other related media. Your DVD can contain several movies, slideshows of digital still photos, music, and animation.

In this chapter, I'll cover the basics of choosing one of iDVD's pre-made themes and working with its integrated elements, such as drop zones, motion menus, and editing text. In the next chapter, I'll get into the specifics of customizing a theme and tailoring it to your own tastes. Like decorating an otherwise functional room, working with iDVD themes can add some flair to the presentation of your movie.

Applying a Theme

When you start iDVD, a theme is already selected for you—either the first one in iDVD's list, or the one that was active the last time you used the program. Applying a different theme is simply a matter of clicking on a new one in the Themes pane. Your buttons and submenus are retained with the look of the new theme applied.

The themes introduced in iDVD 6 are organized in families, so your project can share a consistent look while also providing variation among the menus (**Figure 20.1**).

To apply a theme family:

1. Click the Themes button to display the Themes pane, if it's not already visible.

2. Click a theme family icon to apply the theme to the current menu and any submenus based on it.
   - ▲ If you're working in the Standard (4:3) aspect ratio, iDVD offers to switch to Widescreen (16:9) mode (**Figure 20.2**). Click Keep to leave the mode unchanged (unless you want to switch, of course).
   - ▲ You may also see an Apply Theme Family dialog confirming that you want the theme to apply to all of the submenus attached to the current menu. Click OK.

   After a few seconds, the theme changes in the main window.

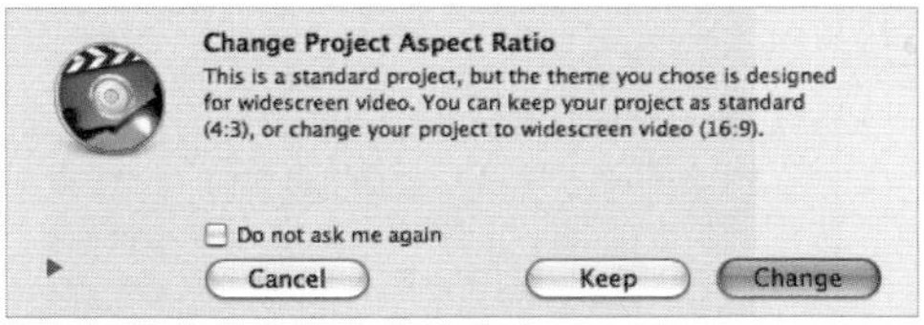

To apply an individual theme:

1. Click the Themes button to display the Themes pane, if it's not already visible.

2. Choose a theme from the list by clicking its thumbnail image. After a few seconds, the new theme is applied.

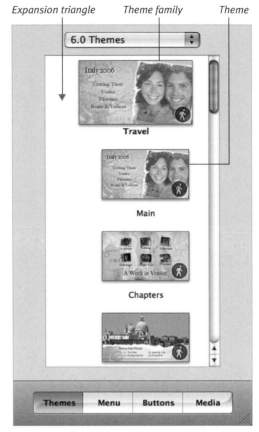

Expansion triangle   Theme family   Theme

Figure 20.1 Click a theme in the Themes pane of the Customize panel to apply it to your menu.

Figure 20.2 This dialog appears whenever you switch standard aspect ratio themes. Click the Do not ask me again checkbox to avoid it in the future.

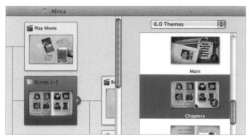

Figure 20.3 Select an icon in the Map view and then click a theme to apply it to that menu.

Before using Apply Theme to Submenus

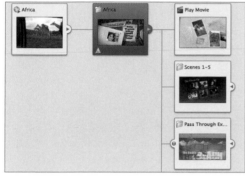

After using Apply Theme to Submenus

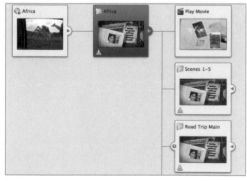

Figure 20.4 When you use the Apply Theme to Submenus command, all submenus are given the same theme. Looking at the Map view, you can see how the menus at the top use different themes. Afterwards, they all share the same theme.

To apply a theme in the Map view:

1. With the Themes pane visible, click the Map button.

2. Click the icon of the menu whose theme you want to change.

3. Click a theme from the Themes pane to apply the change (**Figure 20.3**).

4. Click the Return button to exit Map view.

To apply a theme to every menu in your project:

◆ In any menu screen, choose Apply Theme to Project from the Advanced menu. Every menu in your project now has the same theme.

To apply a theme to submenus:

1. Navigate to a submenu that you wish to change (the Map is a good place to do this; click the Map button, then click the menu you wish to view).

2. Choose Apply Theme to Submenus from the Advanced menu. The theme of every submenu in the current hierarchy is changed (**Figure 20.4**).

✔ Tips

■ Click the popup menu in the Themes pane to select themes from other versions of iDVD (or choose All to view them all in the list).

■ Feel free to mix and match themes within a family; for example, you can use the Extras theme in place of Chapters if you prefer.

■ You can purchase more custom themes from third party developers such as iDVD ThemePak and iDVD Themetastic (see Appendix B).

APPLYING A THEME

Using Motion

Menu items are designed to do more than display a text title or static image. DVDs typically convey video, so why not add some motion to the menus as well?

iDVD uses two types of motion: *motion menus*, which incorporate animated backgrounds, and *motion buttons*, which play movies or abbreviated photo slideshows in place of a generic button icon or still image. (Actually, there's also a third type of motion, audio, which is covered in the next chapter.) Most of iDVD's recent themes incorporate motion because it brings life to menus and makes them more than just pretty pictures. Motion menus include a small icon in the lower-right corner of their thumbnails (**Figure 20.5**).

In this section I cover motion buttons; see "Changing the Background" in Chapter 21 for details on using motion menus.

To activate motion:

◆ Click the Motion button, choose Motion from the Advanced menu, or press Command-J. The Motion button becomes highlighted in blue (**Figure 20.6**), and any animated elements within the theme, such as the background, drop zone, or submenu icons, start to play.

Perform any of the above actions to turn motion off.

✔ Tip

■ Turn Motion off when you're done editing the motion properties of your menu to improve performance while editing other aspects of your project.

Shelves

Motion menus included

Watercolor

Figure 20.5 An icon in the lower-right corner of the theme thumbnail indicates motion.

Figure 20.6 Click the Motion button to activate the motion elements within the menu.

Figure 20.7 The first section of the scrubber bar is the introductory animation, and isn't repeated.

The Introductory Animation

Many themes include an introductory animation before the menu elements appear, indicated by a solid section of the Motion Playhead scrubber bar (**Figure 20.7**). When the total animation finishes playing, it starts over where the vertical bar bisects the scrubber bar. To skip this first animation, deselect the checkbox to the left of the scrubber bar. Some themes also have a concluding animation, too.

Figure 20.8 The Movie slider lets you choose a starting frame for your movie's button icon.

Figure 20.9 These two chapters appear in the same movie, which is why I can set the bottom chapter's button icon to match the top one (not that I'd want to, but you get the idea).

Motion buttons

Any QuickTime movie you add to your menu is a motion button—when motion is turned on, the movie plays within its button icon (except for themes that use only text as buttons, of course). Normally, the first frame of the movie button is the first frame of the movie itself; if you specified a poster frame for the movie file using QuickTime Pro (see Chapter 17), that frame is automatically set as the beginning. You can specify a new first frame, or choose not to play the movie at all and just use a frame of it as a still image.

To set the starting frame:

1. Click a motion button to select it; a Movie slider appears above it. This works whether motion is activated or not.

2. Drag the Movie slider to locate the frame you wish to use as the starting point (**Figure 20.8**). Click outside the button to deselect it.

To turn off movie playback for a button:

1. Click a motion button to select it.

2. Uncheck the Movie checkbox that appears above the button.

   To choose a specific frame as the button's image, set a new starting frame using the preceding steps before turning off movie playback.

✔ Tip

■ The chapters from an iMovie-generated iDVD project all belong to the full movie, so when you're changing the starting frame of the motion button, the slider represents the entire movie, not just that chapter (**Figure 20.9**).

Motion duration

The Loop Duration slider in the Menu pane controls how long your motion elements play before they are reset to their starting points.

To set motion duration:

1. Click the Menu button to view the Menu pane.

2. Drag the Loop Duration slider to change the duration of the motion menu (**Figure 20.10**). The number to the right of the slider represents the total time required to play all motion elements on the menu.

✔ Tips

■ What if you don't want any motion when you burn your project to disc? Set the Loop Duration to 00:00, and disable any motion button movies, and turn off any of a theme's introductory or ending animations.

■ The maximum menu duration used to be 30 seconds in previous versions of iDVD. Now, it's limited by the length of the menu's background movie or audio, whichever is longest, up to 15 minutes. If one ends before the other, it loops to keep the motion effect going.

■ One of my biggest gripes about DVDs is that they don't loop cleanly, either on my projects or commercial DVDs. The motion menu reaches the end and pauses briefly before starting over. However, one feature can help: in iDVD's preferences, click the General icon and enable the option labeled Fade volume out at end of menu loop (**Figure 20.11**).

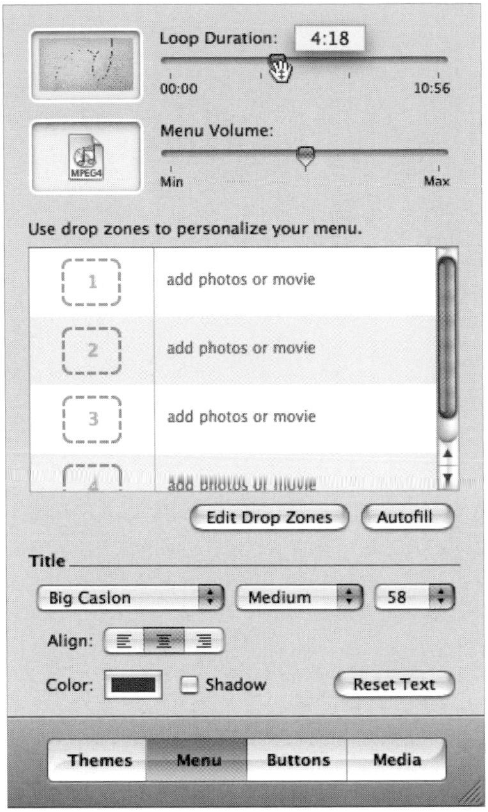

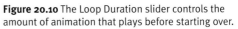

Figure 20.10 The Loop Duration slider controls the amount of animation that plays before starting over.

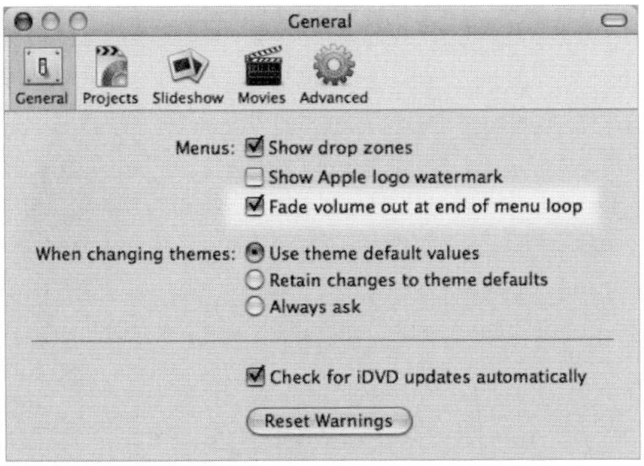

Figure 20.11 Tired of music getting chopped off at the end of a menu's animation? This preference will help.

USING MOTION

Black and yellow border appears when media is over the drop zone.

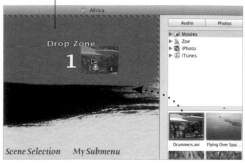

Figure 20.12 Drag a photo or movie from the Media pane to a menu's drop zone.

Drag to set start and end points in the drop zone.

Figure 20.13 Choose which section of a drop zone movie plays in a menu's animation.

Drop Zone Movie Start/End

When you place a custom movie into a drop zone, you can control which portion of it plays during the menu's animation, just like editing the clip in iMovie. Click the movie in the drop zone to display the Movie Start/End control, and then drag the markers (**Figure 20.13**).

Using Drop Zones

To add a bit of visual interest and a personal touch to your menu, add a movie, photo, or collection of photos to the drop zones included with some themes.

To add a movie or photo to a drop zone:

1. Click the Media button to display the Media pane.

2. Click the Photos or Movies button at the top of the pane.

3. Drag a movie, photo, or multiple selected photos to a drop zone, indicated by a yellow border (**Figure 20.12**). iDVD adds the media to that zone.

Or

◆ Drag a movie or photo file(s) from the Finder to the drop zone.

Or

1. Control-click the drop zone and choose Import from the contextual menu.

2. In the Open dialog that appears, locate a movie or photo file on your hard disk, then click the Import button.

To reposition media in a drop zone:

◆ Click and drag the media in the drop zone to control which portions are visible.

To remove media from a drop zone:

◆ Control-click the zone and choose Clear from the contextual menu.

◆ Drag the photo or movie out of the drop zone and release the mouse button.

✔ Tip

■ When repositioning a photo or movie in a drop zone, don't drag too far or else iDVD thinks you're removing the item from the zone.

Working with dynamic drop zones

Some of the latest themes feature dynamic drop zones: one or more drop zones animated within the theme. Individually, they operate as normal drop zones, but you can also control them as a group.

To add movies or photos to dynamic drop zones:

1. Turn off Motion, if it's currently active, by clicking the Motion button. (You can leave it on if you want, but that makes it difficult to add each media item.)

2. Drag a movie or photo to a drop zone; each zone is numbered.

3. Advance the Motion Playhead by dragging it to the right (**Figure 20.14**). (If you don't see it, choose Show Motion Playhead from the Advanced menu.) The animation progresses, revealing more drop zones.

4. Repeat steps 2 and 3 until you've populated the drop zones.

Or

1. Double-click a dynamic drop zone to view the floating Drop Zones palette (**Figure 20.15**).

   You can also click the Edit Drop Zones button in the Menu pane.

2. Drag movies or photos to each drop zone.

3. Click the close button at the upper left corner to go back to the menu.

Or

1. Click the Menu button to display the Menu pane, which is home to the drop zone list (**Figure 20.16**).

2. Drag movies or photos to each drop zone.

Figure 20.14 Drag the Motion Playhead to the right to advance through the dynamic drop zone animation.

Figure 20.15 The Drop Zones palette is an easier way to add movies and photos to multiple drop zones.

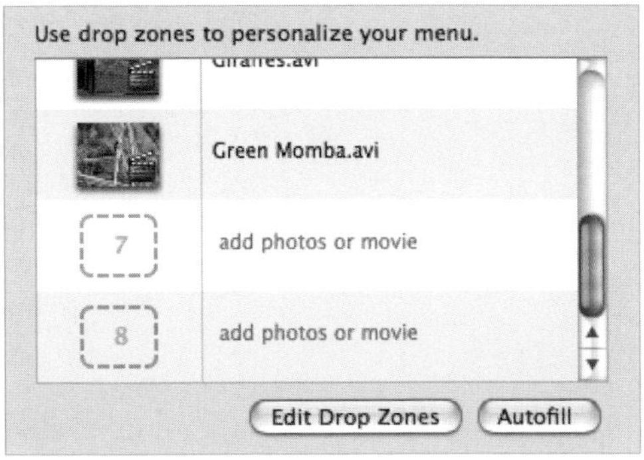

Figure 20.16 The drop zone list in the Menu pane provides yet another area to add media to your zones.

USING DROP ZONES

Figure 20.17 Press the Command or Option key before you drop a media file to direct how it will be added.

To autofill drop zones:

1. Click the Menu button to view the Menu pane.

2. Click the Autofill button. iDVD collects media that you've already used in the project (such as movies added) and fills the drop zones.

✔ Tips

- Consider waiting until you've added more content to your project before using the autofill feature, so that iDVD will have plenty of media to choose from.

- The drag-and-drop approach can be problematic if your aim is poor: a few pixels off and you could find yourself replacing the menu's background image (see "Changing the Background" in Chapter 21). To ensure you're performing the action you want, press the Command or Option key when dragging to view a contextual menu with options for placing the media (**Figure 20.17**).

- You can opt to turn off the "Drop Zone" text in iDVD's General preferences by disabling the Show Drop Zones checkbox. If you turn it off, the words reappear when you drag media onto the menu area.

- Double-click a zone in the Drop Zones palette to center that zone in the menu animation.

- The Drop Zones palette makes it easy to drag content from the Media pane. However, you can also add items from the Media pane to the drop zone list in the Menu pane: just drag from the Media pane to the Menu button, which switches the visible pane, and then drop the movie or photo onto the drop zone list.

Working with multiple photos in a drop zone

When you drag multiple photos to a drop zone, they act as a slideshow within the zone. You can change the order in which they appear, or add and delete photos using the Drop Zone Editor.

To set which photo displays first:

1. Click the zone to make it editable (**Figure 20.18**).

2. Drag the Photos slider that appears above the drop zone to choose a photo. That picture will appear first when the menu plays with motion.

To change the order of the photos:

1. Click the zone to make it editable.

2. Click the Edit Order button, or double click the drop zone. The Drop Zone Editor appears (**Figure 20.19**).

3. Drag the photos to change their order. iDVD numbers each icon to indicate the playback order.

4. Click the Return button to go back to the menu.

To add more photos:

1. Double-click the drop zone to display the Drop Zone Editor.

2. Drag more images from the Media pane or from the Finder.

3. Click the Return button to go back to the menu.

Figure 20.18 Choose a different photo to appear in the drop zone by moving the Photos slider.

Figure 20.19 The Drop Zone Editor displays the photos you've added to the zone and their playback order.

Figure 20.20 Images 1, 4, and 9 are selected and ready to be deleted (or moved; see Chapter 22).

To delete photos from the drop zone:

1. In the Drop Zone Editor, select the photos you wish to remove. Shift-click to select a range of photos, or Command-click to select non-contiguous photos (**Figure 20.20**).

2. Press the Delete key or choose Delete from the Edit menu. The pictures are removed.

3. Click the Return button to go back to the menu (or the drop zone list).

✔ Tips

■ iDVD determines the amount of time a photo appears depending on the number of photos you've given it. The more photos you add, the less time they stay onscreen. The overall time is based on the Loop Duration setting in the Menu pane (see "Using Motion," earlier in this chapter).

■ If you've already added photos in the menu, dragging more to the drop zone replaces the ones you have; it doesn't add them to the existing lineup. Use the Drop Zone Editor to add more pictures.

■ Click the view preference buttons in the upper-right corner of the Drop Zone Editor to display the photos either as thumbnails or as a list (with filenames).

■ It's not possible to resize or crop photos in a drop zone within iDVD, unfortunately. Some themes determine the size of the media by fitting the width of the photo or movie; others base the size on the height.

Editing Text

Not all text needs to be in service of buttons or submenus—edit and add your own text boxes. The following steps apply to changing the contents of text blocks; in the next chapter, I'll cover more settings such as changing the font and style.

To edit text:

1. Click once to select a button or title, and then click again to select the text (**Figure 20.21**). Don't *double-click* the button, however, because that will either play its movie or go to a submenu.

2. Type your text. Hit Return or Enter to break the line—an improvement that frustrated me in early versions of iDVD (**Figure 20.22**).

3. Click outside the text field to deselect it and accept your changes.

To add new text:

1. Choose Add Text from the Project menu, or press Command-K. A new text block appears (**Figure 20.23**).

2. Edit the text as described above.

3. Position the text by dragging it where you want it; unlike the default behavior of buttons and menu titles, which snap to an invisible grid, a new text block can be placed anywhere on the screen. (See the next chapter for more on positioning buttons.)

To delete text:

1. Click a text block once to select it.

2. Press the Delete key, or choose Delete from the Edit menu. The text vanishes in a puff of smoke.

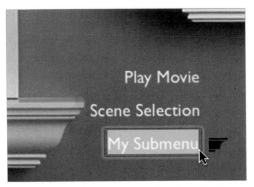

Figure 20.21 Click a button twice (but don't double-click) to edit its text.

Figure 20.22 Create multi-line text boxes by pressing Return or Enter.

Figure 20.23 Add text blocks that aren't buttons or submenus.

EDITING TEXT

TV Safe Area   *Area likely to be cut off*

Figure 20.24 Items placed outside the safe area may get cropped out when played back on a television.

Standard Crop Area

Figure 20.25 The edges of widescreen projects can get hacked off by standard-definition TVs, but it won't matter if you use the Standard Crop Area indicator to position your text.

To insert special characters:

1. Click a text block once to select it, then click again to edit it.

2. Choose Special Characters from the Edit menu. The Character Palette appears.

3. Select the character you want to use in the palette.

4. Click the Insert button to add the character to your text.

✔ Tips

- Some televisions don't display everything that you see in iDVD's screen. To make sure your text will appear, choose Show TV Safe Area from the View menu, or press Command-T, and position the text and buttons within the area that's not shaded (**Figure 20.24**).

- If you're working in widescreen mode, choose Show Standard Crop Area from the View menu, or press Command-Option-T, to see where a standard-definition television showing a full-screen image will crop your menu (**Figure 20.25**).

EDITING TEXT

CUSTOMIZING iDVD THEMES

21

The benefit of iDVD's approach to creating DVD menus is that everything is already in place: the background imagery, animation, typefaces, and navigation structure are all prefab. Your job is to fill in the content.

While that may sound nicely organized to some people, others see it as a collection of limitations. Where's the fun if everything is spelled out for you already? This is where iDVD's theme customization comes into play. It may not be as open-ended as Apple's professional-caliber DVD Studio Pro, but there's enough flexibility built in to let you make your own personal stamp on the menu design.

Editing Text Formatting

A hallmark of the Macintosh has been the capability to change the appearance of text onscreen. Sure, every computer now offers dozens of fonts and styles, but in 1984 that capability was a big deal. So it's sensible that you can change the font, alignment, and color of your menu titles, buttons, and text blocks.

To edit text formatting:

1. Click the text block you want to edit.

2. If you're formatting the menu's title or you selected a text block you created, click the Menu button to display the Menu pane (**Figure 21.1**).

   If you selected a button label, click the Buttons button to display the Buttons pane (**Figure 21.2**).

3. In the Title, Text, or Label area (the name changes depends on what's selected in the menu), set the following attributes:

   ▲ **Family.** Choose a font family from this popup menu to change the font.

   ▲ **Typeface.** Choose the style of font from this popup menu.

   ▲ **Size.** Choose a font size from this popup menu.

   ▲ **Color.** Click the Color field to display the Colors palette and choose a new color (**Figure 21.3**).

   ▲ **Shadow.** Drop shadows are often overused in design, but in DVD menus they often make the text more readable. Click this checkbox to add a subtle drop shadow behind the text.

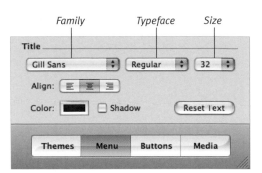

Figure 21.1 Change the formatting of the menu title or stand-alone text blocks in the Menu pane.

Figure 21.2 Button label formatting is handled in the Buttons pane.

Figure 21.3 iDVD uses the Mac OS X Colors palette to choose from the full spectrum of colors.

Figure 21.4 *Could* and *should* are two very different terms. *Restraint* is an even better word.

To reset text to the theme's default formatting:

1. Select the text block you want to change back to the theme's formatting.

2. Click the Reset Text button (Menu pane) or Reset Label button (Buttons pane).

✔ Tips

■ If you want to change the appearance of a menu's title, you don't need to select anything first; the text controls in the Menu pane apply to the title by default.

■ Hooray! In previous editions of this book, I've complained that you couldn't simply choose a standard font size (such as 12 point), but had to rely on an inaccurate slider. Now, in iDVD 6…you can.

■ More good news! iDVD 6 lets you apply formatting changes to each text block or button label independently (**Figure 21.4**). The old restrictions of applying one font for all button labels is gone, gone, gone. However, remember that just because you *can* use all sorts of crazy fonts on your menu doesn't mean you *should*.

Editing Text Alignment and Position

iDVD uses two terms for aligning text: alignment and position. Alignment refers to how the text lines up within its allotted space, or how button labels appear in relation to each other. Position describes where a button's label appears in relation to the button's icon (if it's visible).

Title alignment

The title in each theme is bound to a specific area by default, but you can also opt to place it anywhere within the menu. You can also make it disappear if a title isn't needed.

To set the title alignment:

1. Select the menu title, or make sure nothing is selected (the settings apply to the title if nothing else is selected).

2. In the Menu pane or Buttons pane, click one of the Align options: Left, Center, or Right (**Figure 21.5**). The text is moved relative to the area designated for the title. For example, choosing Center in the Reflection White theme shifts the text to the right of the default position; it doesn't move it to the center of the screen as you might expect (**Figure 21.6**).

    To position the text anywhere you want, simply drag the title elsewhere on the screen; doing so unlocks the title from the theme's placement grid and enables you to drag the title anywhere on screen (**Figure 21.7**).

To remove the menu title:

◆   Select the title and press the Delete key, or choose Delete from the Edit menu. Note that once a title has been deleted, you can't add it back to your page without using the Undo command.

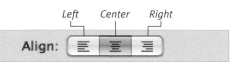

Left   Center   Right

Figure 21.5 Choose a button from the Align options to specify text alignment.

Left alignment

Center alignment

Figure 21.6 A title's position is relative to the area allotted by the theme, not by the overall screen.

Custom positioning

Figure 21.7 You have the freedom to place the title anywhere.

Below   *Center*

Figure 21.8 When a button includes an icon, the Position popup menu includes more options.

Aligned left

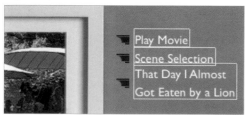

Aligned right

Figure 21.9 You can choose the alignment of text-only buttons.

Button label position

In themes where buttons include an icon, instead of just text, the Position popup menu determines where the text appears in relation to the icon.

To set the position of button text:

1. Select a button in the menu.

2. In the Buttons pane, choose a button label location from the Position popup menu (**Figure 21.8**).

To remove button text:

1. Click the button to select it, then click it again to select the label's text.

2. Press the Delete key or choose Delete from the Edit menu.

Button text alignment

In themes that use only text for buttons, the Align controls specify the text alignment of the buttons relative to each other. (You can also switch normal buttons to text buttons on any theme; see "Editing Buttons" on the next page.)

To set the alignment of button text:

1. Select a text button in the menu.

2. In the Buttons pane, choose the Left, Center, or Right buttons to align the text of the labels to each other (**Figure 21.9**).

✔ Tip

■ Some label position settings don't work well in some themes. For example, using a Left Side position in some themes can make the text run off the screen or onto other buttons. You can move the buttons around, however; see "Editing Buttons" on the next page.

EDITING TEXT ALIGNMENT AND POSITION

Editing Buttons

Buttons are the mechanism by which your viewers interact with the DVD. In addition to changing the buttons' text, you can change their shape, location, and size, plus the highlight color.

To change the button style:

1. Select one or more buttons in the menu.

2. Choose a button shape at the top of the Buttons pane (**Figure 21.10**). To return to the style included with the current theme, choose From Theme.

To reposition buttons:

◆ Drag a button onto another button to swap their locations on the grid. The others move out of your way as you drag.

Or

1. In the Buttons pane, click the Free positioning radio button (**Figure 21.11**). The button is no longer shackled to the grid.

2. Drag the button to a new location within the menu (**Figure 21.12**).

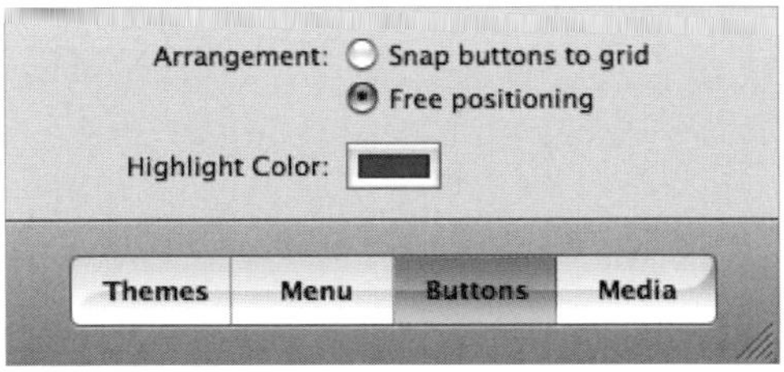

To resize buttons:

1. Select one or more buttons in the menu.

2. In the Button pane, drag the Size slider. This feature becomes useful if you've added lots of buttons to your menu and you want to prevent overlap (**Figure 21.13**).

To change the button highlight color:

◆ In the Buttons pane, click the Highlight Color field and choose a color from the Colors palette.

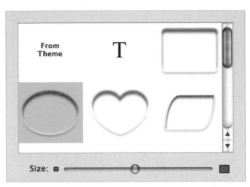

Figure 21.10 Change the appearance of button icons by choosing a new style in the Buttons pane.

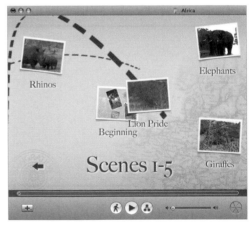

Figure 21.11 You're free, to do what you want, any ol' time, with the Free positioning option.

Figure 21.12 Free positioning allows you to drag buttons to any location within the menu.

EDITING BUTTONS

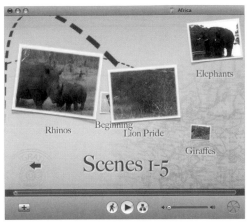

Figure 21.13 The Size slider makes button icons smaller or larger (but not the button text).

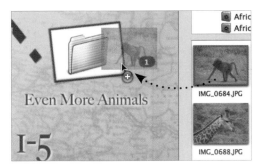

Figure 21.14 Drag a photo or movie from the Media pane to a submenu to change its icon (this works only in themes that use icons, naturally).

Custom icon applied

Figure 21.15 Use the Submenu slider to change from the custom icon back to the generic icon.

To change the appearance of a submenu icon:

◆ In themes that display button icons, drag a photo or movie from the Media pane or the Finder onto the new submenu icon (**Figure 21.14**).

You can switch back to the generic submenu icon, if you want, by clicking the icon and moving the Submenu slider to the left (**Figure 21.15**). Only one photo or movie can be applied to a submenu icon—dragging others just replaces the previous image.

✔ Tips

■ Unlike earlier versions, iDVD 6 lets you change the appearance of each button independently, which means you can have some buttons with image previews and some with just text labels, for example.

■ If you decide to position your buttons freely (without the grid), turn on the TV Safe Area (press Command-T or choose it from the Advanced menu) to make sure the buttons won't get cut off when viewed on some television screens.

■ iDVD doesn't include many different button style choices. If you're looking for something else, check out the iDVD Button Paks sold by DVD ThemePak (www.dvdthemepak.com).

EDITING BUTTONS

Changing the Background

To dramatically alter a theme's appearance, swap the existing background image with your own photo or movie.

To use a photo or movie as the background with no drop zones:

◆ Drag a photo or movie from the Media pane or the Finder and drop it onto the Background well in the Menu pane (**Figure 21.16**). (Drag the photo onto the Menu button to switch to the pane without releasing the mouse button.)

Or

1. From the File menu, go to the Import submenu and choose Background Video.

2. Locate a movie on your hard disk, and click Import.

To use a photo or movie as the background and keep the drop zones:

◆ Drag a photo from the Media pane or the Finder and drop it onto the current theme's background. The advantage of this approach is that you can keep the theme's drop zone (if it has one). If you drag the photo to the Background well, the drop zone is no longer available.

Or

1. Drag a photo or movie file from the Media pane or the Finder to the menu, but don't release the mouse button.

2. Press the Command or Option key to bring up a contextual menu with choices (**Figure 21.17**).

3. Choose Replace background to use your movie file as the background but keep the drop zones; or, to use just the movie file, choose Replace background and drop zones.

Background well in Menu pane

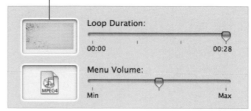

Figure 21.16 Adding a photo or movie to the Background well makes it the theme's background image.

Figure 21.17 Press Command or Option before releasing the mouse button to choose an action.

Click this triangle to view the Start/End control.

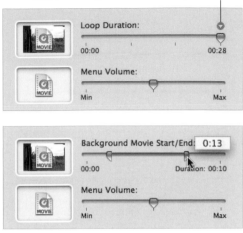

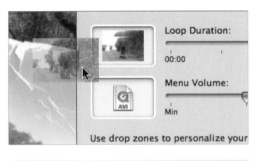

Figure 21.18 Use the almost-secret control in the Loop Duration slider to set the start and end of your background video.

Figure 21.19 Drag a photo or movie file out of the Background well to revert to the theme's original background image. The image disappears in a poof of smoke.

To set the beginning and ending of a background video:

1. With a video set as the background, switch to the Menu pane.

2. Click the small triangle above the Loop Duration slider to display the Background Movie Start/End control (**Figure 21.18**). The triangle appears only when a video is used as the background.

3. Drag the ends of the control to set the start and end of the video.

To remove your background photo or movie:

1. Switch to the Menu pane.

2. Drag the photo or movie out of the Background well (**Figure 21.19**). The theme's default background reappears.

✔ Tips

- For best image quality, export your background movie from iMovie at the Full Quality DV setting (see Chapter 16).

- If the movie is meant as a visual item only, export it from iMovie with the sound disabled, or set at a low volume.

- If you switch to a different theme, your background image or movie is deleted from the project; you'll need to re-import it under the new theme.

- Remember that you won't see your movie in action unless Motion is enabled.

- If you remove a video from the background well, be sure to also remove the audio that the video may have added (see the next page).

- Import video files you shot with a digital still camera by locating them in the Media pane's Photos list.

CHANGING THE BACKGROUND

Setting Background Audio

Being a more visual person, I tend to forget about audio unless it's either (a) highly annoying, or (b) eerily nonexistent. Some themes include background audio, others don't, but you can add an audio file to any of them to customize your menu's sound.

To choose an audio file:

1. Switch to the Media pane, and click the Audio button (if it's not already active). Your GarageBand songs and iTunes music appear (**Figure 21.20**).

2. Locate the audio file you wish to use. To help narrow your search, click one of the playlists in the upper portion of the window, or type a name (song or artist) in the search box at the bottom.

3. Click the Play button if you want to preview the file. Otherwise, click the file to select it.

To add background audio:

◆ With a song selected in the Media pane, click the Apply button.

◆ Drag an audio file from the Media pane or the Finder to the Audio well in the Menu pane (**Figure 21.21**).

◆ Drag an audio file from the Media pane or the Finder to the menu.

Or

1. From the File menu, choose Audio from the Import submenu.

2. Locate an audio file on your hard disk, and click Import.

To change the volume of the background audio:

◆ Drag the Menu Volume slider in the Menu pane.

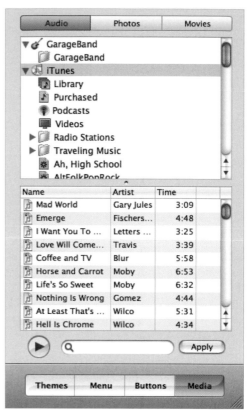

Figure 21.20 The Audio list in the Media pane displays your iTunes and GarageBand songs.

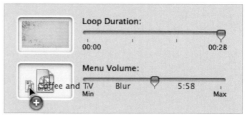

Figure 21.21 Drop a song file onto the Audio well to use that as your background sound.

Protected audio file

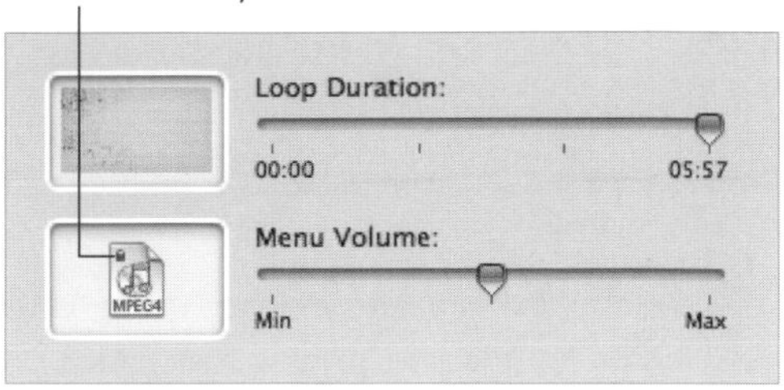

Figure 21.22 The icon in the Audio well can tell you if you're using protected audio content.

To remove background audio:

1. Switch to the Menu pane.

2. Drag the sound file out of the Audio well. The well's icon changes to a generic speaker icon.

✔ Tips

- To play more than one song in the background, select multiple audio files and drag them to the Audio well together.

- If you want the background audio turned down, not off, use the Volume slider at the bottom of the iDVD window. This setting only affects the volume while you work, not the volume of the audio when the project is burned to disc.

- Background audio doesn't need to be music. Spoken-word content or other sound effects work just as well.

- You can drag a QuickTime movie to the Audio well and use only its audio track.

- GarageBand songs need to be saved with an iTunes preview before you can add them to iDVD (see Chapter 14).

- Speaking of GarageBand, that type of audio is great for a DVD menu: you have control over the duration of the song, and it can loop in the background.

- If you add a background movie, then delete the movie from the Background well, the audio stays. You need to also delete the music from the Audio well.

- iDVD recognizes when it's using protected audio files, such as songs you buy from the iTunes Music Store, and displays the file's icon (which includes a small lock image, **Figure 21.22**).

SETTING BACKGROUND AUDIO

Looping Movie Playback

Normally, a movie or scene plays its frames and finishes, moving on to the next scene or returning to the menu. However, you can opt to loop a movie so that once started it will replay until you intervene.

To loop a movie:

1. Click the Map button to switch to the Map view.

2. Select a movie file.

3. Choose Loop Movie from the Advanced menu. A loop icon appears on the movie clip (**Figure 21.23**).

✔ Tips

- When you loop a movie chapter that's part of a larger movie, all of its chapters include the loop icon and the entire movie loops, not an individual chapter.

- This may be too obvious, but never loop an AutoPlay movie. If you do, the DVD will never proceed to the main menu.

- Did I say *never*? Looping the AutoPlay movie might be what you want if you're creating a video that needs to keep playing in a kiosk mode (such as for a convention booth, art installation, or other presentation).

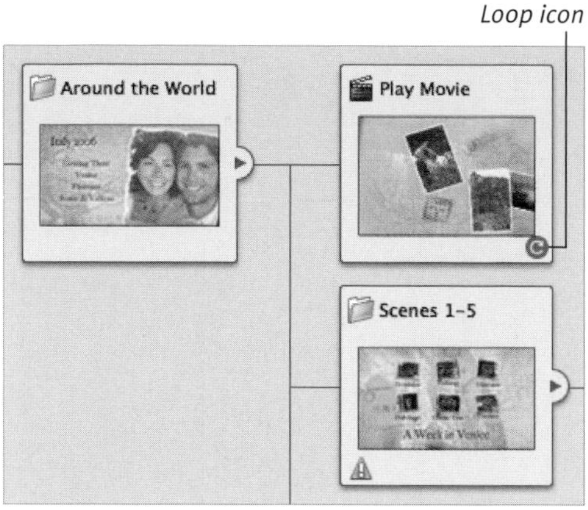

Loop icon

Figure 21.23 A loop icon in the Map view indicates that a movie will replay once it reaches its end.

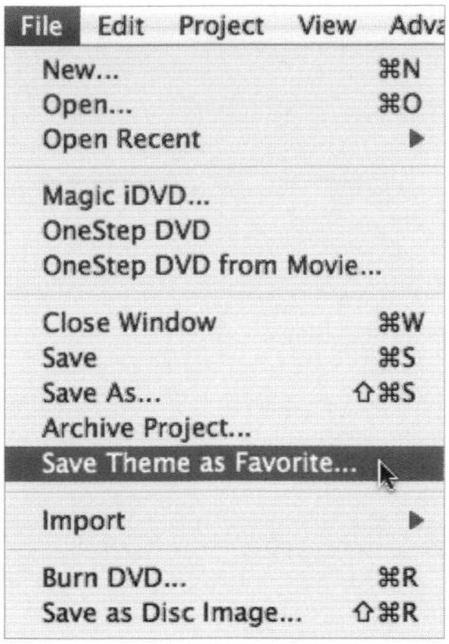

File	Edit	Project	View	Adva
New...				⌘N
Open...				⌘O
Open Recent				▶
Magic iDVD...				
OneStep DVD				
OneStep DVD from Movie...				
Close Window				⌘W
Save				⌘S
Save As...				⇧⌘S
Archive Project...				
Save Theme as Favorite...				
Import				▶
Burn DVD...				⌘R
Save as Disc Image...				⇧⌘R

Figure 21.24 When you're ready to save your theme, choose the Save Theme as Favorite option.

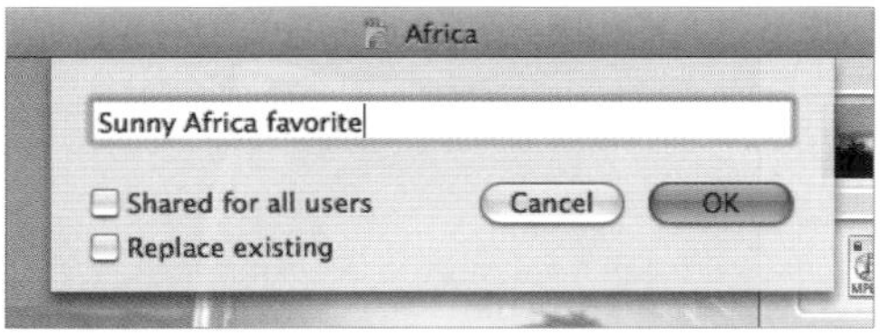

Figure 21.25 Type a name for your new favorite theme, and decide if all users of your Mac can use it.

Favorite icon

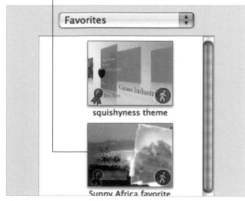

Figure 21.26 Saved themes appear in the Themes pane's Favorites list, and include a custom icon.

Saving a Favorite Theme

You've added a new background, new music, and tweaked the buttons and text to your liking. If you want to keep this setting for future projects, save it as a favorite.

To save a favorite theme:

1. Choose Save Theme as Favorite from the File menu (**Figure 21.24**).

2. In the dialog that appears, type a name for the theme (**Figure 21.25**).

3. To make the theme available for all users on your computer, enable the Shared for all users option.

4. If you're changing a favorite that you've already created and want to save over it, mark the Replace existing checkbox.

5. After the theme is saved, it becomes available in the Themes pane. Choose Favorites or All from the popup menu to view your theme (**Figure 21.26**).

✔ Tips

- If you've arranged your buttons with the Free Positioning option selected in the Button pane, those positions become the basis for the grid when you apply your favorite theme to a new project.

- If you placed a photo or movie in a drop zone before saving the theme as a favorite, that media becomes part of the background image, but leaves the drop zone open for new media.

SAVING A FAVORITE THEME

Deleting a Favorite Theme

Creating a favorite theme is a simple operation, but iDVD offers no similarly direct method of removing a favorite. However, you can do it with a little poking around in the Finder.

To delete a favorite theme:

1. Quit iDVD if it is running.

2. In the Finder, locate iDVD's Favorites folder. There are two; the location of the one you want to delete depends on whether the theme was made available to all users or not.

   ▲ If you enabled the Shared for all users option, go to [Computer] > Users > Shared > iDVD > Favorites (**Figure 21.27**).

   ▲ If you did not enable Shared for all users, go to Home > Library > Application Support > iDVD > Favorites (**Figure 21.28**).

3. Select the file corresponding to the theme you wish to delete, and drag it to the Trash.

4. Re-launch iDVD to see that the favorite theme is now no longer available.

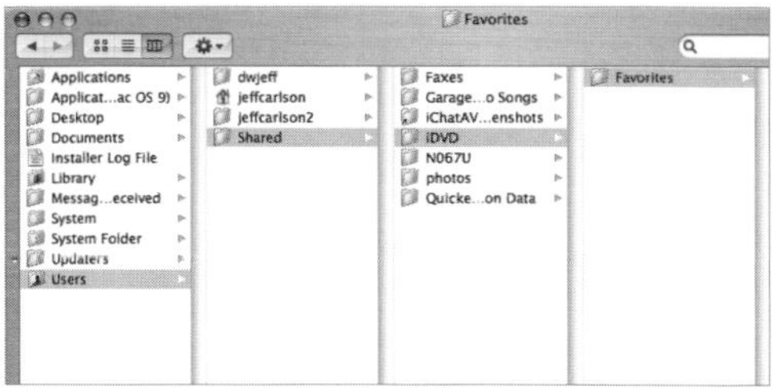

Figure 21.27 A favorite theme shared by all users appears in Mac OS X's Users directory.

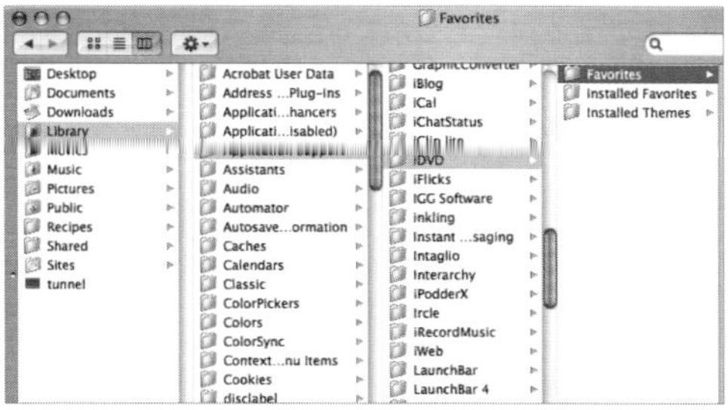

Figure 21.28 If the theme will be used only by you, it's stored within your user Library folder.

SLIDESHOWS

Most of this book centers on video and all of the wonderful things you can do with it. But your digital lifestyle probably includes a lot of still photos, too (either taken with a digital still camera or your camcorder, or scanned from paper originals).

In addition to providing a venue for your movies, iDVD can build slideshows from your photos, including transitions and audio, which can be played back on DVD players.

Creating a Slideshow

The ingredients for a successful slideshow are photos, photos, and more photos (with perhaps a dash of audio thrown in, which I'll address later in the chapter).

To create a slideshow:

◆ Click the Add button and choose Add Slideshow, or choose Add Slideshow from the Project menu (or press Command-L). A new empty slideshow appears in the menu (**Figure 22.1**).

◆ Drag two or more pictures from the Media pane or the Finder to the main window (if you drag only one, then the photo is used as the background image). A new slideshow titled "My Slideshow" is created containing those pictures.

◆ Drag an iPhoto album from the Media pane to the main window (**Figure 22.2**). The slideshow that is created takes the name of the album.

To set the slideshow icon:

1. Click a slideshow to select it. A Slideshow slider appears. (This feature works only in themes where buttons include icons.)

2. Drag the Slideshow slider to choose one of the slideshow's photos (**Figure 22.3**).

3. Click outside the icon to deselect it and apply the change.

To delete a slideshow:

◆ If you want to remove a slideshow, click its button in the main window and press Delete or choose Delete from the Edit menu.

Figure 22.1 When you create an empty slideshow, it appears as a new button in the menu.

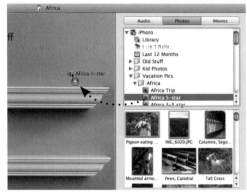

Figure 22.2 Drag an iPhoto album from the Media pane to the menu to create a slideshow containing all of the album's pictures.

Figure 22.3 The Slideshow slider lets you pick a photo to use as the button's icon.

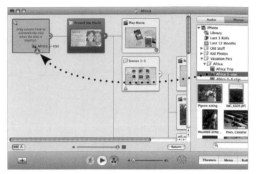

Figure 22.4 When you add photos to the AutoPlay well, the slideshow begins when the disc starts playing.

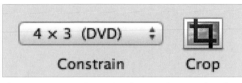

Figure 22.5 Crop photos in iPhoto to the 4 x 3 (DVD) constraint before importing them into iDVD.

iDVD as Presenter

You can use an iDVD slideshow as a presentation tool. Create your presentation in Keynote or PowerPoint, then save each slide as a PDF file. Import those files into iDVD as a slideshow. This puts your presentation on the same disc as other multimedia materials (videos, etc.), which can be played back on any DVD player, not just a computer. At the very least, you'll have a backup of your presentation in case your original file is lost or damaged.

✔ Tips

■ You can also drag photos or albums directly from the iPhoto application to iDVD's menu to create a new slideshow. That applies to folders containing images in the Finder, too.

■ Use the left or right arrow key to view the slideshow icon photos one by one, or if you don't want to drag the slider with the mouse.

■ If you want a slideshow to start as soon as you insert a DVD disc into a player, switch to the Map view and drag your photos to the AutoPlay well (**Figure 22.4**). Double-clicking the well with photos added brings up the AutoPlay Slideshow editor, which features the same options described throughout the rest of this chapter.

■ To ensure that your photos display correctly in iDVD, crop them first in iPhoto. Double-click the photo to enter Edit mode, then choose 4 x 3 (DVD) from the Constrain popup menu (**Figure 22.5**). If your project is widescreen, choose Custom from the popup menu and set the ratio to 16 x 9. Move or resize the selection box so that the image appears as you'd like it to, then click the Crop button. When you bring it into iDVD, it will be in the proper size ratio.

■ An iDVD slideshow displays its photos as static images. If you want to add some movement to them, use the Ken Burns Effect in iMovie or iPhoto and create a movie that contains just the photos you'd use in a slideshow (see Chapter 9). Then, import that movie file as a regular movie. (It's not actually a slideshow in iDVD's eyes, but you get the same overall effect.)

Setting Slideshow Options

Now that you've created a slideshow, use the Slideshow editor to change several settings that pertain to how long each photo appears, whether the slideshow repeats, and more.

To enter the Slideshow editor:

◆ Double-click a slideshow in the menu (or in the Map view) to bring up the Slideshow editor (**Figure 22.6**).

To set the slide duration:

◆ Choose a time from the Slide Duration popup menu to specify how long each photo remains onscreen before loading the next one (**Figure 22.7**).

If you've included background audio in your slideshow (see "Adding Background Audio," later in this chapter), you can also choose Fit To Audio, which divides the total audio playing time by the number of photos to come up with an equal display time for each photo (for example, a slideshow of five photos that contains 60 seconds of audio would display each picture for 12 seconds).

The last option, Manual, requires the viewer to advance the frames using the DVD player's controls. Manual is not available if you add background audio.

To set the transition style:

◆ Choose a transition type from the Transition popup menu (**Figure 22.8**). As with transitions between menus (see Chapter 19), this setting applies only when you're advancing to the next slide; if you switch to the previous image, no transition occurs.

For transitions that can operate in different directions, such as Cube, click a directional arrow to the right of the popup menu.

Figure 22.6 The Slideshow editor contains the options you need to control your slideshow.

Figure 22.7 The Slide Duration popup menu controls how long a photo appears onscreen before advancing.

Figure 22.8 Click the Transition popup menu to choose an effect that plays each time the slide advances.

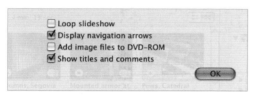

Figure 22.9 Click to type a title and comment for the slide.

Figure 22.10 The Settings dialog provides a few miscellaneous options.

Figure 22.11 The navigation arrows that appear are strictly visual aids. Clicking them serves only to make your index finger sore.

To edit titles and comments:

◆ iDVD copies each photo's title and comments from iPhoto. If you plan to make these visible, click the title or comment area below a photo and type your title and comments (**Figure 22.9**).

To apply miscellaneous settings:

1. Click the Settings button to display the Settings dialog (**Figure 22.10**).

2. Enable or disable the following options:

   ▲ Click the checkbox labeled Loop slideshow to make the show repeat once it reaches the last photo. Your viewers will need to return to the menu using their player's controls.

   ▲ Click the checkbox labeled Display navigation arrows to show a pair of arrows onscreen that indicate more photos are available before and after the current one (**Figure 22.11**). (The first and last photos in a slideshow display only one arrow.)

   These arrows are just decoration; they aren't buttons that can be clicked to advance the slideshow.

   ▲ Click the checkbox labeled Add image files to DVD-ROM to include copies of the image files on the disc so that anyone with a computer can access them (see "Adding DVD-ROM Data" in Chapter 19).

   ▲ Click the checkbox labeled Show titles and comments to display the photos' text during the slideshow.

To preview the slideshow:

◆ With the Slideshow editor open, click the Preview button. You can also go back to the menu, preview the project from there, and then click the slideshow's icon, but previewing from within the Slideshow editor is easier.

To remove photos from a slideshow:

1. Select one or more photos in the Slideshow editor.

2. Press Delete, or choose Delete from the Edit menu.

To exit the Slideshow editor:

◆ Click the Return button to go back to the menu.

✔ Tips

■ You can choose to always include high-resolution slideshow photos on the DVD-ROM portion of your disc. Open iDVD's preferences, click the Slideshow icon, and enable Always add original slideshow photos to DVD-ROM contents.

■ Does a thick black band appear around your photos when you preview the slideshow? iDVD shrinks the images to fit within the TV Safe Area. To turn off this feature (if you're going to view the DVD on a computer, for example), open iDVD's preferences and click the Slideshow icon. Then, disable the option marked Always scale slides to TV Safe area (**Figure 22.12**).

■ Click the list style buttons at the upper-right corner of the Slideshow editor to switch between viewing just thumbnails of your images and viewing them in a list with filenames displayed (**Figure 22.13**).

■ Remember in Chapter 8 when I advised you to trim your footage so that your audience wouldn't get bored? The same applies to slideshows. I know, it's so easy to just drag virtual stacks of photos to iDVD—there's plenty of space on the disc, and it's quicker than sorting through them. Resist that urge: add only the good shots and don't flirt with the limits of your viewers' attentions.

Figure 22.12 Images are usually scaled to fit within the TV Safe Area, but you can turn off this option. Compare this example with the same slide on the previous page.

List style buttons

Figure 22.13 Photos can be viewed in a list, too.

A Pointer about Pointers

When you add a photo from the Media pane, iDVD creates a pointer to the photo's original image file; it doesn't store a new copy. So, if you add a photo to your slideshow, then edit it in iPhoto later (such as cropping it or converting it to black and white), the edited version appears in your slideshow.

This also explains why, if you edit a photo in iPhoto, that picture's thumbnail image isn't updated in your slideshow, even if the correct version appears when you preview the slideshow. iDVD creates a thumbnail image of the photo when it's added to the slideshow.

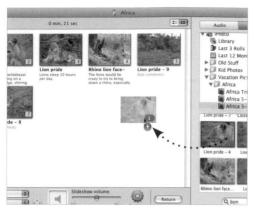

Figure 22.14 Add one or more photos from the Media pane by dragging them to the Slideshow editor.

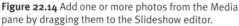
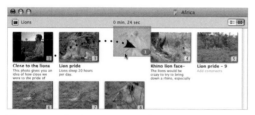

Figure 22.15 Drag one or more photos to a new location in the Slideshow editor to rearrange them.

Before slides arranged   *After slides arranged*

Figure 22.16 The slideshow icon is based on the photo positions within the slideshow. If you've chosen the photo in the number 2 position as the icon (left), and then move a different photo to that position, the new photo becomes the icon (right).

Adding Photos

I never seem to hit upon the right combination of photos when I create a slideshow—there's always one (or two, or twenty) more that *really must* go in. iDVD 6 removes the previous version's 99-photo limit—well, the maximum number is now 9,801 photos, but it's hard to really call that a *limit*.

To add photos to the slideshow:

1. Double-click a slideshow to enter the Slideshow editor (if it's not already open).

2. Drag one or more image files from the Media pane or the Finder to the Slideshow editor (**Figure 22.14**).

To rearrange photos:

◆ Drag one or more images to a new location within the Slideshow editor. The other images are re-ordered to accommodate the change (**Figure 22.15**).

✔ Tips

■ Don't drag new photos to the slideshow's icon in the menu—they'll change the icon, but won't be added to the slideshow. (See "Using Motion" in Chapter 20.) Make sure you're adding them to the Slideshow editor.

■ Rearranging the order of the photos changes the preview icon for your slideshow in the menu (**Figure 22.16**). For example, if the icon is photo number 2 and you move another picture into the number 2 position in the Slideshow editor, the latter photo appears as the icon when you return to the menu.

■ You can add multiple copies of the same photo to a slideshow, in the event that you want an image to repeat later.

Adding Background Audio

Just as audio can play in the background of a menu, slideshows can include audio, too.

To add background audio:

1. Double-click a slideshow to enter the Slideshow editor (if it's not already open).

2. Drag one or more audio files, or an iTunes playlist, from the Media pane to the Audio well (**Figure 22.17**). You can also drag audio files from the Finder.

   When you add audio to the well, the Slide Duration popup menu automatically switches to Fit To Audio, which divides the total audio playing time by the number of photos to come up with an equal display time for each photo.

To set the audio volume:

◆ Drag the Slideshow volume slider to control how loud or soft your background music plays (**Figure 22.18**).

To remove background audio:

◆ In the Slideshow editor, drag the music file out of the Audio well. A gray speaker icon indicates that no audio is set.

✔ Tips

■ You can also drag QuickTime movies to the Audio well; iDVD ignores the video track and plays the audio.

■ Need some visual entertainment in the background at your next party (gotta use that obnoxiously huge widescreen television for something, right)? Load up a slideshow with your favorite images and drag an iTunes playlist to the Audio well. If it's an exceptionally long party, enable the Loop slideshow option. Burn the disc, pop it into your DVD player, and then go mix some martinis!

Figure 22.17 Drag one or more songs from the Media pane to the Audio well to add background audio.

Figure 22.18 iDVD assumes you want softer music behind your slideshow, and sets the Slideshow volume slider to half the maximum volume.

ARCHIVING, ENCODING, AND BURNING

iMovie's purpose is to create a movie, which can be saved back to video tape, transferred to a Bluetooth phone, published to a Web page, sent via email, or distributed in other ways. iDVD's purpose, however, is to create a project that can be burned to a DVD disc. It contains high-quality video and audio that will play on a consumer DVD player. Without the disc-burning step, iDVD is pretty much just an interesting exercise in customizing a user interface.

True to form, the process of burning a disc is simple: click the glowing Burn button, insert a recordable DVD disc (DVD-R, DVD-RW, DVD+R, or DVD+RW), and go outside to enjoy the sunshine for a few hours. But getting to that point, while not difficult, involves a few choices that determine the amount of data that can be stored on the disc and the quality of the finished project.

Creating a Project Archive

Burning a DVD takes a lot of hard disk space and processing power. Some people choose to build a project using one Mac (such as a laptop), and then burn the DVD on another computer (such as a desktop Mac, which boasts a speedier SuperDrive and a faster processor). Or, perhaps your Mac doesn't include a SuperDrive. In these situations, create an archive of your project that can be copied to another machine.

If you're planning to burn a disc on your computer but don't need an archive, skip two pages ahead to "Choosing an Encoding Setting."

To create a project archive:

1. Choose Archive Project from the File menu. If your project isn't saved, iDVD asks you to save it. To continue, click OK in the dialog that appears; otherwise, click Cancel.

2. In the Save dialog that appears, choose a location for the archive and, optionally, change its name (**Figure 23.1**).

3. Enable or disable the following options. The estimated size of the archive appears to the right and changes based on your choices.

   ▲ **Include themes.** If your project uses themes that aren't likely to be on another computer (such as third-party themes you purchased, or favorite themes you designed), enable this option to copy the necessary information to the archive. If you leave this disabled, but your project contains custom elements, an error dialog appears on the other computer when you open the archive (**Figure 23.2**).

Figure 23.1 When you save your project as an archive, the Save dialog contains archive-specific options.

Figure 23.2 Choose Include themes when saving an archive to avoid an error dialog like this one.

External Burners

Until iDVD 6, the only official way to burn a DVD was to do it on a Mac that contained an Apple-supplied internal SuperDrive. Now, at long last, that restriction is history: you can burn to external DVD burners directly from iDVD.

Figure 23.3 If you have protected audio files in your project, you need to authorize the computer with your iTunes Music Store ID and password.

Name	Size
Africa Archived.dvdproj	4.43 GB
Africa.dvdproj	204.4 MB

Figure 23.4 An archive is significantly larger than an iDVD project file because it stores all of the media, rather than including just pointers to the data.

▲ **Include encoded files.** iDVD can encode material in the background, which reduces the time it takes to burn the disc (see "Choosing an Encoding Setting" on the next page). Including these files means it will take less time to burn the project on another machine, but it also makes the archive size larger.

4. Click Save. After a few minutes, depending on the size of your project, a new archive file is created.

✔ Tips

■ An archive contains all the data your project needs—except fonts. If your project contains a font that may not be on the computer to which you're sending the archive, be sure to also send a copy of the font.

■ If you've included any protected audio files (such as songs purchased from the iTunes Music Store) in your archive, you won't be able to open the project on another computer unless that machine is authorized by you. A warning dialog appears (**Figure 23.3**), and then opens iTunes so you can input your iTunes Music Store identification and password.

■ So why not just copy the project file? To save disk space while you're working, iDVD includes pointers to the media and other data in your project, not the data itself. Copying just the project file to another machine wouldn't include that information. An archive packs it all into a nice tidy package (**Figure 23.4**).

Choosing an Encoding Setting

iDVD employs two different encoding methods: Best Quality and Best Performance.

To choose an encoding setting for the current project:

1. Choose Project Info from the Project menu or press Command-I.

2. For the Encoding setting, click the radio button beside the type of encoding you wish to use (**Figure 23.5**).

To choose an encoding setting for new projects:

1. Open iDVD's preferences and click the Projects icon.

2. For the Encoding setting, click the radio button beside the type of encoding you wish to use.

Best Performance

Best Performance provides up to 60 minutes of video and shorter burn times than Best Quality. iDVD can encode the video while it's running, whether you're doing something else in iDVD or working in another program.

To enable or disable background encoding:

1. In iDVD's preferences, click the Project icon and click the checkbox labeled Enable background encoding.

2. Close the preferences window.

3. Choose Project Info from the Project menu. In the Encoding area, the progress bars to the right of the assets indicate how much of the video is encoded (**Figure 23.6**). If disabled, the progress bar remains blank.

Figure 23.5 The encoding options are located in the Project Info window, as well as in iDVD's preferences.

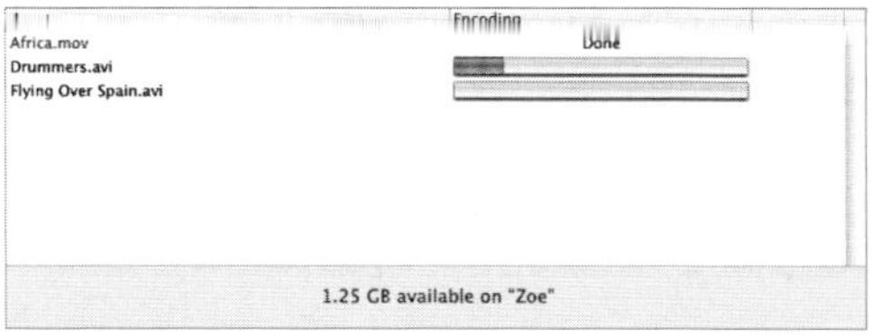

Figure 23.6 With the Best Performance and Background Encoding settings enabled, iDVD encodes movies in the background. The Project Info window reports on the progress.

Encoding and Burn Times

To give you a rough idea of how long it takes for iDVD to encode projects using the two encoding settings, here are two examples of projects I created.

Using Best Performance, burning a project containing a 48-minute movie took roughly 50 minutes on my (still trusty) 1.25 GHz PowerBook G4.

Using Best Quality, a separate project of mine with a 118-minute movie took 4 hours and 40 minutes to burn.

Best Quality

Best Performance

Best Quality

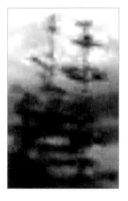

Best Quality

Best Performance

Best Performance

Figure 23.7 When is Best Quality not best quality? These examples come from a 118-minute project (Best Quality) and the same footage in a 48-minute project (Best Performance). More motion and noise gets more compression (top), resulting in pixelation around the trees (detail). However, when there is less motion, the two encoding styles look very much alike (bottom, with detail).

Best Quality

If your project exceeds 60 minutes, or you want to make sure you're getting the highest quality encoding that iDVD can offer, use the Best Quality mode. After you start the burn process, iDVD examines the video to determine where it can apply different levels of compression.

✔ Tips

- If you're using Best Performance and Background Encoding is enabled, wait until the assets are finished encoding in the Project Info window before you burn.

- Best Quality does not encode video in the background the way Best Performance does. Instead, it performs its calculations during the burning phase. So, don't stare at the Background Encoding area of the Status pane waiting for the encoding to finish, because it hasn't started.

- As projects get longer than 60 minutes, their image quality is more likely to decrease due to the additional compression that needs to be applied. If higher image quality is important to you, try not to skirt that two-hour border with your project sizes (**Figure 23.7**).

- After you burn a project using Best Quality, iDVD holds onto the files it encoded. However, if you remove any assets from the project and want to burn it again, be sure to first choose Delete Encoded Assets from the Advanced menu to force iDVD to re-scan the footage and choose the best compression settings.

- The DVD Capacity figure in the Project Info window is based on the type of encoding you've specified. If iDVD is set to use Best Performance but the capacity exceeds 4.2 GB, switch to Best Quality—iDVD changes its estimate.

Burning the DVD

Before you click the Burn button, make sure you have enough hard disk space available: at least twice the amount the project occupies. You can view your project's size and the free space on the hard disk that contains your project by choosing Project Info from the Project menu.

Figure 23.8 In the Project Info window, change the name of the disc when it's inserted in a computer.

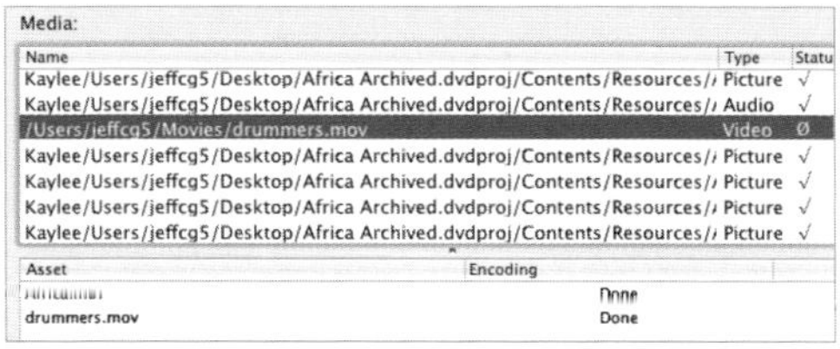

To change the name of the burned disc:

1. Choose Project Info from the Project menu, or press Command-I. The Project Info window appears (**Figure 23.8**).

2. Type a new name in the Disc Name field. After the disc is burned, this name is used when the DVD is mounted on a computer's desktop.

3. Close the window to apply the change.

To locate a missing asset:

1. Choose Project Info from the Project menu, or press Command-I to display the Project Info window.

2. Scroll through the asset list to find entries with a zero (0) in the Status column (**Figure 23.9**).

3. Double-click the missing asset to bring up the Missing Files dialog.

4. Select a file in the dialog and click the Find File button.

5. Locate the file and press OK. The Status column displays a checkmark. Note that for missing imported videos, you need to re-link the video and audio portions (just point to the same file).

6. Click OK to exit the dialog.

Figure 23.9 Use the Project Info window to locate missing assets.

How to Fix Missing Assets

The Project Info dialog tracks everything you've added to the project, even assets that you've deleted. If the file cannot be found, iDVD will not proceed when the time comes to burn.

I learned this the hard way when I dragged a JPEG image file to a menu background, decided it didn't look good, and then deleted it from the Background well in the Menu pane. Since the image no longer appeared in the project, I deleted it from my hard disk.

There are two solutions:

◆ Double-click the item in the Project Info window and choose another image.

◆ Go to the Map view and delete the asset entirely.

BURNING THE DVD

Normal   *Activated*

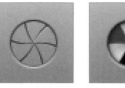

Figure 23.10 In iDVD 6, you need to click the Burn button only once to start the process (some earlier versions required two clicks). So, really, there's no good reason to hide the button behind the safety iris—except that it's cool.

Figure 23.11 If errors are found before burning, iDVD gives you the opportunity to fix or ignore them.

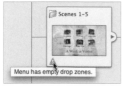

In the Map view, position your mouse pointer over a warning icon to locate potential burn problems.

Figure 23.12 The disc burning process goes through five stages of encoding and writing data to disc. The small preview helps you determine how far along the process has advanced.

To burn the DVD:

1. Click the Burn button; the iris reveals the glowing Burn button that's been hiding under iDVD's interface (**Figure 23.10**).

   If any assets are missing, iDVD displays a warning dialog (**Figure 23.11**). The Map view also displays potential burn problems.

   Otherwise, the program asks you to insert a blank recordable DVD disc.

   (The "closed" Burn button is like the bright red safety cover that's always mounted over The Big Important Button—the one that launches the missiles, opens the airlocks, or initiates the self-destruct sequence that destroys the villian's secret underground lair in all those movies.)

2. A progress dialog appears that identifies the stages of the process (**Figure 23.12**):

   ▲ **Stage 1: Prepare.** iDVD ensures that it has everything it needs to continue burning.

   ▲ **Stage 2: Process Menus.** Buttons, motion menus, and other menu interface elements are rendered and encoded.

   ▲ **Stage 3: Process Slideshows.** Slideshow photos are resized and compressed as needed. If you've specified slideshow transitions, they are rendered separately during this stage.

   ▲ **Stage 4: Process Movies.** Depending on which encoding method you've chosen, this stage usually takes the longest.

   ▲ **Stage 5: Burn.** The footage is *multiplexed*, which combines the audio and video data into a single stream that can be read by DVD players. Burning is when the laser actually etches your data into the surface of the disc.

✔ Tips

- If you've specified Best Performance, wait for asset encoding to finish before starting the burn process.

- Remember that the total space occupied on the disc includes motion menus, slideshows, etc. So if your movie is 56 minutes long, you may still get an error message that the project is too big.

- Earlier versions of iDVD required you to enable the Motion button to include motion on the disc, but iDVD 6 renders the motion elements whether the **Motion** button is highlighted or not. To burn a project with no motion, set the Loop Duration slider in the Menu pane to zero (00:00).

- I frequently burn test copies of a project to a rewriteable DVD-RW disc, so I'm not throwing away a bunch of shiny platters. When you insert such a disc that already has data on it, iDVD gives you the option to erase it before continuing with the burn process (**Figure 23.13**).

- Including transitions between menus or within slideshows adds time to the burning process.

- Did you create a widescreen movie in iMovie, but it's not appearing as widescreen in your DVD player? Check to see if the player has a 16:9 or letterbox feature...some models (such as mine at home) play the movie full frame if it doesn't detect a flag on the disc instructing it to letterbox the picture.

- Wondering at what speed your Super-Drive is burning the disc? The answer is found in Mac OS X's console.log file. After you burn a project, open the file, located at [Computer]/Library/Logs/Console/.

Figure 23.13 If you insert a rewriteable disc that contains data, iDVD can erase it during the burn stage.

File	Edit	Project	View	Adva
New...			⌘N	
Open...			⌘O	
Open Recent			▶	
Magic iDVD...				
OneStep DVD				
OneStep DVD from Movie...				
Close Window			⌘W	
Save			⌘S	
Save As...			⇧⌘S	
Archive Project...				
Save Theme as Favorite...				
Import			▶	
Burn DVD...			⌘R	
Save as Disc Image...			⇧⌘R	

Figure 23.14 "Burn" a disc image to your hard drive.

Figure 23.15 Drag a disc image to Disk Utility to burn its contents to a DVD disc.

Burn Disc In: MATSHITA DVD-R UJ-816

Waiting for a disc to be inserted...

Burn Options

Speed: Maximum Possible ☐ Test Only

☐ Erase disc before burning
☐ Leave disc appendable

After Burning
☑ Verify burned data
◉ Eject disc   ◯ Mount on Desktop

Close   Cancel   Burn

Figure 23.16 After clicking the Burn button in Disk Utility, insert a blank DVD disc to start burning.

Saving as a Disc Image

Until iDVD 5, you needed to own a Mac with an Apple-supplied SuperDrive to burn iDVD projects. It wouldn't work with third-party external burners.

Now, that restriction is gone. However, there are still occasions when you want to save the project as a disc image, which effectively "burns" your project to the hard drive. For example, you may want to burn a DVD disc from that disc image on another computer, or mount the image on your desktop and preview the final project using the DVD Player application.

To save as a disc image:

1. Instead of clicking the Burn button, choose Save As Disc Image from the File menu, or press Command-Shift-R (**Figure 23.14**).

2. Choose a location on your hard disk to save the disc image; make sure you have plenty of free space.

3. Click the Save button. iDVD follows the same procedure as when it burns a disc.

To burn a DVD disc from a disc image:

1. Launch Disk Utility (located in Applications > Utilities).

2. Drag the disc image from the Finder to the left-hand column (**Figure 23.15**); or, choose Open from the Images menu.

3. Select the disc image in Disk Utility and click the Burn button.

4. Insert a recordable disc (**Figure 23.16**).

To play a disc image using DVD Player:

1. Double-click the disc image to mount the disc as if it were a physical DVD.

2. Launch the DVD Player application.

After the Burn

When the burning process is complete, iDVD spits out the DVD disc and asks if you'd like to make another copy (**Figure 23.17**). If so, insert a new disc; otherwise, click Done.

Here are a few other suggested things to do while you're in your cooling down period.

Test your project

Just because you have a shiny disc in hand doesn't guarantee that it works. Test it on your own machine using DVD Player. Test it on friends' Macs and PCs, and insert it in your consumer DVD player. Test, test, test, or you may find yourself singing, "To every season, burn, burn, burn...".

Delete encoded assets

If you don't need to burn another disc, you can free up some hard disk space by deleting the project's encoded assets, which are stored in the project file.

Create an archive of the project for offline storage to make sure you have all of the original footage.

To delete encoded assets:

◆ From the Advanced menu, choose Delete Encoded Assets.

Make duplicates

If you want to make copies of the DVD without going through the iDVD burning process, use Disk Utility or other software such as Roxio's Toast (www.roxio.com).

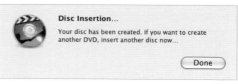

Figure 23.17 If you're creating multiple copies of the same disc, burn them in succession so you don't have to go through the encoding stage each time.

TROUBLESHOOTING

Software is never perfect, and unfortunately iMovie 3 had more than its fair share of "challenges," as an optimistic friend of mine likes to say. iMovie 4 was a big improvement, but many people reported performance problems and other glitches. I'm happy that iMovie HD versions 5 and 6 are much more polished—but no software is without issues.

My first bit of troubleshooting advice is to make sure you're running the latest versions of iMovie and iDVD; check the iLife page at Apple's Web site (`www.apple.com/ilife/`) or run Software Update (in your System Preferences or from the Apple menu).

Also, check Apple's online support discussion forums for iMovie HD and iDVD (`discussions.info.apple.com`) to see if other users have found solutions or work-arounds to a problem you may be experiencing. And check some of the resources in Appendix B for up-to-the-minute reports and troubleshooting. iMovie and iDVD users make up a dedicated community, and I owe a great debt to many folks online who have prodded the program to find answers.

Finally—and perhaps most important—*give Apple feedback* (`www.apple.com/feedback`). It's the best way to communicate what needs fixing (and yes, the developers do listen).

iMovie HD 6 and iDVD 6 Troubleshooting

iMovie HD seems to prefer lots of memory and fast processors, but even on powerful Macs you might see sluggish behavior. Try the following suggestions to improve performance.

Change the playback preference

In iMovie's preferences, click the Playback icon and choose a different Quality setting (**Figure A.1**).

Make iMovie window smaller

Use the resize handle on the bottom-right corner of the iMovie window to make it as small as it will go.

Quit other running applications

This frees up more memory for iMovie to use. Although Mac OS X manages memory better than Mac OS 9, I've seen iMovie and iDVD gain some pep if they're not competing with other processes.

Remove third-party plug-ins

Try paring down iMovie to its essentials. Remove any third-party plug-ins, such as those from a previous version, from [Home]/Library/iMovie/ (they may also be in a Plug-ins folder in that iMovie folder, too).

Defragment your hard disk

You can run into performance issues if your hard disk space is severely fragmented—there aren't enough open stretches of disk space available to write entire files, so the files are broken up into pieces to fit the available free locations.

The best way to defragment a disk is to make a complete backup copy of it, erase the drive, and then restore the data.

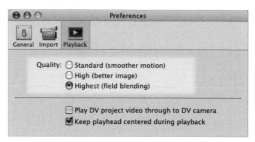

Figure A.1 If iMovie playback is stuttery, try using a different Quality setting.

Trash iMovie or iDVD preferences

If the program's preferences get corrupted, it places a load on the program's operation. iMovie and iDVD re-create the files they need the next time you launch the program.

To trash iMovie or iDVD preferences:

1. Quit the application. (You may want to quit all running applications, too.)

2. Go to your preferences folder at [Home]/Library/Preferences/, and delete the following files (you may not have all of the iMovie files):
   - ▲ iMovie Preferences
   - ▲ com.apple.imovie.plist
   - ▲ com.apple.iMovie3.plist (this is used by iMovie 4, too)
   - ▲ com.apple.iDVD.plist

Turn off FileVault

FileVault is a technology introduced in Mac OS X 10.3 that creates an encrypted version of your Home directory. However, iDVD and iMovie store their project files in the Home directory, which means that when FileVault is active, the computer is constantly encrypting and decrypting massive quantities of data on the fly. Turn it off in Mac OS X's Security preference pane.

Fixing out of Sync audio/video

If your audio and video are out of sync in a video clip, try extracting the clip's audio track, which locks the audio to the video (see Chapter 10).

Also, make sure your audio was recorded at 16-bit, not 12-bit. See the following article for more information: http://docs.info.apple.com/article.html?artnum=61636.

Disc Burning

Here are some things to check if your discs are turning into drink coasters (or if you're not even getting to the burn stage).

Have lots of disk space

Make sure you have plenty of hard disk space available. Figure at least twice the size of your iDVD project as being a good starting point. You may have to copy your project to another disk (such as an external FireWire drive) and run it from there; iDVD stores its working files and encoded media within the project file, so even if you have a drive with lots of free space, iDVD will ignore it if the project file is not located there.

Ensure disk is formatted correctly

If you're using an external drive, make sure it's formatted as a Mac OS Extended (Journaled) volume. Some drives are pre-formatted for Windows or Unix operating systems, and although the Mac can read and write to them, iMovie and iDVD need to use Mac OS Extended (Journaled). Use Disk Utility to erase and reformat the drive.

Delete encoded assets

Some previously-encoded material could be causing problems. From iDVD's Advanced menu, choose Delete Encoded Assets, which deletes any rendered footage and forces iDVD to re-encode the material from scratch.

Check DVD media

Unfortunately, sometimes the problem is the blank DVD disc you're trying to burn onto. This can happen with less expensive discs purchased in bulk, but has been known to affect reputable manufacturers' discs, too. If you're getting errors, try a new media brand, such as the discs sold and certified by Apple.

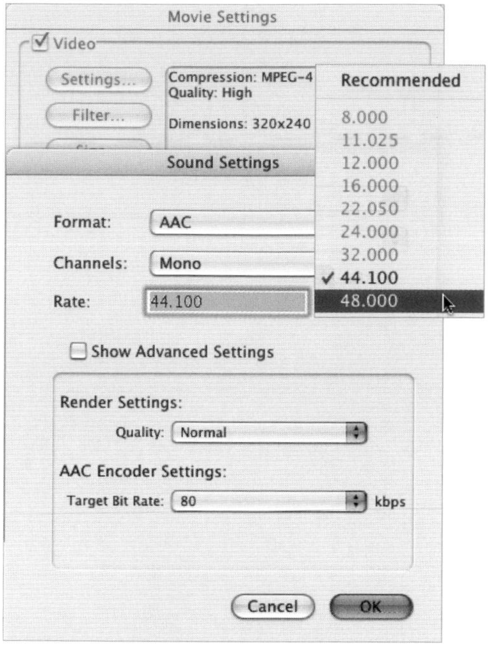

Figure A.2 Audio set to 44.100 kHz (12-bit) has been known to cause problems in iDVD. Change it to 48.000 kHz (16-bit) by exporting a QuickTime movie from iMovie using Expert Settings.

Clean your SuperDrive

A tiny laser burns pits into a disc, resulting in data that a computer or DVD player can read. If your SuperDrive has accumulated dust, it can throw off the beam and ruin your burn. Spray a little compressed air into the slot (but don't go crazy with it).

Set Energy Saver settings

Disc burning is processor-intensive. Go to the Energy Saver preference pane in Mac OS X's System Preferences and set the processor performance to Highest and the hard drive to never spin down. Also make sure that the computer won't go to sleep after a period of inactivity.

Burn during the day

It's convenient to start a burn late at night so the process will complete while you're sleeping. However, Mac OS X performs some nightly system maintenance at approximately 3 a.m., which can interfere with burn performance. Burn your project during the day to see if this is the culprit.

Change audio quality

iMovie and iDVD use audio set to 48.000 kHz (16-bit). However, some audio sources may record at 44.100 kHz, which has been known to cause burning problems.

To change a movie's audio quality:

1. Export your movie from iMovie to a QuickTime file using Expert Settings (see Chapter 16).

2. In the Movie Settings dialog, under Sound options, click the Settings button.

3. Click the Rate popup menu and choose 48.000 (**Figure A.2**).

4. Export the clip, then import it into iDVD.

DISC BURNING

267

General System Troubleshooting

Sometimes the problem isn't iMovie or iDVD, but something in Mac OS X that's not behaving well. Try these steps, especially if you're seeing problems in other applications.

Repair Mac OS X permissions

For whatever reason, some of the thousands of files that Mac OS X relies on wind up with improper permissions. I've found that fixing permissions is often a good general cure-all for when my Mac starts getting flaky.

To repair Mac OS X permissions:

1. Open Disk Utility, which is located within the Utilities folder of your Applications folder.

2. Select your main hard disk (your "boot drive") from the list at left.

3. Switch to the First Aid tab.

4. Click the Repair Disk Permissions button (**Figure A.3**). The process can take several minutes.

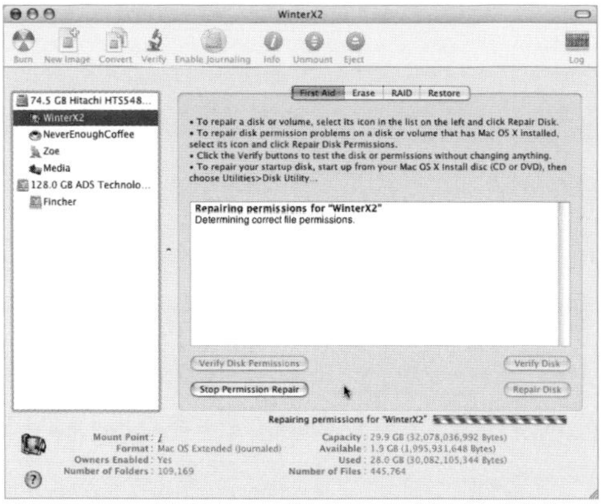

Clean house with Onyx

Onyx (`www.titanium.free.fr`) is a splendid little utility that can perform all sorts of Mac OS X housecleaning chores, such as deleting cache files and performing daily maintenance routines. And it's free!

Figure A.3 Repair disk permissions using Disk Utility to help improve performance.

B

RESOURCES

Essential Information

iMovie HD & iDVD for Mac OS X: Visual QuickStart Guide companion Web site

http://www.jeffcarlson.com/imovievqs/

Apple iLife

http://www.apple.com/ilife/

Canon Digital Camcorders

http://www.canondv.com/

Sony Digital Camcorders

http://www.sonystyle.com/
digitalimaging/H_Camcorders.shtml

JVC Digital Camcorders

http://www.jvc.com/

Panasonic Digital Camcorders

http://www.panasonic.com/
consumer_electronics/camcorder/

Recommended Books

The Little Digital Video Book, Michael Rubin (Peachpit Press, 2001)

Real World Digital Video, 2nd Edition, Pete Shaner and Gerald Everett Jones (Peachpit Press, 2004)

continues next page

The Macintosh iLife '06, **Jim Heid
(Peachpit Press, 2006)**

http://www.peachpit.com/

*Take Control of Making Music with
GarageBand* **and** *Take Control of
Recording with GarageBand,* **Jeff Tolbert
(TidBITS Electronic Publishing, 2006)**

http://www.takecontrolbooks.com/

The Computer Videomaker Handbook,
by the editors of *Computer Videomaker
Magazine* **(Focal Press, 2001)**

http://www.videomaker.com/

*Killer Camera Rigs that You Can
Build,* **by Dan Selakovich (Angel Dog
Entertainment, 2004)**

http://www.dvcamerarigs.com/

*Behind the Seen: How Walter Murch
Edited Cold Mountain using Final
Cut Express and What This Means
for Cinema,* **by Charles Koppelman
(Peachpit Press, 2004)**

http://www.peachpit.com/

Online Tutorials and Reference

HD for Indies Weblog

http://www.hdforindies.com/

The "Unofficial" iMovie FAQ

http://www.danslagle.com/mac/iMovie/

Matti Haveri's List of iMovie HD Bugs

http://www.sjoki.uta.fi/~shmhav/
iMovie_HD_6_bugs.html

Ken Tidwell's "Unofficial" iDVD FAQ

http://www.kentidwell.com/idvd4/

MyMovieFest.com

http://www.mymoviefest.com/

RESOURCES

Cyber Film School

http://www.cyberfilmschool.com/

DVcreators.net

http://www.dvcreators.net/

2-pop.com

http://www.2-pop.com/

Post Forum

http://www.postforum.com/

iMovie Plug-ins

eZedia

http://www.ezedia.com/

GeeThree

http://www.geethree.com/

Virtix

http://www.virtix.com/

Stupendous Software

http://www.stupendous-software.com/

cf/x

http://www.imovieplugins.com/

BKMS

http://plugins.bkms.com/

Audio Editing Applications

SoundStudio

http://www.felttip.com/products/
soundstudio/

SndSampler

http://www.sndsampler.com/

iDVD Themes

iDVD ThemePak

http://www.idvdthemepak.com/

Blue Fusion iDVD Themetastic

http://www.idvd-themetastic.com/

Other iMovie-Related Software

Still Life

http://www.grantedsw.com/still-life/

Photo to Movie

http://www.lqgraphics.com/

iStabilize

http://www.pixlock.com/

Royalty-Free Audio Clips

Freeplay Music

http://www.freeplaymusic.com/

Killersound

http://www.killersound.com/

Sound Dogs

http://www.sounddogs.com/

SmartSound

http://www.smartsound.com/

INDEX

INDEX

S

INDEX

INDEX